Inventory Management

Advanced methods for managing inventory within business systems

Geoff Relph and
Catherine Milner

KoganPage

LONDON PHILADELPHIA NEW DELHI

Publisher's note
Every possible effort has been made to ensure that the information contained in this book is accurate at the time of going to press, and the publishers and authors cannot accept responsibility for any errors or omissions, however caused. No responsibility for loss or damage occasioned to any person acting, or refraining from action, as a result of the material in this publication can be accepted by the editor, the publisher or either of the authors.

First published in Great Britain and the United States in 2015 by Kogan Page Limited

2nd Floor, 45 Gee Street
London EC1V 3RS
United Kingdom
www.koganpage.com

1518 Walnut Street, Suite 1100
Philadelphia PA 19102
USA

4737/23 Ansari Road
Daryaganj
New Delhi 110002
India

© Geoff Relph and Catherine Milner, 2015

The right of Geoff Relph and Catherine Milner to be identified as the authors of this work have been asserted by them in accordance with the Copyright, Designs and Patents Act 1988.

ISBN   978 0 7494 7368 6
E-ISBN   978 0 7494 7369 3

British Library Cataloguing-in-Publication Data

A CIP record for this book is available from the British Library.

Library of Congress Cataloging-in-Publication Data

Relph, Geoff.
   Inventory management : advanced methods for managing inventory within business systems / Geoff Relph, Catherine Milner.
      pages cm
   ISBN 978-0-7494-7368-6 (paperback) – ISBN 978-0-7494-7369-3 (ebk)   1. Inventory control.
2. Production management.   I. Milner, Catherine.   II. Title.
   TS160.R425 2015
   658.5–dc23
                                                                                               2015008790

Typeset by Graphicraft Limited, Hong Kong
Print production managed by Jellyfish
Printed by CPI Group (UK) Ltd, Croydon CR0 4YY

CONTENTS

This book is dedicated to June and Simon,
our patient other halves.

Our thanks to all the staff at Kogan Page for their help
and support during the process of writing this book.

Also our thanks to all the case study sources for
granting permission to quote them in this book.

Introduction

What this book is about

This book is intended as a manual for operations management professionals who are looking to improve the effectiveness of the inventory management and Material Resource Planning (MRP) functions within their organizations. We hope you will find it a useful guide. You will know that the availability of software is such that from small businesses upwards MRP systems are now used to manage companies' materials and production planning. To do this, three decisions need to be made:

1 How much to buy and how often.

2 How to protect against variations in supply and demand.

3 How long it will take to make/deliver the item.

All of these decisions affect the inventory level that the system and the planners will deliver. What is a little disturbing is that, despite many decades of research, business systems still provide very little support to the planners in the form of optimizing techniques. Research by Relph (2006) showed that:

- only 50 per cent of business systems provided automatic mathematical models for determining cycle and safety stock; and

- even when offered they were rarely used by planners.

These conclusions are further confirmed by Jonsson and Mattsson (2006), whose analysis of companies from 1993 to 2006 stated:

> It could be thus concluded that a common way of determining parameters such as order quantities and safety stocks is by general judgement and experience. Only a minority of companies applied formal calculations and optimisations. Parameters used in materials planning methods are reviewed rather infrequently, typically once a year or less often in over half the companies.

If you are concerned that your company is not managing its planning parameters well and that you are lagging behind the industry, these conclusions offer a crumb of comfort: you are not alone.

In our many years of experience we have come across numerous companies that have struggled with the problem of managing their planning parameters. The inventory budget is set in the boardroom as a simple financial amount or percentage, but operations managers know that the decisions of what inventory to hold have to be taken at a detail level – what items, where, when, what quantity? Thus achieving a 20 per cent inventory reduction is simple to say but complex to put into action.

This book is based on our many years of operational, consulting and academic experience working with small and large companies. It sets out tools and techniques that have been used successfully to help companies simplify this complex task of managing many thousands of parameters and achieving inventory targets set by senior management. The book will provide a step-by-step guide on how to simplify the approach to determining the optimal parameters for each item and will provide a simple linkage between the business budget decisions and the item level parameter settings.

How the book works

There are a number of threads in the book that look at the problem from both the philosophical level as well as the practical. There is a general narrative of issues and current thinking and best practice, examples of theory/formulae, with worked examples which are built on throughout the book. Each technique is explained and, where possible, formulae are shown in both academic form as well as being expressed in an Excel format. Reading this book, you will be able to create Excel models to test and gain an understanding of each tool. The tools will build into a comprehensive working model that will enable you to analyse and plan inventory. The development of the model through Chapters 4 to 6 will show how high-level targets can be broken down and developed into a coherent plan.

All the Excel sheets that we work through in the book are available to download at **koganpage.com/imresources**
In the Excel sheets reproduced in this book, cells displaying the *result* of a formula are shown with a grey fill. The formula to be entered in each cell is shown below the Excel sheet.

The use of Excel

The book can be read without the added use of Excel should you so wish. We believe there is great value in the reading of the book without investigating the calculations in any depth. However, there is the additional benefit, should you wish to use it, of creating a plan using the step-by-step Excel exercises.

The use of Excel within business is both a blessing and a curse. The ease with which data can be extracted and manipulated means that often planners prefer to plan with Excel and as a result do not use the planning system (eg in MRP). The intention in this book is to allow the reader to create a plan whose results can be transferred back into the planning system, which will encourage more effective use of it. There is a presumption that you will be familiar with Excel and have a good working knowledge of the basic features and some knowledge of more advanced features.

You should be comfortable using the following Excel features:

- VLOOKUP;
- CHOOSE;
- DSUM;
- Complex IF statements;
- FILTER; and
- pivot tables.

The use of the formulae is entirely the reader's responsibility: no liability for use/misuse will be accepted. If the reader does not understand what the function is doing they should not use it in a business situation, unless they have fully understood the input and output of the model. The examples are intended to assist in guiding the user in the correct use of the tools.

This is how the book is arranged:

Chapter 1 Introduction to inventory management: This chapter looks at the essentials of inventory management. It breaks down inventory management into the three key components: planning; control; and balancing. The chapter then looks at how planning systems are used to support the planning and balancing of inventory. It concludes with surfacing the supply/demand planning dilemma.

Chapter 2 Business systems and business: This chapter begins by looking at a brief history of business systems and why we need them today. It then considers the basic business processes and the guidelines for implementation and management of the business systems.

Chapter 3 The complexity of inventory management within business systems: The essence of this chapter is to examine why inventory management has become so complex, where the real problems lie and what the simple approaches are to successful management. At the conclusion of this chapter the reader will have a good understanding of the problems facing an operations manager and the planner.

Chapter 4 Traditional thinking in inventory optimization: This is the first of the technical chapters that look in detail at the current tools available for planning the optimum inventory level. It covers the planning of the cycle stock and the safety stock and concludes by looking at techniques that can be used for aggregate planning. In this chapter the reader will begin to build working inventory models that can be utilized within their own businesses.

Chapter 5 k-curve methodology: This chapter will show how the economic order quantity (EOQ) and Pareto techniques were combined to create the *k*-curve methodology. It shows how *k*-curve methodology builds on traditional approaches and addresses the weakness of EOQ and Pareto approaches. As with Chapter 4, the reader will be able to build inventory models: these can be experimented with to aid understanding and appreciation of the techniques.

Chapter 6 The practical application of k-curve: This chapter builds on Chapter 5 to show how the *k*-curve approach can be used as part of an inventory planning process. It takes as an example the case of planning a 20 per cent reduction of a company with £9 million inventory spread across 5,000 parts with a turnover just short of £100 million. By the end of the chapter the reader should be able to apply the technique to their own business data.

Chapter 7 Case study examples and what to do next: The final chapter looks at the issues of implementing *k*-curve successfully: what are the steps, who needs to be involved and learning from case studies of successful implementations.

It will discuss what it is about the *k*-curve approach that makes it so relevant to the pressures of business operations today. It will look at the inexorable drive to reduce inventory, drive cost down and increase service ability and in particular why these three measures are often in direct conflict. It will show how to decide when to stop reducing inventory.

The final chapter and the book conclude with suggested next steps for anyone eager to improve their inventory management.

Notes

Jonsson, P and Mattsson, S (2006) A longitudinal study of materials planning applications in manufacturing companies, *International Journal of Operations Production Management*, **26**, pp 971–95

Relph, G J (2006) *Inventory Management in Business Systems*, PhD thesis, Manchester University

Introduction to inventory management

Introduction

Almost all organizations use computer systems of one sort or another to help manage their business. Most of them also have a good deal of cash tied up in inventory, from which they need to get a good return on the ongoing investment. This chapter brings together these two fundamental business concerns – effective use of business systems and getting value from money tied up in inventory – and considers how to optimize inventory within the business system.

Inventory (or stock) covers all the goods and materials that an organization owns or holds, and to which a business intends to add value before selling. The dichotomy of inventory is that inventory held ties up working capital (because it costs money and therefore less is better) but it is needed in order to have something to add value to and sell (because we need the inventory to ensure product availability).

Business systems are designed to help to manage inventory, but need to be given precise instructions in order to do so. All too often these instructions are generalized or delegated to individuals within the organization and not coordinated or aligned to the business goals. Many businesses fail to effectively synchronize the vision and strategy of their business to the detailed inventory management decisions needed to define the system parameters. This is precisely the challenge that this book sets out to meet.

Availability of software is such that from small businesses upwards these systems will be used to manage the company. These systems will need to use either simple re-order point (ROP) logic or Material Resource Planning (MRP) logic for purchasing and inventory planning. Whichever one is used, three decisions need to be made: 1) how much and how often to purchase raw material; and 2) how to protect against variations in supply and demand and 3) how long it will take to make/deliver the item.

All these decisions produce inventory. And inventory costs money.

The inventory budget is typically set in the boardroom as a financial amount as part of a business plan. The decisions of what inventory to hold has to be taken at a detail level – what items, where, when, what quantity? Determining the link between the boardroom budget and the item level decisions has been the challenge for operations managers and planning teams for many decades.

It is this critical linkage that this book sets out to examine. We first consider the issues facing operations managers, then move on to review the tools and techniques used today and finally show how they can be extended to utilize the proven k-curve methodology (KCM).

KCM was conceived in the 1990s through research between IBM and Aston University. The approach was used by IBM in its manufacturing plant in Havant, and subsequently used by the IBM consultants working with IBM's major clients. The IBM research centre in Zurich developed software to support the consulting teams in early 2000. When Geoff Relph left IBM and set up Inventory Matters he continued the research work and used KCM to support his clients in the understanding and management of inventory. Inventory Matters' own software was developed in 2007.

This book provides a step-by-step guide on how KCM achieves the linkage between the business budget decisions and the detail level on parameter settings at item level. The reader will be able to construct a working KCM model that will, in a simplified form, enable you to analyse and plan inventory using this approach. This chapter sets the stage for that approach:

- We first discuss the fundamental principles of inventory management.

- Second, we examine the issues and relationships between the business systems designed to manage inventory and the problems of achieving the business goal.

- And finally, we examine the essential costs and the need for flexibility within business operations.

Inventory and inventory management

Inventory is the stock of any item held in an organization. The aim is, naturally, to have the right amount, in the right place, at the right time and the right cost.

Inventory management sets out to achieve just that. It is the process of directing and administering the holding, moving and converting of raw materials through value-adding processes to deliver finished products to the customer. The efficient and effective management of inventory (or stock) is important to almost every organization.

Ordering and managing inventory is nothing new. It is known to date back at least as far as the ancient Egyptians, as shown by inventory management records on papyrus fragments held by the Louvre in France:

> The solar temple... sent goods from various agricultural centres or services to the funerary temple... Three columns [in the table] were devoted to each product: the expected quantities to be delivered, the actual amount delivered, and the remainder due. (Bernadette Letellier)

In simple terms, inventory management:

- is the set of policies and controls that monitor levels of inventory;
- determines what levels of each product should be maintained;
- identifies when stock should be replenished; and
- decides how large orders should be.

Figure 1.1 shows the optimum inventory tightrope that operations professionals have to walk. Inventory management in daily life is challenging, especially when identifying and achieving the optimum amounts to hold:

- Holding *too little inventory* of the required products often leads to customer orders being unfulfilled on time, or perhaps lost altogether. This can put the business at risk since *lost orders* may lose a customer altogether, and dissatisfied customers often complain about the lack of availability. If this dissatisfaction spreads, the long-term impact causes a reduction in profitability. Another problem when too

FIGURE 1.1   Optimum inventory tightrope

Too little inventory
Lack of availability
Lost orders
Firefighting

Too much inventory
Overstock
Money tied-up
Slow to react

little inventory is held is the time and energy then needed to manage the shortage. *Firefighting*, although often accompanied by a feeling of success, uses a great deal of time and energy. Wherever possible, the upfront management of inventory to ensure that sufficient product is being held is a far more valuable use of time.

- Holding *too much inventory* – being 'over-stock'– is also problematic. Money is not only tied up in the purchase of unnecessary stock, but is also spent on the holding and managing of that inventory. If too much working capital is tied up for too long then cash flow may be affected, and buying-in of inventory of other much needed products may be compromised.

    Over-stock also impacts on the space where inventory is held, whether on the shop floor or in a warehouse. The over-stock items need space to be stored, space that cannot then be used for the normally rotating products, and in extreme situations additional warehousing space may need to be bought.

    Another problem when too much inventory is being held is that an organization will find it more difficult to *react to changes quickly*. The change may be to demand in the marketplace where requirements may change very quickly. Alternatively, the change may be in engineering or design, which may happen because of health and safety or quality reasons, or due to an upgrade in development. When large amounts of inventory are held, the number of parts that need to have changes made to them is correspondingly large and changes cannot be made through the system quickly.

For every part held within an organization there is an ideal quantity of inventory which lies within an optimum range. The ideal range is based on a wide range of factors, for example: demand; variability of the demand; unit cost of the item; size of the product; shelf-life (if any) and the time it takes to supply/manufacture the product. Determining this ideal is explored further in later chapters when the inventory saw-tooth and the economics of stock balancing are discussed.

It is quite usual for demand to vary within an expected range in many businesses. Unexpected changes in customer demand or product supply will affect inventory plans, which in turn may push inventory holdings out of the ideal range. The sooner a business knows about changes in supply or demand, either within its own organizations or elsewhere in its supply chain, the quicker it can react and calculate the impact of those variations, and the closer it will be able stay to the new ideal volumes.

The three pillars of inventory management

Inventory can be held in many places within an organization – for example, raw materials, components and finished goods in warehouses, work-in-progress and feed-stock on the shop floor. Wherever it is held it needs to be managed.

Inventory management has three key pillars, as shown in Figure 1.2:

- inventory planning – determining the optimum level;
- inventory control – managing the integrity of the stock;
- inventory balancing – balancing the ongoing supply/demand relationship.

FIGURE 1.2 The three pillars of inventory management: plan, control and balance

any weakness and the whole fails!

Reproduced by kind permission of Inventory Matters Ltd

Inventory planning

Inventory planning is about determining the optimum levels of inventory both for today and the future.

- The purpose of creation of the plan is to identify the optimum inventory levels. This will involve understanding demand patterns, what value-add is needed for each product (eg manufacturing requirements, retail volumes and sales locations, military and medical consumption levels), and deciding what inventory categories each product should be in.
- The inventory plan must aim to match the high level business needs with what is possible at the detailed item level, ie in order to meet the expected demand for the products to be sold by the business, what products should be held, where and in what volumes, and at what cost?

- A key feature of the plan is to identify and manage the parameters that need to be set within the business systems, which are needed to balance future stock levels (eg order frequencies, safety stock policies, minimum order quantities and lead times).

Inventory planning is the main focus area of this book.

Inventory control

Inventory control is about managing the integrity of the stock. Data accuracy is essential:

- Inventory moves through a physical process. The physical movements need to be tracked by system transactions to accurately reflect *where inventory is* in the process and *in what quantities*.
- It is necessary to ensure that the system records of each product match the physical inventory held.

Inventory control is also, obviously, about the management of the physical inventory. This is a critical and essential part of inventory management. As Gwynne Richards (2013) says: 'Warehouses are now seen as a vital cog within today's supply chain.' This is well covered in his *Warehouse Management*. This is a large topic in itself.

Inventory control is a broad topic. The management of both the data integrity and of the physical stock are of fundamental importance and more can be read about it in Richards (2013) and elsewhere.

Inventory balancing

Inventory balancing is required to manage the success of the inventory plan on a daily or weekly basis:

- Is the rate of supply (eg goods-in) as expected?
- Is the rate of demand (eg goods-out) as expected?
- Is the flow of inventory through the process as expected?
- Is the process in balance from the supply to the through-put to the fulfilment of customer demand?

Inventory balancing is about supply/demand management:

- The daily managing of the ongoing supply/demand relationship.
- Is the inventory flowing properly today?
- Is the plan working?

Inventory balancing is normally managed by the business systems. When systems manage inventory balancing well, they are based on:

- good inventory planning, for example clear categorization of parts and correct setting of parameters;
- good inventory control, for example accurate data and good management of the physical stock; and
- good performance measurements, for example good exception management.

Inventory balancing examples will be used in later chapters in this book to show how the business systems calculations are made within MRP/MPS systems.

Inventory planning pyramid

Inventory reduction is seen as a good route to:

- increase profitability;
- reduce costs; and
- become more agile and responsive.

An instruction from senior management within a company to 'reduce inventory by 25 per cent' gives a clear direction of *what* is wanted, but without necessarily a clear indication of *how* it can be achieved.

The relationship between these different views, and the process flows that link them, is shown in the inventory planning pyramid in Figure 1.3.

The following areas of a company will be interested in inventory availability and therefore affected in different ways by a significant reduction in it:

- sales and marketing;
- customer service;
- after sales;
- warehousing and logistics;
- manufacturing; and
- finance.

We will now look at this important relationship and the process steps in the inventory planning pyramid in more detail.

FIGURE 1.3 The inventory planning pyramid

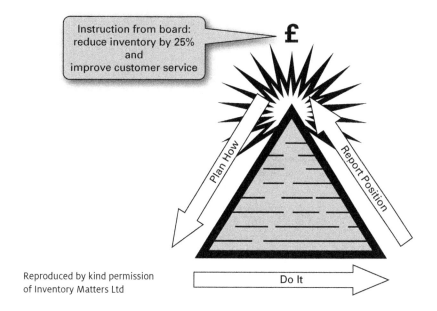

Reproduced by kind permission
of Inventory Matters Ltd

Report position

The first step in the inventory planning pyramid is to 'report the current position':

- Has the previous plan achieved the required reduction?
- What is the impact on customer service and product availability?
- Are there critical inventory items that were needed, and why?
- What items am I short of, what do I have too much of?
- What do my customers want?

Instruction from the board

Senior management often sees good inventory management as a critical part of the effective way of managing a business. However, there is often a call from the board to reduce inventory volumes and costs without any real understanding of the impact at a part level, and the impact this might have on product availability for customers. This is the responsibility of the operations management people, who have to consider how this could be done and report back on the consequences of any reductions.

FIGURE 1.4   Breaking down the inventory planning pyramid

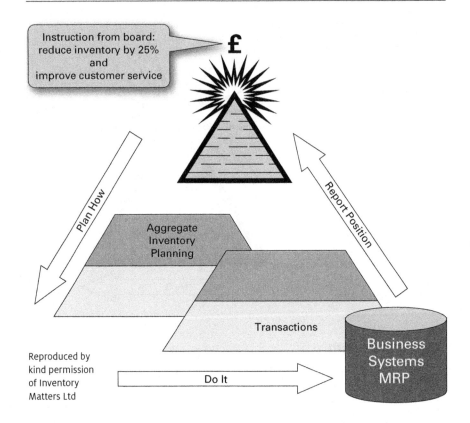

Reproduced by kind permission of Inventory Matters Ltd

Plan how

The next step in the inventory planning pyramid is to *plan how* to achieve the reduction. To plan this reduction the operations manager will need to decide which of the many parts (often 10,000 and frequently more) can have their stock levels reduced. This will involve a detail understanding of not only the part's value, but any issues related to its supply and demand, and its relative importance to the business. We will look in detail at ways of doing this in Chapters 4, 5 and 6.

Do it

Once the 'plan how' is decided, the next step can be started. To do this, instructions need to be given to the planning and control systems within the business system, for example Master Production Scheduling (MPS) or Manufacturing Resource Planning (MRP or MRPII). The MPS or MRP use these instructions to perform a series of planning calculations. Systems often give planners the opportunity to try this out in a what-if scenario:

- The instructions are given in the setting of a number of parameters (for example, lead-time, minimum batch size, safety stock) which result in suggested order quantities.

- The planning system uses these parameter settings to calculate orders and thus volume of inventory that will be produced as a consequence.

- The ability of the system and the business processes to continue to satisfy customers with the reduction in inventory levels can be measured with key performance indicators (KPIs) such as stock availability measured against demand, non-compliance, etc.

This book sets out the process and tools needed to enable the use of the inventory planning pyramid which can be used to link the high-level financial instruction to reduce inventory, with the detailed implications of that reduction at an item by item and parameter by parameter level.

We have also talked about the process flow in the planning pyramid. Managing processes well is of fundamental importance in a successful business. We will examine the way in which companies can effectively manage the

FIGURE 1.5   Translating financial saving to detailed items in the inventory planning pyramid

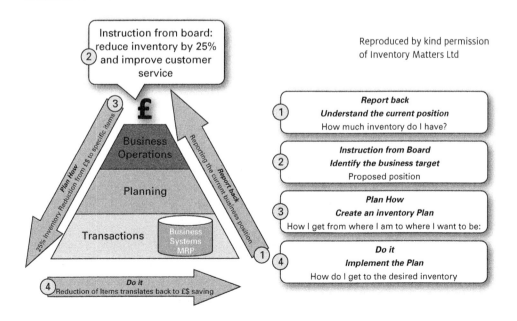

relationship between their processes, their organization (and people), and their technology (or systems) in Chapters 2 and 3.

Understanding the inventory planning pyramid allows a company to address the following questions, and determine 'how' to carry it out and what the implications are likely to be:

- Does your company have too much money tied up in stock?
- Does it make sense to reduce your inventory by 25 per cent?
- Would you like to understand where you'd be at risk?

Management of inventory in business systems

As we have already said, all organizations plan and most use business systems to help them. It is essential to be able to create the best inventory plans in such a way that they work with the business systems in an organization. These planning and control systems help manage all three elements of the three inventory pillars of planning, control and balancing.

Planning

Materials requirement planning is the principal tool used to manage inventory planning. It utilizes BOMs (bills of materials) to define what is needed and the MPS (Master Production Schedule) to define what is wanted and when. When the optimal parameters are defined (by the planners) the MRP system will drive the business towards the optimal inventory.

Control

By capturing all the transactions made (ordering products, receiving goods, moving though processes, storing locations within the process) the systems enables the control needed to facilitate tracking and finding stock. Accurate records ensure that when MRP plans it is based on an accurate foundation of what is in stock, what is needed and what is on order.

Balancing

As the demand (inevitably) changes these MRP planning systems will re-calculate requirements. MRP has to take account of the differences with the original plan and to make adjustments to the stock levels, and to the order due dates in order to reflect the increase and decrease in demand. The system will output instructions to the planners detailing which orders are to be brought forward, pushed back and if needed cancelled.

An overview of the importance of inventory management within business systems is considered here, with Chapter 2 looking at the planning engine within business systems in more detail.

A good, well-installed system will help people within a business to make speedier and more well-informed decisions. Vollmann *et al* (2005: 4) say that the 'system does not make the decisions or manage the operations – managers perform those activities. The system provides the support for them to do so wisely.'

As shown in the inventory planning pyramid in Figure 1.5, it is essential to be able to link between the different levels within a business:

- Communicating in a meaningful way is essential from the very top of an organization to the shop floor and back again. This is no different whether the message being communicated is about new products, business success and direction, profitability or cost of inventory held. The difference with inventory is often that the communication on inventory from the top of a business is in a different language to that used by planners and on the shop floor, and needs translating from financial amounts into parts held, and back again. The inventory communication goes from company vision to strategy to tactical planning to operational planning to transactional execution and back again.

- The ability to communicate the inventory requirements and implications between the different levels in a meaningful way is essential for businesses, and is a key topic for this book.

Process flow

Organizations tend to follow the same process flow (see Figure 1.6): forecast (identifying future demand and future requirements), plan and execute:

- Forecast: this is deciding what future requirements need to be met.
- Plan: this is the determination of how to do it.
- Execute: this is about putting the plan into action and ensuring that what is achieved will correctly meet the business need.

FIGURE 1.6   Process flow from forecast to execute

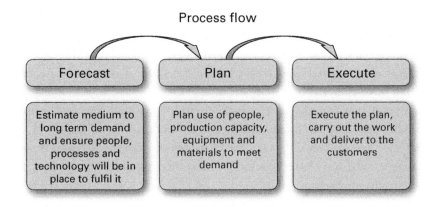

Transactions within the planning engine

Many of the transactions within the planning engine of a business system are involved with inventory. Accurate data and careful management of these activities is essential to allow the planning engine to calculate a meaningful output.

Vollmann, Berry and Whybark (1998: 2) identified inventory related tasks within the planning engine:

- Plan for materials to arrive on time in the right quantities needed for product production.

- Maintain appropriate inventories of raw materials, work in progress, and finished goods: in the correct locations.

- Track material, people, customer's orders, equipment, and other resources in the factory.

- Communicate with customers and suppliers on specific issues and long-term relationships.

- Meet customer requirements in a dynamic environment that may be difficult to anticipate.

- Respond when things go wrong and unexpected problems arise.

- Provide information to other functions on the physical and financial implications of the manufacturing activities.

This list gives a clear idea why it is essential that good inventory planning and inventory control is in place before the system performs its calculations and transactions.

Business planning systems

The planning engine within a business system calculates production requirements based on the known or estimated future demand. The planning engine may be based on a reorder point (ROP) calculation, or on a manufacturing requirements planning calculation.

The business system may be called an enterprise requirements planning (ERP) system. The key elements and the differences between ERP, MRPI and MRPII are shown in Figure 1.7.

Reorder point logic, according to the APICS body of knowledge, is defined as:

> A reorder point is calculated for each independent demand item. When inventory levels drop to the reorder point, a signal is sent to replenish inventory in a fixed quantity amount. The reorder point is equal to the expected demand during lead time plus safety stock to cover demand in excess of expectations.
>
> (APICS, 2014)

The difference between MRP logic and ROP is that MRP is time-phased and based on future demand, whereas ROP is based on an average of past demand.

Business planning systems are discussed further in Chapter 2.

Lean and JIT

Lean and 'just in time' (JIT) processes are not based on business systems but are philosophies, processes or techniques used by companies. Lean and JIT were popularized in the 1980s when exported from Japan following their success at reinvigorating the Japanese industry post-WWII. Lean and JIT are process-driven approaches, although transactions such as Kanban triggers are not incorporated into some ERP systems. Where JIT production techniques are employed there tends to be a reduced need for all operations to be recorded within the business system, although some recording will still be necessary. The processes are designed to self-regulate the management of inventory levels and movement. The effect that Lean and JIT have on inventory will be considered in more detail in Chapter 2.

FIGURE 1.7 MRP to MRPII to ERP

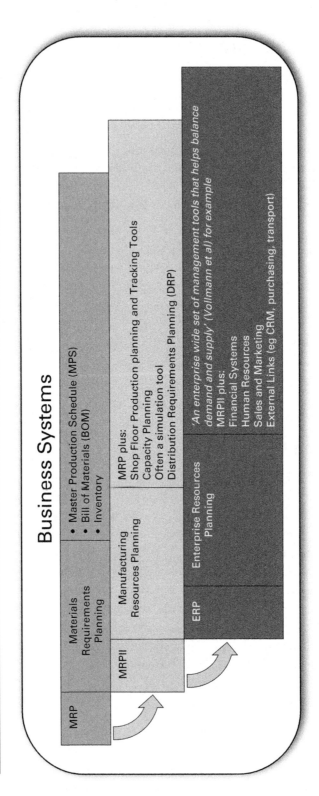

Business Systems

MRP	Materials Requirements Planning	• Master Production Schedule (MPS) • Bill of Materials (BOM) • Inventory
MRPII	Manufacturing Resources Planning	MRP plus: Shop Floor Production planning and Tracking Tools Capacity Planning Often a simulation tool Distribution Requirements Planning (DRP)
ERP	Enterprise Resources Planning	'An enterprise wide set of management tools that helps balance demand and supply' (Vollmann et al) for example MRPII plus: Financial Systems Human Resources Sales and Marketing External Links (eg CRM, purchasing, transport)

The cost of inventory and the ability to react to change

Cost of inventory

Inventory has four main costs:

- Unit price cost of the inventory: this is the price paid per unit for the volume of product bought. It is fairly common for large orders to attract a reduction in the unit price paid. 'Price breaks' are often offered for different order volumes (for example, to buy a quantity of 100 T-shirts @ £8.00, 500 @ £5.00, 1000 @ £4.00). Unit price is a reasonably obvious number because it is the price paid when the items arrive or leave the business.

- Cost of ordering inventory/cost of set-up.
  Cost of ordering inventory: there is a cost associated with order placement, including the cost of placing the order as well as the cost of packaging and transporting the order, and the cost of receiving or issuing materials. This is less easy to calculate than the unit price cost, and is explored further in Chapter 4 when economic order quantity is discussed (EOQ).

  Cost of set-up: there is a cost to set up a machine or workstation when changing over from producing product A to product B. This set-up time will take × minutes or hours, and the cost of set-up is then allocated to the number of items in the production run (for example, if the set-up time is two hours and the production run is 120, one set-up minute has been spent per item; alternatively, if the set-up time is two hours and the production run is 12, ten set-up minutes have been spent per item). A common approach used to improve/reduce the set-up times is known as SMED (Single Minute Exchange of Die), developed by Shigeo Shingo.

- Cost of holding inventory: the cost of holding inventory is more difficult again to calculate. This cost includes warehousing and handling costs (renting, heating, lighting, insurance, and personnel), the cost of having the money tied up in inventory (working capital costs), risk costs (eg obsolescence, deterioration, shrinkage or evaporation) and opportunity costs (the lost opportunity to invest elsewhere, etc.)

- Cost of shortage: there is another inventory cost which may be considered. The cost of shortage or lost sales. This cost is the loss of the revenue opportunity when a business has been unable to meet demand, and the known or estimated unmet demand is allocated a cost. The evaluation of this cost is very difficult because it is not always possible to know when you have failed to deliver. This is considered in Chapter 4 where safety stock considerations are discussed.

The supply/demand dilemma

It is very important for businesses to be able to react to changes in the marketplace within their supply chains. This is possible where: there is a desire to make changes; there are clear market signals; there is good information available within the supply chain; and when optimum amounts of inventory are held.

The ability to react to change

An example of this was demonstrated in the automotive industries in the United States in the Great Depression of the late 1920s and 1930s. General Motors was able to remain profitable during this time, while Ford was losing money during the 1930s 'because it was disorganized' (O'Brien, 1990):

'What accounts for this exceptional record [of paying dividends throughout the 1930s] in a period when many durable-goods producers failed or came close to bankruptcy? ... I think that ... we had simply learned how to react quickly. This was perhaps the greatest pay-off of our system of financial and operating controls.' (Alfred Sloan quoted in O'Brien, 1990)

This lesson is one that repeated itself with the economic downturn in 2008 and the severe impact on the automotive industries in the United Kingdom. The following quotes show how purchasing of cars fell drastically at this time and how the car manufacturers reacted.

From end Jan 2009 'carmaker Honda... shut its British factory for four months' because in December 2008: 'In Britain, the number of cars rolling off production lines nearly halved.' (Kollewe, 2009)

Toyota dealt with the economic downturn in a slightly different way:

[Toyota] put its European workforce on a three-day week as it forecasts the biggest slump in car sales for 35 years... Thierry Dombreval, chief operating officer, said 'it would be "foolish" to take short-term decisions to close plants needed in the longer term. These are assets for the future.' (Gow, 2009)

In addition to taking a long-term view, Toyota was also aware that they wanted to avoid building inventory levels too high, since they were confident that they would easily be able to increase production levels once sales started to take off again.

Both car companies reacted to the change in demand from the market by reducing the rate at which they were producing their end products. Since the products were not selling they had an urgent need to stop building up excess stocks of inventory. This reaction to the economic shock of 2008 was repeated across a wide range of industries. The industries have, over the past 50 years, developed very tight and reactive supply chains which have increased their capabilities to react to economic shocks.

An example of a non-automotive company which worked hard to reduce their number of suppliers and create truly strategic partnerships is the Boeing Dreamliner. The strategic decision to involve suppliers in the design and production of the Boeing 787 Dreamliner was made partly as a way of reducing design time, reducing costs and ensuring total commitment from a single-source supplier. There was, however, an unexpected consequence when there was a major production disruption following the 2011 earthquake in Japan. The Japanese manufacturers at that time were producing '35 per cent of the 787, 20 per cent of the 777, and 15 per cent of the 767. What they build can't be duplicated anywhere else, and Boeing can't call in a new supplier to make one piece if it runs short' (Ray, 2011).

The natural disaster demonstrated one of the risks of running a Lean supply chain: when this happens the low volumes of inventory held means that there is a very small buffer of components and sub-assemblies to keep production going. The benefits of a single source supplier needs to be balanced with a good risk analysis of what to do if it all goes wrong.

This example show how at the strategic level the drive for Lean business can expose a business's ability to cope with catastrophic shocks. This dilemma is summarized in Figure 1.8.

Inventory management in the supply chain

The implication of inventory management should be considered not just within a single organization but across the whole supply chain. Managing the steps in the journey of inventory throughout the supply chain is the responsibility of many different organizations, (ie the sequence of steps from initial raw material via a series of value-adding processes to end customer and beyond) but the information on the steps in the journey can be shared.

FIGURE 1.8 Supply demand planning dilemma

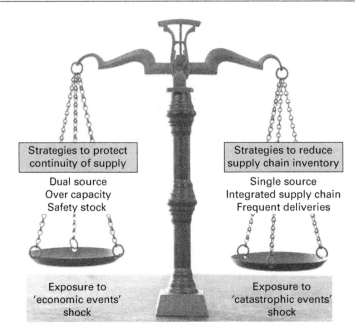

Reproduced by kind permission of Inventory Matters Ltd

The supply chain, logistics and operations management are all linked. Operations management is the organizing of value-adding activity within a business. Logistics is the placement of inventory throughout the supply chain at the right time and in the right place: transporting and warehousing of stock has to be managed both within an organization (eg bins of nuts and bolts at a work station, or work-in-progress awaiting machine availability) and between organizations (eg tins of tomatoes being transported – in one or many stages – from a manufacturer to a retailer).

The supply chain is the linking of the businesses and the processes involved with producing a product from the raw material to the end customer, and beyond to recycling or disposal for many products. *Supply chain management* therefore is the management of this supply chain, defined by Mentzer (2001) as:

> the systemic, strategic coordination of the traditional business functions and the tactics across these business functions within a particular company and across businesses within the supply chain, for the purposes of improving the long term performance of the individual companies and the supply chain as a whole.

Sharing supply and demand information throughout the supply chain can have huge implications on the cost of creating a product (see study below).

Inventory management in the extended supply chain and 'the Beer Game'

We know that sharing supply and demand information throughout the supply chain can have huge implications and benefits on the cost of creating and manufacturing a product. The importance of developing the view of inventory management beyond the walls of a single organization and into the extended supply chain is well understood. One place where this was demonstrated was in research by Kevin Permenter of the Aberdeen group in 2013, which focused on supply chain collaboration in consumer markets: these were identified as having a particularly high market pressure to perform well, in addition to an increasingly complex global customer–supplier network. One of the respondents to the 'Supply Chain Collaboration in the Consumer Markets' research is quoted in support of extended collaboration as saying:

> It is a no-brainer that collaboration can decrease material or distribution costs... and working with our suppliers and partners to react quickly and proactively to deal with packaging disclosure changes has been a huge boon to our cost structure.

> (Permenter, 2013)

The research concludes that collaboration – in both the external and the internal supply chains – and the speedy sending and receiving of information between the customers and suppliers along the supply chain are the way forward.

It is also possible to find examples of where increased collaboration along the supply chain has resulted in major problems for some or all of those involved. One example is the company GTAT, which was driven to bankruptcy and ceased trading on 15 October 2014 (Arthur, 2014), when it failed to deliver sapphire for screens to Apple. Another example is the Boeing Dreamliner. The message here is that extended collaboration along the supply chain needs to be entered into carefully by all parties, with an understanding of the risks as well as the benefits.

Less controversial is the benefit of speedy exchange of information up and down the supply chain. Despite being less controversial, a true understanding of the dangers of not taking this seriously may be hard to achieve within an organization. Alick Chia, MD of global company SKF Logistics, addressed this issue when he spoke about 'Logistics Challenges Today' at the Singapore Institute of Management on 27 November 2014, saying that he had used 'The Beer Game' to great effect in his company to instil a real understanding of the importance of communicating along the extended supply chain and the perils of not doing so.

The Beer Game was developed by the Massachusetts Institute of Technology (MIT) in the 1960s to demonstrate the impact of the Bullwhip or Forrester Effect (first documented by JW Forrester and identified by him in the 1950s), that is:

> an extreme change in the supply position upstream in a supply chain generated by a small change in demand downstream in the supply chain. Inventory can quickly move from being backordered to being excess. This is caused by the serial nature of communicating orders up the chain with the inherent transportation delays of moving product down the chain. The bullwhip effect can be eliminated by synchronizing the supply chain. (APICS, 2014)

The Beer Game, which has had several spin-off games, is a training technique developed to demonstrate the Forrester Effect. It gives the participants in the game first-hand experience of the confusion that can arise along a simple supply chain where demand varies only slightly but where there is a lack of communication. This results in wildly varying amounts of inventory being built and held and normally a feeling of chaos, mistrust and bewilderment.

A spin-off Beer Game developed by the Warwick Manufacturing Group (WMG) at Warwick University doesn't stop at the end of the initial stage by which point confusion has normally reigned, but has an interesting second and third stage:

- In the second stage, the teams are rearranged to gather together a single member of each of the 'companies' from the game's first stage. The new teams then collaborate in managing the supply chain, calculating the inventory and production needed with the variation in demand from the end customer.

- In the final stage, there is a further degree of control. The variation in demand is input directly into an Excel program which calculates the requirements along the whole supply chain to meet the change in demand. This final stage takes minutes to calculate, compared with the hour or more that the first stage of the game will have taken. It also demonstrates one of the benefits of using a computer system to assist in managing the information flow along the supply chain.

The benefits of sharing supply and demand information throughout the supply chain, with collaboration where there is sufficient trust and ability, are available to those companies who can make it work. The question of 'what do we have to do?' can be added to 'how do we do it?' by electronic communications between business systems. The Beer Game helps people experience the problems of the Forrester Effect for themselves in a risk-free environment, to perhaps assist towards greater integration in the extended supply chain.

Summary

Chapter 1 has given an overview of the three pillars of inventory management: planning; controlling; and balancing. We have outlined what inventory and inventory management is, the importance of good inventory planning and why it is essential to be able to translate the high-level financial inventory needs of the business into what this means at an item level, and back again. On a practical level in the majority of businesses, it means that the results of inventory planning decisions need to be routinely fed into the business systems. We have outlined the types of systems available and how using these business systems on a daily basis to execute both purchase and works orders can ensure inventory is well managed and optimum levels achieved. Finally, we have looked at the costs that are involved when making these inventory management decisions and the supply–demand dilemma that faces every business when planning inventory. The following chapters discuss how this can be done in practice.

Notes

APICS (2014) www.apics.org/dictionary. Retrieved from www.apics.org: www.apics.org/dictionary/dictionary-information?ID=471.0 and www.apics.org/industry-content-research/publications/ombok/apics-ombok-framework-table-of-contents/apics-ombok-framework-5.9

Arthur, C (2014, 14 November) The desperate struggle at the heart of the brutal Apple supply chain, retrieved from www.theguardian.com/: www.theguardian.com/technology/2014/nov/14/sapphire-gt-advanced–brutal-apple-supply-chain

David, C and Lane, J D (2011) Profiles in operations research: Jay Wright Forrester, in *Profiles in Operations Research: Pioneers and innovators*, ed S G Assad, pp 363–86, Springer, New York

Gow, D (2009, 3 March) Retrieved 29 August 2014, from www.theguardian.com: www.theguardian.com/business/2009/mar/03/toyota-car-crisis-europe

Kollewe, J (2009, January) www.theguardian.com/business. Retrieved August 2014, from www.theguardian.com: www.theguardian.com/business/2009/jan/30/honda-swindon-shutdown

Letellier, B (nd) www.louvre.fr. Retrieved August 2014, from www.louvre.fr/en/oeuvre-notices/inventory-and-accounts-temple-abusir

Mentzer, J T (2001) Defining supply chain management, *Journal of Business Logistics*, **22**(2), 1–25

Mr Alick Chia, M O (2014, 27 November) Logistics Challenges Today. (C Miner, Interviewer)

O'Brien, A P (1990) *Industrial Dynamics in a Historical Setting*. Retrieved August 2014, from www.cliometrics.org/conferences/ASSA/Dec_90/OBrien.shtml

Permenter, K (2013, March) *Supply Chain Collaboration in the Consumer Markets*. Retrieved from CH Robinson White Paper – Aberdeen Group Research: www.aberdeen.com/research/8391/ai-supply-chain-collaboration/content.aspx

Ray, S A (2011, 24 March) *The Downside of Just-in-Time Inventory*. Retrieved October 2014, from www.businessweek.com: www.businessweek.com/magazine/content/11_14/b4222017701856.htm

Richards, G (2013) *Warehouse Management: A complete guide to improving efficiency and minimizing costs in the modern warehouse*, p7, Kogan Page, London

Vollmann, T E, Berry, W L and Whybark, D C (1998) *Manufacturing Planning and Control Systems* (4th edn), Irwin/McGraw-Hill, Bolton

Vollmann, T, Berry, T, Whybark, D C and Jacobs, F R (2005) *Manufacturing Planning and Control for Supply Chain Management* (5th edn), McGraw Hill, Singapore

Business systems and business

Introduction

Inventory management doesn't exist separately in a business but is integral to the organization. In this chapter we look at how businesses utilize their systems and the basic architectures that are used to help to understand and design effective organizations.

Inventory management and business systems exist within the wider context of the business itself. At the highest level a business will have a vision and a mission statement. These need to be translated into strategic, tactical and operational actions, and you also need to consider their influence on the key business elements of process, organization (including people) and technology. The technology or business systems architecture that manages the business activities has three simple steps – forecast, plan and execute. We look at how these simple steps evolved as systems have developed from MRP to the all-encompassing ERP. We will also examine the importance of the sales and operations planning process and where responsibility for inventory rests within an organization. The chapter will conclude by looking at business system development, how Lean and JIT processes interact with the business systems and the part inventory plays in the business processes and business systems.

The business

An organization exists to deliver something – perhaps an aeroplane, or a packet of peas, a music festival, a guide dog, healthcare, sports facilities, or the defence of the realm – to someone or to another organization. They all add value to a raw material to create products or services for a customer, whether they belong to the public sector, the private sector or if they're a charity.

Vision, mission and action plan

All organizations have a vision, a mission and an action plan at their start and foundation. These are essential to keep a business focused in a clear direction. A company's vision (what) and mission (how) statements tell us what the company intends to be and to do today and in the future. A clear strategy and high-level action plan are necessary to identify what objectives need to be achieved in what markets and in what timescales.

Some examples of several well-known companies' vision and mission statements are given in Figure 2.1.

FIGURE 2.1   Examples of vision, mission

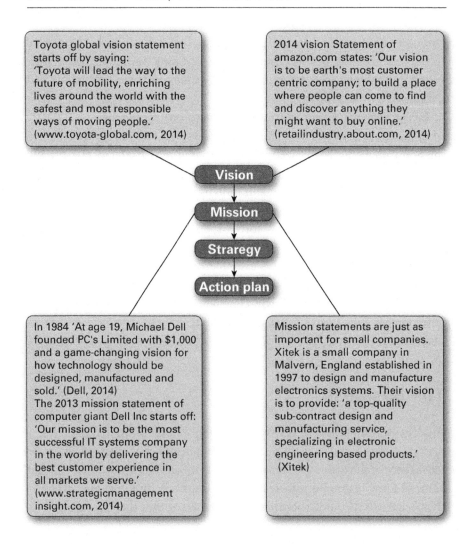

Toyota global vision statement starts off by saying: 'Toyota will lead the way to the future of mobility, enriching lives around the world with the safest and most responsible ways of moving people.' (www.toyota-global.com, 2014)

2014 vision Statement of amazon.com states: 'Our vision is to be earth's most customer centric company; to build a place where people can come to find and discover anything they might want to buy online.' (retailindustry.about.com, 2014)

Vision

Mission

Straregy

Action plan

In 1984 'At age 19, Michael Dell founded PC's Limited with $1,000 and a game-changing vision for how technology should be designed, manufactured and sold.' (Dell, 2014)
The 2013 mission statement of computer giant Dell Inc starts off: 'Our mission is to be the most successful IT systems company in the world by delivering the best customer experience in all markets we serve.' (www.strategicmanagement insight.com, 2014)

Mission statements are just as important for small companies. Xitek is a small company in Malvern, England established in 1997 to design and manufacture electronics systems. Their vision is to provide: 'a top-quality sub-contract design and manufacturing service, specializing in electronic engineering based products.' (Xitek)

FIGURE 2.2 Purchasing at strategic, tactical and operational levels

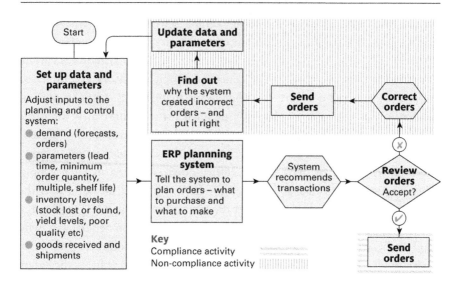

Reproduced by kind permission of Inventory Matters Ltd

Working at strategic, tactical, operational and transactional levels

Organizations manage long-, medium- and short-term objectives and needs by operating at strategic, tactical and operational levels. Figure 2.2 shows how purchasing activities work at:

- a strategic level (eg what products and items need to be brought in for the business to be able to sell the goods it intends to sell, or whether strategic supplier partnerships are to be created);

- a tactical level (eg supplier specification, partnership agreements, what level of automation is desirable and achievable, how the order process will flow with the suppliers, and longer-term price, quantity and delivery schedule agreements); and

- operational and transactional levels (eg order placement and payment).

Inventory management at strategic, tactical, operational, transactional levels

Inventory management will be affected by strategic, tactical and operational decisions and activity too. As shown in Chapter 1 in the inventory planning pyramid, there is an involvement at a strategic level in setting the inventory holding budget. There are also key decisions at a strategic level that are critical to inventory management, for example selection of strategic supplier partnerships, risk management and meeting industry regulatory requirements. As we discussed in Chapter 1 the supply demand dilemma requires careful consideration as there is no right answer. Often inventory is purchased to 'protect' against a future risk that never materializes. Catastrophic or economic shocks can never be truly planned for and survival is often the result of the dedication of the staff within the business to react swiftly and creatively. The legacy of each shock/risk will drive the organization to either invest in inventory or drive the inventory down, focusing in Lean supply. This see-saw is reflected at all three levels: at the strategic level it is the choice to be single or dual source; at the tactical level it will be whether the sales department, who tend to be optimistic, or production department, who tend to be pessimistic, will drive the manufacturing volumes; and at an operational level it will be whether the planner adds or reduces the safety stock on individual parts.

The business performance measures (what measurements are reported and what the figures show) will indicate how successful the inventory planning is and how well the strategic, tactical and operations plans are being adhered to although they do not always show the underlying detail which is crucial when wanting to change direction. The translation of strategic measures into detail operational measure is achieved by a number of management tools, such as Hosin Kanri, which are discussed in more detail in Chapter 6.

The choice of business systems and how they are implemented will be very important for inventory management. Decisions made during implementation will impact how inventory planning is carried out at a tactical level; for example, a decision at the implementation stage whether inventory replenishment should be calculated using a fixed quantity or a fixed interval method. The reason for choosing the latter of these two options is discussed in more detail in a later chapter.

In addition, the decisions made in the strategic and tactical levels in the development of the action plan will determine the type and number of transactions (eg purchase order (PO) placement) carried out: for example, whether the POs will be created completely automatically or have some manual involvement, or whether a form of supplier replenishment – eg vendor managed inventory (VMI) – is used instead, removing the need for PO transactions.

Completely automatic creation of POs aims to increase both data accuracy and speed of placing the orders. The following considerations are important:

- a system that is capable of handling automatic order placing;
- a process that enables automatic order placing and does not require additional human input or checking;
- established supplier partnerships with agreed pricing, lead times etc; and
- a process that alerts the user if a problem arises.

Semi-automatic creation of POs allows for the order to be raised automatically but it is only sent when the user actions it. A benefit of this manual intervention is that orders can be changed before sending if necessary. However, the underlying cause of the mistakes must also be rectified, and making this correction is all too easy to put off until later. Meanwhile more incorrect orders may be raised due to the same mistake. An example is that a delivery lead time may need to be decreased in the system, causing purchase orders for parts to be raised too early.

The volume of transactions is a critical measure when considering the capability of the business process and of the system, and will be revisited in later chapters.

Inventory is the responsibility of the whole organization, including:

- Board – visions and mission, strategic, long-term implications.
- Senior management – tactical importance, translating strategic decisions into medium- to long-term plans.
- Management – operational, medium-term plans.
- Planners – operational, short to medium-term actions.
- Systems – transactional, consequences of all the above levels of inventory management, translation into a high level of detail.

Process, organization (including people) and technology

For an organization to be successful it will need to manage business processes, the organization (eg people and products) and technology (eg business systems such as enterprise resource planning (ERP) systems). The three all need to be present, and much like a three-legged stool in Figure 2.3, if one leg were missing it would be impossible for the stool to remain standing.

FIGURE 2.3   Process, organization and technology (POT)

Reproduced by kind permission of Inventory Matters Ltd

The following paragraphs consider process, organization and technology in more detail.

A process is:

- a series of connected actions with an end goal;
- the way in which raw materials are converted into more valuable items;
- where inputs are transformed into outputs; and
- a way of describing something we do and the deliverables we produce.

Processes should not be considered to be static since the environment a business works in is constantly changing: process review should be carried out routinely (for example, comparing 'our' business with best practice in operations management), and change made where necessary.

Organization is concerned with:

- people with the right abilities and experiences; training where new skills are needed;
- product: R&D, engineering, design, manufacture; and
- culture: the values and practices of an organization and how its people interact with each other and with customers and suppliers. Companies with 'adaptive' cultures find change easier to manage.

Technology includes:

- the systems and hardware needed for effective and efficient business management; and
- ERP, financial control, engineering management, planning and control.

These are looked at in more detail in the following section.

Business system development

According to Klassen and Menor:

> Offering desirable customer service at a reasonable cost requires an efficient flow of materials and services while simultaneously managing the organization's resources that direct and form these flows. Effective planning and coordination ensures that all resources required to deliver services or produce goods are available in the right quantity and quality at the right time. (Klassen, 2005)

It is not an easy task for most organizations to deliver goods or services in the right quantity, place and right time at reasonable cost. This has driven the need for business systems.

A brief history of planning systems

Business system development initially grew because of the need to manage manufacturing (see the timeline in Table 2.1). As we saw in Chapter 1 inventory management was used in ancient Egypt to record stocks and overdue

TABLE 2.1   An overview of business system evolution

Timeline	Development
Early 1900s–1920s	Re-order point and economic order quantity
1960s	Early computer based production planning Toyota Production System/Just In Time developments continue
1970s	Materials Requirements Planning (MRPI)
1980s	Manufacturing Resource Planning (MRPII) Lean Manufacturing introduced in James Womack's book
1990s	Enterprise Resource Planning (ERP)
2000s	Cloud-based ERP systems, Software as a Service, Customer Resources Management
2010s	ERP developments continue: integration (eg with SCM, CRM), platforms and connectivity (eg web options and mobile devices)

orders of food and goods. From the early twentieth century more sophisticated methods were developed:

- Reorder-point/reorder-quantity (ROP/ROQ) methods were used by early manufacturing industry.
- Economic Order Quantity (EOQ): the model and formula, originally developed by Ford Whitman Harris in 1913 was used in the 1920s by Wilson.

From the 1960s computers started to be used in production planning. Over the following decade Materials Requirements Planning (MRPI) was championed by Joseph Orlicky. MRPI was designed to plan manufacturing, inventory, purchasing and shipments to customers. Forecast or actual demand was used to plan production of finished products (known as 'independent demand'), and bills of materials identified the relationship the finished products to all the components and items required to create the final product. MRPI was first used in 1964 by Black and Decker.

In the 1980s Oliver Wight developed MRPI further into MRPII (Manufacturing Resource Planning), which introduced capacity planning and master scheduling. MRPII also started to link with other areas of an organization such as cost accounting.

In the 1990s MRPII continued to link with other areas of the business – human resources, financial management – to create Enterprise Resource Planning (ERP). ERP is defined by APICS (APICS, APICS Definitions) as:

> Framework for organizing, defining, and standardizing the business processes necessary to effectively plan and control an organization so the organization can use its internal knowledge to seek external advantage.

ERP systems were not all developed from the basis of the MRPII production systems. There were already sophisticated financial control packages in existence, as well as maintenance or human resources systems, and software development companies built out from their strengths in their various offerings. By the mid-1990s there were several ERP systems which addressed and linked these core functions together in a single system, typically having the following: a common database which is shared by and built to support all applications and an integrated system operating in 'real time'.

ERP is 'not a revolutionary conceptual breakthrough' according to Hicks and Stecke (1995). It has been attributed to the Gartner Group of Stamford, Connecticut, US. Hicks and Stecke go on to say about ERP that:

> It is not a major technological advance, nor is it even a truly new idea. It is however, a pretty useful paradigm, and it stems from the recognition that you can't make good decisions in a vacuum.

FIGURE 2.4   ERP systems application architecture
(Slack *et al*, 2010)

Essentially, ERP is concerned with making sure that a firm's manufacturing decisions are not made without taking into account their impact on the supply chain, both upstream and downstream. (Hicks and Stecke, 1995)

Continue by looking to the future and predict the rise of ERP cloud applications describing a vision of EDI or internet ordering from system to system without human intervention. With production being managed by computer-based order release onto the shop floor. In fact, many scheduling systems used by servicing companies and taxi firms utilize computerized or intelligent scheduling to direct the engineer/taxi driver to the next job at the point that they become free, rather than being planned the day or even a couple of hours ahead.

In the first decade of the 21st century ERP moved from just being offered as an 'on-premise' system (ie installed and maintained on the customer's own sites), to being offered through the internet. Often called 'cloud ERP' this comes in many forms, all accessible to many users in similar or diverse locations. Cloud ERP aims to benefit users with lower upfront and operating costs, with faster implementation and upgrades, as well as with improved accessibility and mobility. The major ERP software suppliers (SAP, Infor, Oracle, Microsoft) all offer various forms of cloud-based ERP packages as well as 'on-premise' or hosted ERP. There are now a number of ERP cloud packages which were originally developed in the cloud (rather than starting as 'on-premise' packages), such as that offered on the Salesforce platform: Salesforce originated as a customer relationship management (CRM) package. The move from on-site to cloud-based applications has enabled businesses to implement systems faster and at lower costs, however it is still important to heed the warnings of Wilson (2003) and Oliver Wight International Inc (2010) who both focus on avoiding the technology trap by getting the business process right before implementing technology. This is discussed in more depth in Chapter 3.

The development of Just in Time (JIT) occurred differently to the MRPI ERP journey. JIT started in Toyota as the Toyota Production System (TPS) and was developed from 1949 into the 1970s. JIT is based on the elimination of waste. A JIT production system is often called a 'pull'; this is where parts are only made when the existing stock has been used up by the production processes. This is in direct contrast to MRP or 'push' where the product is made to a planned date even if the requirement has changed in the meantime. JIT uses stocks that is delivered to the production line 'just in time' but more importantly in direct response to the customer demand. The phrase 'sell one make one' is often used to describe the real benefit of JIT. The automotive industry is a well-known user of JIT.

Taiichi Ohno, Shigeo Shingo and Eiji Toyoda are jointly credited with developing the TPS (Inc). TPS is both a management philosophy and a way of working. In post-WWII Japan industry had been devastated and visionaries like Toyoda Kiichiro, president of Toyoda Motor Company said: 'Catch up with America in three years. Otherwise, the automobile industry of Japan will not survive' (Ohno, 1978). Ohno decided that establishing production flow and a way to maintain a constant supply of raw materials was the way of Japanese production.

The concept of Lean manufacturing was well suited to both the culture of Japan as well as the physical infrastructure as described in the book *The Machine that Changed the World* by James Womack, first published in 1990. Lean manufacturing is based on waste elimination and follows the JIT philosophy closely, introducing 'tools' to assist in the elimination of waste. The US and the Western economies still find it difficult to migrate away from the 'large batch' mentality and move to the JIT approach.

Choosing the most appropriate system

The choice of whether to use MRPII, ERP, JIT or another control system depends on the type of business a company runs. The relationship between industry type and the different systems is shown in Figure 2.5.

FIGURE 2.5 Choosing the most appropriate system for the business (Vollmann *et al*, 2005: p 10)

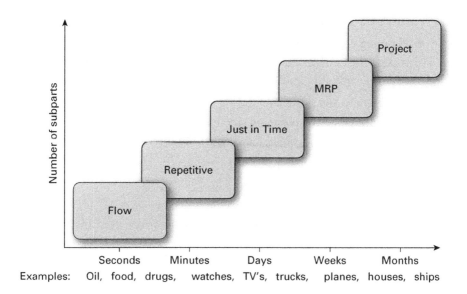

Figure 2.5 shows us clearly that:

- there is a large overlap between the systems, making it difficult to always identify what is the 'best' system;
- there is no guarantee of success by choosing well; the system must also be carefully implemented according to the needs of the business; and
- it may be appropriate for a company to implement more than one system:
  - the rate of flow and the number of subparts may well vary greatly in different parts of the business in a larger company; and
  - many batch firms run MRP with JIT.

The building blocks of MRPI, MRPII and ERP

The process flow: forecast, plan, execute

The process flow of forecast, plan and execute was already mentioned in Chapter 1. This will now be developed to show how the process flow informs the business systems:

- Forecasting includes quantitative or qualitative forecasting, customer order management and manufacturing planning and the processes objective is deciding *what* to do – It will involve validating the customer demand before passing into the planning process.

- Planning is the second step and its objective is determining *how* to do it and who is involved; this will look at both the manufacturing to confirm capability and supply to ensure continuity of supply.

- Execution is the third step and the objective is to carry out the plan as described by the planning step to ensure that manufacturing and purchasing are coordinated to deliver the forecast to the customer.

This is shown schematically in Figure 2.6.

These are the fundamental building blocks of MRP.

Companies, whether manufacturing or providing services, must forecast, plan and execute in a cost-effective way. To do this they must manage, efficiently and effectively, to:

- move materials through the business;

- choose and use the best people for the tasks;

- co-ordinate with suppliers; and

- serve their customers.

FIGURE 2.6   Process flow from forecasting to execution

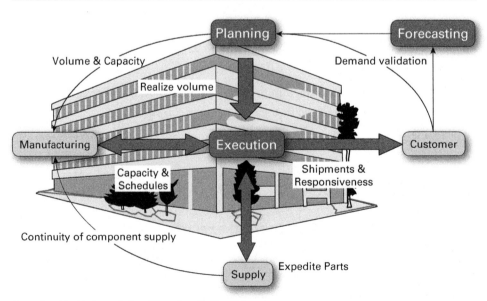

Reproduced by kind permission of Inventory Matters Ltd

Material requirements planning

Material requirements planning (MRPI) works to bring the right amount of raw material and other supplies into the business to support production at the right time. MRPI includes a master production schedule (MPS) of what needs to be done to satisfy the expected demand, a bill of materials (BOM) identifying what items are required to be able to produce each product, existing stock levels of raw materials, components and finished goods, and order information for planned manufacturing and purchases from suppliers. MRPI, however, makes the false assumption that there is unlimited capacity. The MRPI basic configuration is shown in Figure 2.7.

Manufacturing resource planning (MRPII)

Manufacturing resource planning (MRPII) was developed at least in part to satisfy the lack of capacity constraints in MRPI. In addition to the MRPI functionality, MRPII adds rough cut and detailed capacity planning, shop floor production planning and tracking, financial information, and a what-if simulation to understand the consequences of different possible production plans. MRPII plans materials, machines and people. The basic MRPII configuration is shown in Figure 2.8.

FIGURE 2.7 Basic MRPI (Materials Requirements Planning) configuration

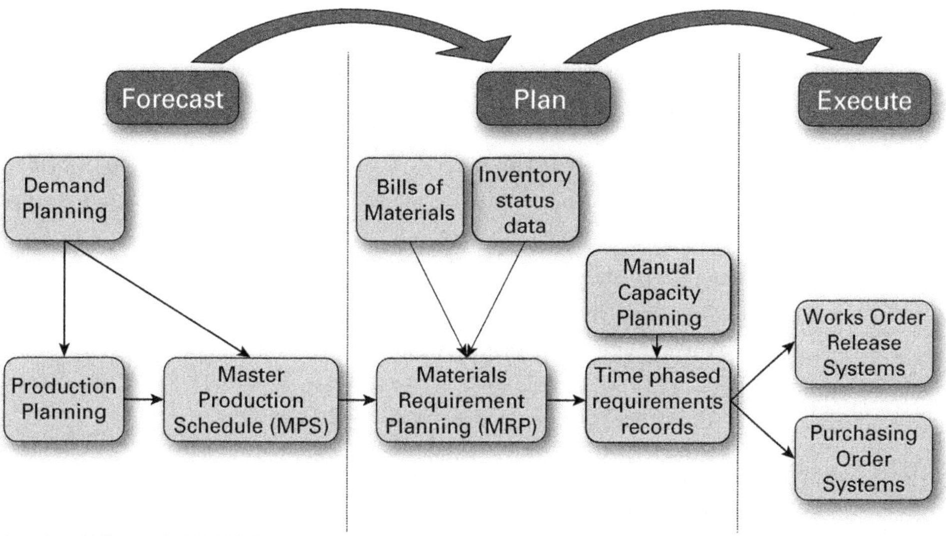

Based on Vollman *et al* (2005:8)

FIGURE 2.8   Basic MRPII (Manufacturing Resource Planning) configuration

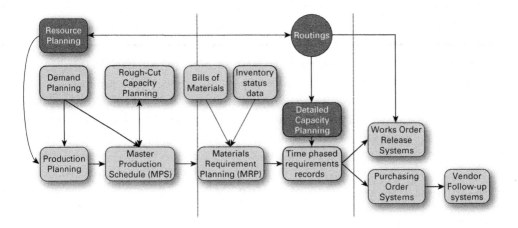

Enterprise resource planning (ERP)

Enterprise resource planning (ERP) systems integrate all functions within a company, as already shown in Figure 2.8. The planning and purchasing engine sits at the heart of the ERP system in the manufacturing industry. The large size and complexity of ERP means that it can be offered and installed as different modules. Figure 2.9 shows the how the basic MRPI and MRPII has been extended to cover all the business functions, such as Finance, Quality and Engineering for an all-encompassing ERP configuration.

Forecast: the first step in the process flow

An organization needs to know or to estimate the future demand of its products or services. This information is then used to create an action plan for the work that will be needed to meet that predicted or known future demand, and in accordance with its own strategy and vision.

The first step in the process flow is labelled 'forecast'. In this we include all the work carried out by an organization to estimate future demand and to identify the capacity and resources needed to meet this demand.

Sales and operations planning (S&OP)

S&OP is a part of medium- to long-term planning and is carried out at a tactical level. It combines predicted sales with an understanding of the ability to achieve those sales.

FIGURE 2.9   Basic Enterprise Resource Planning (ERP) configuration

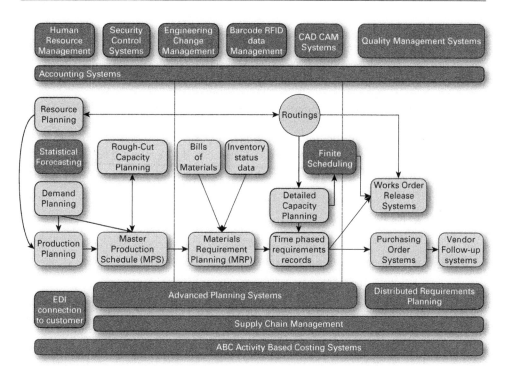

APICS defines S&OP as:

> a process to develop tactical plans that provide management the ability
> to strategically direct its businesses to achieve competitive advantage on a
> continuous basis by integrating customer-focused marketing plans for new and
> existing products with the management of the supply chain.

ERP assists the S&OP operation greatly because of the shared current and
historical data, as well as a clear indication of the production and operational
capability to achieve the future demand. The process of agreeing the predicted
demand through the sales and operations planning (S&OP) review is a wide-
ranging task and needs to include the following parts of an organization:

- sales and marketing;
- production;
- operations, including:
  - order processing and customer service;
  - purchasing;

   – production planning; and

   – logistics and warehousing.

Depending on the issues raised, there may need to be input from:

- finance and cash flow;
- human resources; and
- product design, engineering and R&D.

It is essential for sales and marketing to work closely together with operations and production to combine knowledge to make best use of resources and at the least operating cost. To produce the best S&OP good communication is essential to identify:

- best estimates and plans for medium and long horizon sales predictions;
- understanding what level of sales are needed by the organization;
- calculating whether the existing production capacity is sufficient; and
- identifying where the skills of the current employees may need additional training or lead to new hires.

Figure 2.10 shows the linkage of the S&OP process to the company vision and the different levels of the predicted future demand, working through the strategic, tactical and operational levels and thereby across the different time scales and horizons.

Sometimes, however, predictions of future demand can be wildly incorrect. Tom Watson, while IBM chairman in 1958, is famously alleged to have said: 'I think there is a world market for about five computers.' Whether this quote is accurate or not it goes to show that there are frequently big changes in the environment, product development and the marketplace which are hard to predict. It is important to ensure that the S&OP process delivers a single agreed plan that is linked to the company vision as shown in Figure 2.10. The 'single' plan is important since MRP needs to be given a forecasted demand that it can plan materials against. If the plan is too optimistic then the sales will not consume the production, and if it is too pessimistic then the production will fall short of the customer demand leading to lost opportunities. This balance is extremely difficult to achieve and will have a significant impact on the inventory held by the business.

On a tactical level and in the medium to long term the sales and operations planning (S&OP) will identify what the likely demand levels will be

FIGURE 2.10 Linking the company vision to the operational plan

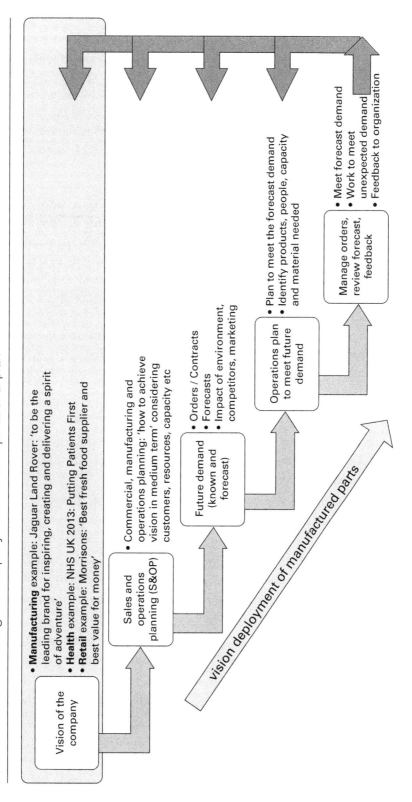

and how to meet that demand. This will take into account production capacity, inventory management, outsourcing efficiencies, purchasing options etc, but not, at this stage, at a high level of detail.

In summary, S&OP brings the different demand forecasts together, reconciling the difference between the demand forecast and the manufacturing plan in a business planning process meeting. The MPS is the result of the S&OP process and is critical to the management of ERP/MRP systems.

Forecasting unknown future demand

For some industries there may be partly or fully known future demand. For the rest the only way of reliably predicting the future demand is to use forecasting tools. Forecasting tools assist in predicting future demand, which it recognizes is unknown. Forecast will invariably be 'wrong' so it is important to manage the process with the correct expectation and building in protections, and check and balances to minimize the effects when inevitably the forecast is not realized.

Forecasts need to consider both quantitative information (ie statistical forecast based on past sales) and qualitative information.

Quantitative forecasts:

- Produced by many systems, single exponential smoothing is the most common.

- Forecasting systems will often calculate several possible forecasts, compare them against historical sales and produce a 'best fit' forecast.

- Seasonality is included: some products sell more in summer (eg garden products, bottled water, ice cream), and others in winter (eg chocolates and turkeys around Christmas time).

- Trend is calculated: have sales increased or decreased over time? Measuring forecast inaccuracy is essential since the amount and direction of error should be used to assist in inventory management. Common measurements include:

  - Forecast error: how inaccurate is the forecast? Often used are both a rolling percentage over a number of weeks and the error of the most recent week are used.

  - Forecast bias: is the forecast significantly above or below the actual sales?

  - Exception measurement: the system should alert the planners when the forecast measures go outside agreed acceptance limits.

Qualitative forecasts which are not usually generated by the system since they relate to external influencers:

- Marketing plans: identifying and communicating marketing plans to the rest of the organization. It is important to understand how these marketing plans will affect demand. For example:
  - which items are to be promoted;
  - what additional advertising is planned;
  - any specific markets or prospective clients being targeted;
  - the resulting increase in demand is to be expected.

- Market intelligence: knowledge the organization has about external influences on the market and expected demand. This will include understanding the activity and plans of the competition.

- External environment: risks and opportunities that might arise from changes in the external environment should be considered and analysed. For example, changes in the climate/weather happening unexpectedly may cause challenges in demand and supply (eg excessive, unexpected and perhaps prolonged heat/cold; tsunami; hurricanes or tornadoes). Other problems or opportunities may be caused by legislation changes or health concerns.

Master production scheduling

The MPS is developed at a tactical level, and shows what products should be produced, in what quantity and by when. Calculating the MPS is a key activity within the S&OP process since it confirms (or otherwise) that the sales plan can be met by production. Strategically it will consider high-level production plans. A long horizon plan will be developed for:

- production, and the people, components and materials needed to achieve that production;
- cost predictions: production costs, inventory costs, etc;
- meeting the identified future sales at minimum cost;
- an agreed length of time; and
- at an aggregate level.

The MPS can be tested for validity by using Rough Cut Capacity Planning (RCCP) which will examine at an aggregate level the key capacities, ie machines and people in critical manufacturing processes.

Plan: the second step in the process flow

The first of the three steps in the process flow – forecast – has already been considered. In this section we will consider the second step – planning – and look at the following:

- planning the supply/demand relationship;
- the master production schedule: using the MPS to drive the MRP planning;
- bills of materials; and
- parameters.

Planning for a balanced supply/demand relationship

There are three key supply/demand relationships, each of which results in a different inventory management process:

- Supply can follow demand variation, resulting in a need to only hold minimum inventory.
- Supply cannot match demand at peak periods (eg products with seasonal variation). This results in the need to manage inventory build-up before the season starts and reduction after the season (for example, garden products for which there is a far greater demand in the spring and early summer).
- Supply is constrained and cannot meet demand, resulting in the need to manage both demand and inventory (for example, when a highly popular new smartphone is first released).

It is essential to identify the correct inventory management processes for each type of product. A business may have all the different supply/demand relationships within a business. It is necessary to understand the forecast and orders for each item or group of items to develop a picture of the relevant inventory management process.

The situation shown in Figure 2.11 exists in many types of standard batch manufacture where there is little variation in supply or demand. This relationship means that it is possible to operate with minimal inventory, keeping inventory management costs to a minimum. The forecast will be stable and orders should be automated, with appropriate alerts set in case the situation changes unexpectedly.

This situation can be managed well with MRP without significant consideration to capacity. The orders/forecast can be used to drive the demand within the MRP process.

FIGURE 2.11   Supply matches demand: MRP

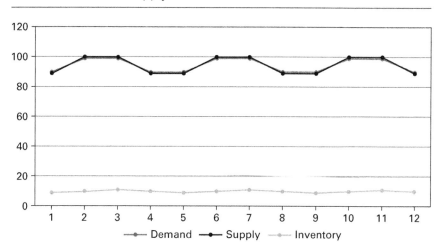

The situation in Figure 2.12 exists where there is a seasonal/cyclic element to the demand for the product. Where this exists the maximum production capacity is below that required to satisfy the peak demand. The situation is managed by building up the inventory held before the period of peak demand. This relationship means that it is necessary to operate with more inventory, resulting in higher inventory management costs, than in Figure 2.11 where supply matches demand. The forecast will be volatile and can be affected by the weather. The management of the forecasted demand becomes critical, for example when the weather is a certain temperature above or below the

FIGURE 2.12   Demand periodically > Supply needs balancing: MPS

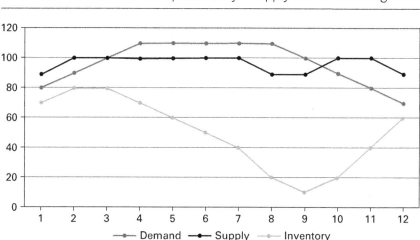

seasonal average, it will need to be carefully managed. By the end of the peak demand period there needs to be a careful management of the reduction in inventory in preparation for the low season.

This situation needs an MPS-based inventory plan.

An example of this type of supply/demand relationship is sales of bottled water. Sales are higher in the summer and lower in the winter. Bottled water supplies are increased in the spring anticipating higher sales in the summer. When summer temperatures are hotter than usual, more water is sold, but if it is a cool summer then sales of fizzy drinks eats into the bottled water market.

The situation shown in Figure 2.13 exists where there is either a fixed supply which is lower than demand (eg from a steel furnace), or where there is a much higher ongoing demand than the supply is able to meet and there is no alternative supply (eg new technology products). Production departments will ideally want to run the business on a level schedule to increase the efficiency of the manufacturing operations; there is always a risk that if this focus prevails that while the manufacturing operations are seen to be efficient, the inventory may be driven up as a consequence.

Where the product is a commodity then price can be used as a lever to dampen or stimulate demand. Price of the product to the customer may also be increased if it is a seller's market, which in turn can drive demand up further. It is common in the technology industries to use market allocation, particularly when new products are released. The MPS schedule is the key tool in helping the S&OP process determine the appropriate responses.

FIGURE 2.13 Supply controls demand: allocation

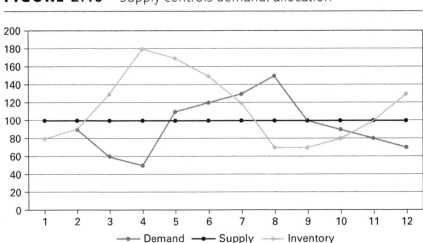

FIGURE 2.14 Simple supply/demand exercise

Period	1	2	3	4	5	6	7	8
Forecast Demand	20	30	25	25	30	20	25	30
Supply/Delivery	25							
Projected Inventory Initial stock on hand = 15	20							

When forecasting these products is important to understand if the high demand will continue or even increase as the variation of capacity is very difficult.

Supply/demand/inventory mechanism

When preparing for an S&OP review it is possible, given that we know our capacity, to create a supply/demand/inventory projection. The scenarios described above can be modelled to support the decision-making process. The example in Figure 2.14 is a simple supply/demand example, where there is a fixed supply situation whereby 25 units are delivered every week.

If supply is fixed at 25 units per period and stock on hand at the beginning of period 1 is 15 units, what is the projected inventory (PI) at the end of period 8?

The first step is to understand what is happening in period 1:

Period 1: stock on hand is 15 items at the beginning of the period. Since demand is forecast at 20 units, and there will be a delivery of 25 units, the projected closing inventory in the period will be (+15–20+25) = 20

Following the same logic, as shown in Figure 2.15:

Period 2: projected stock on hand is 20 items at the beginning of the period. Since demand is forecast at 30 units, and there will be a delivery of 25 units, the projected closing inventory in the period will be (+20–30+25) = 15

Period 3: projected stock on hand is 15 items at the beginning of the period. Since demand is forecast at 25 units, and there will be a delivery of 25 units, the projected closing inventory in the period will be (+15–25+25) = 15

Period 4: projected stock on hand is 15 items at the beginning of the period. Since demand is forecast at 25 units, and there will be a delivery of 25 units, the projected closing inventory in the period will be (+15–25+25) = 15

FIGURE 2.15 Simple supply/demand exercise: step 2

Period	1	2	3	4	5	6	7	8
Forecast Demand	20	30	25	25	30	20	25	30
Supply/Delivery	25	25	25	25	25	25	25	25
Projected Inventory Initial stock on hand = 15	20	15	15	15				

Using this logic it is possible to calculate the projected inventory at the end of period 8. (Answer is given at the end of this chapter.)

This is a simple example of the calculations carried out within MRP on the thousands – often tens of thousands, sometimes hundreds of thousands – of parts planned and managed within the system. It is useful to understand the basic logic used within the system.

The master production schedule (MPS)

The MPS shows what products should be produced, in what quantity and by when. Calculating the MPS has already been considered in the discussion of the S&OP.

The MPS is translated by MRP into 'time phased net requirements and orders for each component needed to implement this schedule. MRP replans net requirements and coverage for changes in MPS, design, processing or inventory status' (Plossl, 1994).

Dependent and independent demand

Most businesses have products that have independent demand as well as components that have dependent demand. These are defined by Slack (Slack *et al*, 2010) as follows:

> Dependent demand – demand that is relatively predictable because it is derived from some other known factor.

> Independent demand – demand that is not obviously or directly dependent on demand of other products or services.

An airplane is an example of independent demand, and the parts that go into the building of the aircraft are mainly dependent demand. Thus it is known that for every airplane sold, there will be dependent demand for wings (see Figure 2.17). There will be some parts that will have both dependent

FIGURE 2.16 Treating demand differently with independent demand at decoupling points

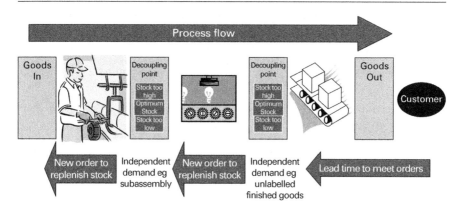

FIGURE 2.17 Simplistic representation of the first level of a BOM for an aeroplane

1 overwing 2 engines wheels & tires tail fin fuselage

Reproduced by kind permission of Ian Young, Madhouse Designs

and independent demand. For example, an aircraft will be produced with one or more engines and during production these are identified as dependent demand. However, if an airplane is in service and new tires need to be fitted, at this point the demand for the tires on the airplane will be independent demand.

The management of the dependent and independent demand in MRP

The use of MRP planning systems is critically dependent on a known or forecast future demand. Customer orders and sales forecasts allow us to be able to use MRP logic to manage independent demand for these finished goods. MRP then calculates the requirements for the components and subassemblies needed to produce these finished goods, ie the dependent demand.

Demand-driven MRP (DDMRP) considers independent and dependent demand differently. DDMRP is a revision to traditional MRP and is discussed in the recent update of Orlicky's MRP book (originally published in 1975 and updated by Ptak and Smith (2011)). The key elements of DDMRP in Figure 2.16 show decoupling points where traditional dependent demand becomes independent demand. In a simplistic way it operates similarly to Kanban with individual plans at intermediate levels in a simplified way, and has these steps:

- Initially forecasts are used to plan at an aggregate level.
- Decoupling points are then identified in the production process, and stock holding levels at these intermediate points calculated.
- A buffer is then built at the decoupling point, often an inventory buffer.
- Customer orders are fulfilled in a short lead-time, for example from a complete-to-order stock-on-hand (eg final labelling and packing) to shipping.
- When the stock at this part of the process falls to a specified level, demand is then passed back along the process using a Kanban style message, to replenish this stock.
- This build order then initiates production in the preceding step of the process.
- At each decoupling point the need to replenish the stock holding is treated as independent demand. One consequence of this is that the buffer gives some protection from possible forecast volatility to the earlier stages of the process.

This process builds on Eli Goldratt's 'Theory of Constraints', Lean theory and JIT, and MRP. Although the stock held at the different decoupling points is considered to have independent demand, there will be a known relationship between the various levels.

Bill of materials

The *bill of materials* (BOM) is the list of items required to manufacture or assemble a product or to deliver a service. A BOM for an airplane will have many levels in it – the first level of the BOM will be the major structure subassemblies: in Figure 2.18 these major sub-assemblies at the first BOM level are shown as a fuselage, tail fin, engines and wings. As mentioned previously, these assemblies are part of the dependent demand, with the airplane itself being the independent demand.

The shape or type of the BOM varies for different industries: an aircraft manufacturer has a very different type of BOM (one product, subassemblies, numerous components) from a company making plastic items for use in the garden (eg nozzles to go on garden hoses for watering the garden) where there are very few raw materials used but these are converted into a wide range of end products. In the petrochemical industry the BOM is sometimes referred to as a recipe: much as when baking a cake, in petro chemicals the ingredients are offered up to different heat treatment and chemical processes.

The type of BOM has an important impact on operations management, something that is frequently underestimated in organizations.

BOMs and part numbering

We will explore the BOM for a simple product – the snow shovel as shown in Figure 2.18. It has five parts at the first level down of the BOM, as clearly shown in Figure 2.19, with a further four parts at the next level down, and three at the third level.

FIGURE 2.18 A snow shovel

Every separate assembly, subassembly, component and raw material in the bill of material must have a part number to uniquely identify it. The product may be as a result of an assembly process, ie fitting the aluminum edge to the scoop, or as a result of a manufacturing process, ie cutting a tube to length

FIGURE 2.19   Bill of Materials for Shovel for N123456

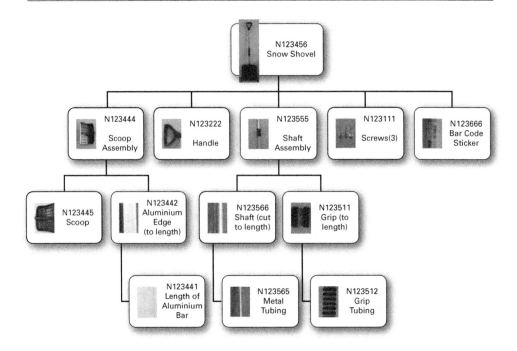

to make the shaft. Part numbering methods vary, occasionally being creatively generated by an organization. The most well-known examples are:

- GS1 – Global standards for barcodes.
- NATO Stock Numbers (NSN) Military Coding System.
- Library (ISBN) National and International Coding for Books/Maps.

Part numbers are also known as stock keeping units (SKUs), item or product or stock or article numbers. These are usually a computer generated random or sequentially allocated number, useful in inventory management as well as being usable for bar codes and radio frequency identification (RFID) tags.

In increasingly rare cases, the part numbers contain a form of description in its number sequence, known as the British System of Component Classification.

Listing parts within the bill of materials structures

Once all parts are numbered they need to be applied to the bill of material structure. Figure 2.19 is a useful visual depiction but not so useful within an ERP planning system. The parts could be listed simply as in Table 2.2:

TABLE 2.2   Snow shovel BOM as a simple parts list

- N123456 Snow Shovel
- N123444 Scoop Assembly
- N123445 Scoop
- N123442 Aluminium Edge (cut to length)
- N123441 Length of Aluminium Bar
- N123222 Handle
- N123555 Shaft Assembly
- N123566 Shaft (cut to length)
- N123565 Metal Tubing
- N123511 Grip (cut to length)
- N123512 Grip Tubing
- N123111 Screws (x3)
- N123666 Bar Code Sticker

Reproduced by kind permission of Inventory Matters Ltd

unfortunately this wouldn't demonstrate how the product should be assembled, since there is no differentiation between the assemblies, subassemblies, components, etc and no clear indication of the relationship between the parts.

It is more useful to use an indented BOM. Each level one is shown with one indentation, each level two with two indentations etc. The groupings of the parts show how the different parts gradually go together to assemble the snow shovel. The number of indentations levels demonstrates the complexity of production, and the BOM determining the material requirement.

Parameters: What they are and how they affect the way MRPII works

These sub-sections only identify the types of parameters that are used in an MRPII system: the calculations will be looked at in Chapter 4.

Figure 2.20 shows the standardized inventory saw tooth diagram. This shows a simplistic inventory plan of how stock levels vary over time. The minimum and maximum stock levels are given and the replenishment or cycle stock (ie the stock that is brought in to meet expected demand, which

TABLE 2.3   Indented BOM for snow shovel

- N123456 Snow Shovel
  - N123444 Scoop Assembly
    - N123445 Scoop
      - N123442 Aluminium Edge (cut to length)
        - N123441 Length of Aluminium Bar
    - N123222 Handle
  - N123555 Shaft Assembly
    - N123566 Shaft (cut to length)
      - N123565 Metal Tubing
    - M123511 Grip (cut to length)
      - N123512 Grip Tubing
  - N123111 Screws (x 3)
  - N123666 Bar Code Sticker

Reproduced by kind permission of Inventory Matters Ltd

FIGURE 2.20   The standardized inventory saw tooth diagram for MRP logic

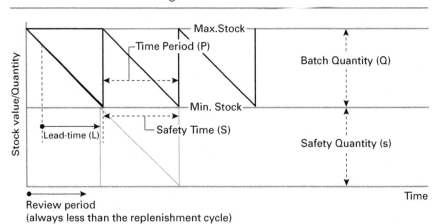

is then consumed over time, until a new delivery is received to replenish the stock levels again) is planned to move between these two values. Safety stock sits underneath the minimum stock level, guarding against unexpected changes in supply or demand.

Figure 2.20 shows pictorially a number of the parameters which need to be managed to enable MRPII to calculate the correct recommendations and create an accurate transaction. The key parameters are:

- cycle stock;
  - fixed order quantities;
    minimum order quantity (MOQ);
    multiple order quantity (Multi);
    economic order quantity (EOQ);
    maximum order quantity (Max);
  - period order;
    order period days (OP);
- safety stock;
  - safety quantity (SSQ);
  - safety time (ST);
- lead-time: total lead time is the sum of:
  - manufacturing lead-time (MLT);
  - purchase order lead-time (PLT);
  - order administration time (AOT);
  - inspection/good-in lead-time (GI);
- yield: whether there is an expected reduction in acceptable product output/delivery.

This shows the large number of parameters to be managed for each product. Good business practices are essential for ensuring the parameters are well managed and kept up to date. Without these the system will start to 'silt-up' and the planning engine will lose its effectiveness. Although BOMs are not parameters, it is imperative that these are also carefully managed and kept up to date.

MRP management and maintenance

Measurements, system produced alerts and business reporting help instill and maintain good quality ERP operations. Measurements should include both the desired outcomes as well as the quality of the MRP process.

Typically, outcome measurements would include:

- on-time delivery to customer order;
- on-time delivery from supplier orders;
- on-time delivery from works orders; and
- number of parts rejected.

The measures that are less frequently reported are those that measure the process quality, for example:

- number of short lead-time orders;
- number of orders modified by the planner/buyer (non-compliance).

The non-compliance measure is a very useful indicator of the health of the system and how well the data and parameters are being managed. If all the data in the system is correct and all the parameters are maintained, the works orders and purchase orders the system produces should be correct. If the person with responsibility for these products makes a change to the system-generated order this is referred to as *non-compliance*. Figure 2.21 shows the compliance/non-compliance process in operation.

When non-compliance happens there are two actions that are needed (as shown in Figure 2.21): one is to correct and place the order; the second is to identify why the system raised an incorrect order, and correct the cause

FIGURE 2.21   Compliance MRP quality process

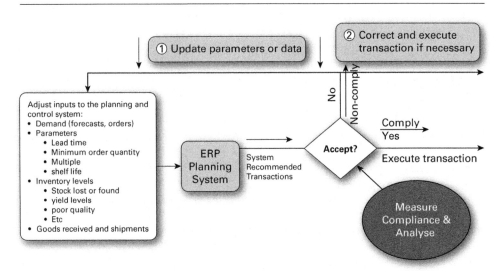

(ie change parameter settings, ensure the data inaccuracy is corrected). It is the second step that is harder to complete, especially with the pressures of daily work, but is essential nonetheless since the aim is for the system to produce the correct order the next time around. Typical causes for non-compliance include:

- unable to meet recommended date;
- bill of material errors;
- statistical group error;
- stock errors;
- order errors;
- forecast errors; and
- batch size incorrect/inappropriate.

Very few organizations measure the non-compliance; the planner will always complete first action to correct, but rarely have time to complete the second.

Execute: the third step

After the planning stage, MRP is 'run' and the next stage executed (eg manufacture, purchase, etc). The complications and examples of doing this, and trying to achieve this in as close to real time as possible are considered in the next chapter in detail.

ERP implementation and management

ERP implementations were a significant activity in business in the late 1990s and the first decade of the 21st century. There are a number of well-documented analyses of failures in ERP implementations which have identified the key critical success factors (see Table 2.4). It is helpful to learn from previous failures in implementations, and to consider where key implementation decisions later hampered the smooth working of the operations process.

It is even more useful to know how to implement ERP correctly. To this end we will briefly consider the Oliver Wight ERP implementation and management guide.

TABLE 2.4 Analysis of critical success factors for implementing ERP

Critical Success Factor	References cited in support of CSF	
Top management support	Anderson *et al* (1981) Wilson *et al* (1990) Callerman *et al* (1986)	Al-Mashari *et al* (2003) Umble *et al* (2003) Zhang *et al* (2002) ElSayed *et al* (2013)
Business plan and vision		Loh and Koh (2004) Schwalbe (2000) Somers and Nelson (2004) Nah (2003)
Re-engineering business process		Davison (2002) Hammer and Champy (2001) Somers and Nelson (2004) Nah (2003) Murray and Coffin (2001)
MRP requires a new way of managing	Anderson *et al* (1981) Burns and Turnispeed (1988) Wilson *et al* (1990) Cox and Clark (1984)	ElSayed *et al* (2013)
Effective project management and project champion	Anderson *et al* (1981) Burns and Turnispeed (1988) Cox and Clark (1984) Wilson *et al* (1990)	Zhang *et al* (2002) Somers and Nelson (2004) Remus (2006) Loh and Koh (2004) ElSayed, *et al* (2013)
Teamwork and composition		Loh and Koh (2004) Al-Mashari *et al* (2006) Remus (2006) Nah (2003) Rosario (2000)
MRP requires a strong commitment to the computer resource and data accuracy	Anderson *et al* (1981) Burns and Turnispeed (1988) Cox and Clark (1984) Wilson *et al* (1990) Ang *et al* (1984)	
ERP system selection		Wei and Wang (2004) Shehab *et al* (2004) Everdingen *et al* (2000) Sprott (2000)

TABLE 2.4 *continued*

Critical Success Factor	References cited in support of CSF	
User involvement		Esteves *et al* (2003) Zhang *et al* (2002)
Education and training	Callerman *et al* (1986) Cerveny and Scott (1989) Cox and Clark (1984) Wilson *et al* (1990) Ang *et al* (1984)	Woo (2007) Nah *et al* (2003) Zhang *et al* (2002) ElSayed *et al* (2013)

Reproduced by kind permission of WMG.

Oliver Wight was instrumental in the development of MRPII in the 1980s. He continued to work implementing MRPII and later ERP, moving from IBM in 1969 to set up his own company Oliver Wight International Inc. He created two key approaches which are still used today:

- The implementation process guide, called: 'The Proven Path.'
- An ERP management and ongoing maintenance guide called: 'ABCD Checklist.'

'Proven Path' for ERP implementation

This is a brief summary of the 'Proven Path' described by Landvater (1997: 245–281).

Phase 1: Build the case

This phase concerns the establishment and documentation of the business case for implementation. Among other aspects, it will be key to involve and educate the executive and operating management, to have a clear vision statement which is shared with the whole organization, and to understand the time that will be needed for the implementation and what additional capabilities are needed within the enterprise.

Phase 2: Engage the company

Phase 2 is project organization. A strong, full-time project leader will be needed, together with a project team and a project plan. These changes must be driven from the top of the organization and engage employees at every level to achieve buy-in.

FIGURE 2.22   Simplified diagram based on Landvater proven path

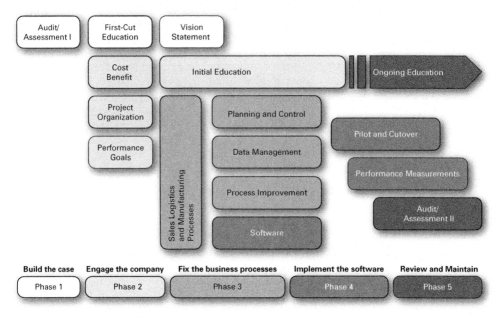

Adapted from Landvater (1997)

Phase 3: Fix the business processes

An existing company will have an existing business process, whether it is written down or not. Business process analysis of the 'as-is' (ie current process) and a clear, detailed objective of the 'to-be' business process (ie what the company feels is the best new process after the system implementation) is essential. As Wilson stated:

> Technology applied to a poor business process will only result in the automation and embedding of inefficiencies which lead to the technology trap. It is essential that processes are improved to remove non value adding activities and any process breakages before technology is applied. (Wilson, 2003)

Fixing the business process in advance of the ERP implementation is essential and has four simple steps:

- Definition of the 'as is' process.
- Development of the 'to-be' process.
- Consensus for the 'to-be' process.
- Creation of the implementation plan, including a detailed plan for the management of the data transfer/creation in the new system including both: unforgiving data (must be right), eg BOMs, routings,

inventory, receipts; and forgiving data (should be right), eg forecasts, item master, parameters.

Phase 4: Implement the software

Phase 4 is the selection and implementation of the software. Once the system is selected and phases 1–3 completed, key steps involved in phase 4 include:

- Test environment, test and resolution process.
- Pilot identified for initial cut-over – there may also be a module by module phased implementation.
- Training materials identified and training carried out.
- Clearly identified implementation and process measurements, including the achievement of the original business case and vision for the new system.

Phase 5: Review and maintain

Implementing a new business process and an ERP system in larger companies can take several years. Once complete, the organization should audit the system and process to assess what has been achieved, including whether the initial business case for implementation is complete. This will identify what may still be left to do, and what has been learnt, including:

- One of the important factors is to ensure that the company and the people operating the system are in control of the system.
- A rolling education programme is needed for new employees and to refresh existing users.
- A review of the business, the system and the processes should be carried out routinely to ensure that the ERP system and the processes being carried out are still suitable for the business.
- Ongoing maintenance is essential. Processes and systems need to be maintained to prevent them from clogging up and thus losing effectiveness.
- Parameters must be kept up-to-date (eg cycle stock, safety stock, bills of materials). This should be carried out at a routine review of key parameters, process measurements and system management to ensure the system continues to operate correctly.

Key learning points of the Proven Path

ERP implementations are continuing in small, medium and large organizations. The Oliver Wight 'Proven Path' implementation process is just one method that can be followed. There is a huge amount of disruption that can be caused to a business by a bad ERP implementation although with so many examples of 'what not to do' these problems should be minimized with new implementations.

ERP management and maintenance

Once an ERP implementation is up and running, a company will begin the improvement of the system and the business processes. It is important for a company to know how well it is performing initially, and to identify what the 'best practice' is that it would like to get to (for example, in operations management), and how to get there.

'ABCD Checklist': a guide to achieving business excellence

One method of achieving business excellence, with the assistance of the newly implemented ERP system, is the use of the Oliver Wight 'ABCD Checklist'. The aim of using the checklist is to identify what level (A, B, C or D) the company is at, and how to progress to being an Class A company.

Achieving business excellence as a Class 'A' Company

One benefit of using the Oliver Wight Class A Checklist (Oliver Wight International Inc, 2010) is that it provides a clear checklist. This is intended to be used by a company to consider how well they are performing and how to progress to the next level, and their ongoing journey to excellence. Measures to be considered include the following high-level areas (as taken from the Oliver Wight Class A Checklist (Oliver Wight International Inc, 2010)):

- managing the strategic planning process;
- managing and leading people;
- driving business improvement;
- integrated business planning;
- managing products and services;
- managing internal supply; and
- managing external sourcing.

Some key areas in the checklist to help achieve best practice for operations management include:

- *Dedication*: a computer system is a tool that can assist with but not independently solve a company's problems. MRPII is simple in concept but its performance can be affected by many people in the organization (for example, the sales team will help to forecast demand, management must help determine the policy decisions, the warehouse operators are responsible for the inventory record accuracy etc). Inventory sits at the core of the MRP and all functions have a responsibility to ensure their part is played. MRPII therefore requires a great amount of support and understanding throughout the company.

- *Understanding*: many people have an input to make to the system. It is essential they know the importance of their input and understand the consequences if they get it wrong. For example, during assembly a component may be found to be faulty and another one not immediately allocated. If the assembly operator takes the component required from another kit or from stores, but doesn't record this transaction on the system, the immediate problem is resolved but the computer records are now incorrect. A shortage of the component will occur in the future unless the error is rectified.

- *Realistic production/maintenance schedules*: if the available capacity in a factory is incorrectly identified (in respect to both people and machines) the production schedule will either be impossible to achieve (resulting in high levels of work in progress and planned customer orders delivered late) or too easy to achieve (meaning that there is a danger of underutilizing capacity, and possibly spending money unnecessarily on outsourcing production that could have actually been carried out in-house).

- *Accurate bills of material*: **the** bill of materials sits at the centre of the planning engine. If the BOM is incorrect materials that are needed may be ignored, and material that is not needed may continue to be bought even when there are large stocks of it. BOMs are frequently subject to high levels of change (eg product specification may be changed). In many complex products, the volume of data can be enormous and difficult to maintain.

- *Accurate and timely data recording* – data accuracy is essential. The planning results and orders raised will be the result of the system calculating the needs of the business, based on the data recorded in the system. The well-known saying of 'garbage in means garbage out' applies here.

The implementation and ongoing management and improvement of an ERP system is no easy task. It is a costly undertaking which does not directly add value to the products offered to customers. However, most large companies need a system to record their data and assist with planning (where huge numbers of calculations are needed), and would not be able to operate without it. For those companies who are the leading users of ERP systems there are many benefits according to the Aberdeen Group (Jutras, 2010):

- 22% reduction in inventory
- 97% inventory accuracy
- 96% manufacturing schedule compliance
- 98% on time delivery

Additional benefits were shown in the same report, based on a survey (Jutras, 2010: 6), that best-in-class firms were:

- 111 per cent more likely to be able to quantify the business benefits [what gets measured gets done];
- best in class used take advantage of 39 per cent more ERP functionality (use it or lose it); and
- the top 20 per cent [of best-in-class users] in terms of aggregate performance scores also enjoy an 83 per cent advantage in full visibility to their business.

Summary

This chapter has considered how inventory doesn't exist separately from a business but is integral to the whole organization. We have considered how inventory management and business systems exist within the wider context of the business itself, and how essential it is to the health of the company that they are both well implemented and well maintained. The way that the planning process works in ERP and MRP was looked at in some detail from considering the role of the S&OP process, together with the importance of parameter setting, BOMs, and the maintenance of the supply and demand relationships that will enable the systems to work efficiently and effectively. And finally, the use of non-compliance as a key measurement of the health of the system was discussed. These are intended to provide a good foundation to understand the complexities of inventory management in business systems in the following chapters.

Answer to the supply/demand balancing exercise

The answer is that there is a projected inventory of 10 items at the end of period 8.

FIGURE 2.23　Answer to the supply/demand balancing exercise

Period	1	2	3	4	5	6	7	8
Forecast Demand	20	30	25	25	30	20	25	30
Supply/Delivery	25	25	25	25	25	25	25	25
Projected Inventory Initial stock on hand = 15	20	15	15	15	10	15	15	10

Period 5: projected stock on hand is 15 items at the beginning of the period. Since demand is forecast at 30 units, and there will be a delivery of 25 units, the projected closing inventory in the period will be (+15–30+25) = 10

Period 6: projected stock on hand is 10 items at the beginning of the period. Since demand is forecast at 20 units, and there will be a delivery of 25 units, the projected closing inventory in the period will be (+10–20+25) = 15

Period 7: projected stock on hand is 15 items at the beginning of the period. Since demand is forecast at 25 units, and there will be a delivery of 25 units, the projected closing inventory in the period will be (+15–25+25) = 15

Period 8: projected stock on hand is 15 items at the beginning of the period. Since demand is forecast at 30 units, and there will be a delivery of 25 units, the projected closing inventory in the period will be (+15–30+25) = 10

Notes

Al-Fawaz, K, Al Salti, Z and Eldabi, T (2008) *Critical Success factors in ERP implementation: a review*, BURA, Dubai

Anderson, J C, Schroder, R G, Tupy, S E and White, E M (1981) *Materials Requirements Planning: A study of implementation and practice*, APICS

Ang, J S, Sum, C C and Yang, K K (1984) MRPII company profile and implementation problems: A Singapore experience, *International Journal of Production and Economics*, **34**, pp 35–45

APICS (2014, October) APICS. Retrieved October 2014 from www.apics.org: www.apics.org/dictionary/dictionary-information?ID=1414.0

APICS (nd) APICS Definitions. Retrieved September 2013 from www.apics.org/dictionary/dictionary-information?ID=1294

Burns, O M and Turnispeed, D (1988) Critical success factors in manufacturing resource planning implementation, *International Journal of Operations and Production Management*, **11**(4), pp 5–19

Cerveny, R P and Scott, L W (1989) A model for Materials Requirements Planning implementation, *International Journal of Operations and Production Management* (Third Quarter), pp 31–34

Chen, I J (2001) Planning for ERP systems: analysis and future trend, *Business Process Management Journal*, 7, 374.

Cox, J F and Clark, S J (1984) Problems in implementing and operating a manufacturing resource planning information system, *Journal of Management Information Systems*, 1, pp 81–101

Dell (2014) www.dell.com. Retrieved October 2014 from www.dell.com/learn/us/en/uscorp1/birth-of-company?c=us&l=en&s=corp&cs=uscorp1

ElSayed, M S, Hubbard, N J and Tipi, N S (2013) Evaluating Enterprise Resource Planning (ERP) post implementation problems in Egypt: findings from case studies of Governmental, Multinational and Private Egyptian organisations, Logistics Research Network

Harris, F W (1913) How many parts to make at once, *Factory, The Magazine of Management*, 10(2), 10, pp 135–36, 152

Hicks, D A and Stecke, K (1995) The ERP Maze. IIE Solutions (August), 12–16

Inc, S (nd) www.strategosinc.com/toyota_production.htm. Retrieved 2014 from www.strategosinc.com: www.strategosinc.com/toyota_production.htm

Jutras, C (2010) ERP in manufacturing 2010 – measuring business benefit and time to value, Aberdeen Group, Boston

Klassen, R D (2005) *Cases in Operations Management*, SAGE Publications, London

Landvater, D V (1997) *World Class Production and Inventory Management*, Wiley, New York

Ohno, T (1978) www.kellogg.northwestern.edu/course/opns430/modules/lean_operations/ohno-tps.pdf. Retrieved 2014 from www.kellogg.northwestern.edu/course/opns430/modules/lean_operations/ohno-tps.pdf

Oliver Wight International Inc (2010) *The Oliver Wight Class A Checklist for Business Excellence* (6th edn), Wiley

Plossl, G W (1994) *Orlicky's Material Requirements Planning*, McGraw-Hill Inc, New York

Ptak, C A and Smith, C J (2011) *Orlicky's Material Requirements Planning* (3rd edn). McGraw-Hill, New York

Ray, S A (2011, 24 March) The Downside of Just-in-Time Inventory, Retrieved October 2014 from www.businessweek.com: www.businessweek.com/magazine/content/11_14/b4222017701856.htm

retailindustry.about.com (2014) http://retailindustry.about.com/od/retailbestpractices/ig/Company-Mission-Statements/Amazon-com-Mission-Statement.htm.

Slack, N, Chambers, S and Johnston, R (2010) *Operations Management*, Financial Times/Prentice Hall, London

Thomas_J._Watson (nd) http://en.wikipedia.org/wiki/Thomas_J._Watson. Retrieved 2014 from http://en.wikipedia.org/wiki/Thomas_J._Watson

Vollmann, T, Berry, T, Whybark, D C and Jacobs, F R (2005) *Manufacturing Planning and Control for Supply Chain Management* (5th edn), McGraw Hill, Singapore

Wilson, F (2003) Walk don't run, *Manufacturing Engineer*, 2003 (June/July), 20–22

Wilson, F, Desmond, J and Roberts, H (1990) Success and failure of MRPII implementation, *British Journal of Management*, 5(1990), 221–40

www.strategicmanagementinsight.com (2014) www.strategicmanagementinsight.com/mission-statements/dell-mission-statement.html Retrieved October 2014 from www.strategicmanagementinsight.com/mission-statements/dell-mission-statement.html

www.toyota-global.com (2014) www.toyota-global.com. Retrieved October 2014 from www.toyota-global.com/company/vision_philosophy/toyota_global_vision_2020.html

Xitek (nd) www.xitek.co.uk/ Retrieved 2 November 2014

You do the maths

Supply planning

FIGURE 2.24

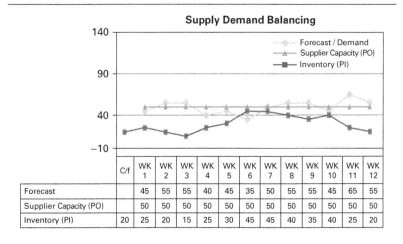

	C/f	WK 1	WK 2	WK 3	WK 4	WK 5	WK 6	WK 7	WK 8	WK 9	WK 10	WK 11	WK 12
Forecast		45	55	55	40	45	35	50	55	55	45	65	55
Supplier Capacity (PO)		50	50	50	50	50	50	50	50	50	50	50	50
Inventory (PI)	20	25	20	15	25	30	45	45	40	35	40	25	20

You are the planner for Snow Shovel and the demand is as shown in Figure 2.24. The forecast has now been refreshed and has increased by 30 units across the next 12 weeks. The supplier capacity is 50 units, however the supplier can increase/decrease capacity by a maximum of 10 per cent (ie by five units) if given four weeks' notice (ie from beginning of week 5). The stock position is 20 units available. The management requirement is to keep a minimum stock of 10 units available, however the stock should not exceed a maximum stock of 20 units. Where practical, the stock position must be the same at the end of the plan period.

TABLE 2.5   Worksheet 1

	wk 1	wk 2	wk 3	wk 4	wk 5	wk 6	wk 7	wk 8	wk 9	wk 10	wk 11	wk 12
	Month 1				**Month 2**				**Month 3**			
Forecast / Demand	50	60	50	45	55	60	50	60	50	55	45	50
Standard	50	50	50	50	50	50	50	50	50	50	50	50
10% Flexibility												
Supplier (PO)												
Inventory (PI)												

Your task is to re-plan the delivery schedule for the Snow Shovel based on the changed forecast, taking into account the change in the forecast. Determine the new delivery schedule needed to meet the new customer orders. What are the critical issues with the supply plan?

Hints:

- Minimize increased deliveries.

- Maintain stock level of 20 if possible.

- Calculate shortfalls and end period stock first.

Part 2

Time has moved on and we are now at the beginning of week 3. See Table 2.6. The forecast has been refreshed and has reduced by 15 units overall. The supplier's capacity is unchanged at 50 units and you can increase/decrease capacity by a maximum of 10 per cent given four weeks' notice. The stock is 10 units at the end of week 3. As before, a minimum stock of 10 units and maximum stock of 20 units must not be exceeded. The stock position must be same at the end of the plan period (20 units).

The second stage of the task is to recalculate the new delivery plan. You will need to consider any changes to the existing orders. Will the supplier accept the changes? What are the critical issues with the supply plan?

Hints:

- Minimize deliveries.

- Maintain stock level of 20 if possible.

- Calculate shortfalls and end period stock first.

TABLE 2.6   Worksheet 2

	Month 1		Month 2				Month 3				Month 4	
	wk 3	wk 4	wk 5	wk 6	wk 7	wk 8	wk 9	wk 10	wk 11	wk 12	wk 13	wk 14
Forecast / Demand	50	45	55	60	45	50	50	55	50	55	55	45
Standard	50	50	50	50	50	50	50	50	50	50	50	50
10% Flexibility (Figure 2.25)			5	5	5	5	5	5				
Supplier (PO)												
Inventory (PI)												

The key is the increase the supply as soon as possible (week 5) and only reduce when the stock is over 20 units.

Here the demand reduction needs to be accounted for by a supply reduction weeks 8 to 10, however there is an increase in the last two weeks to achieve the required end stock.

FIGURE 2.25

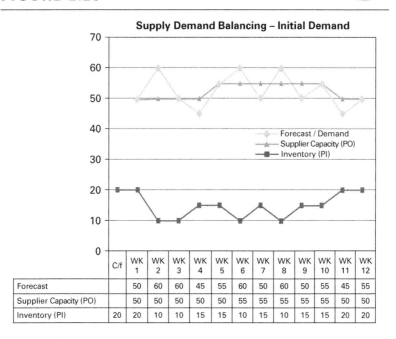

Supply Demand Balancing – Initial Demand

	C/f	WK 1	WK 2	WK 3	WK 4	WK 5	WK 6	WK 7	WK 8	WK 9	WK 10	WK 11	WK 12
Forecast		50	60	60	45	55	60	50	60	50	55	45	55
Supplier Capacity (PO)		50	50	50	50	50	55	55	55	55	55	50	50
Inventory (PI)	20	20	10	10	15	15	10	15	10	15	15	20	20

FIGURE 2.26

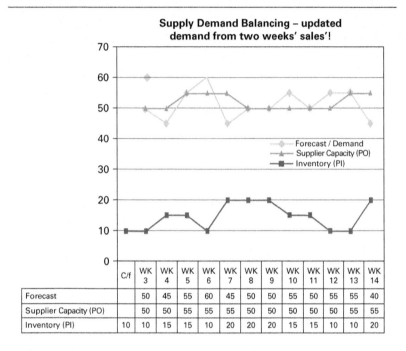

Supply Demand Balancing – updated demand from two weeks' sales'!

	C/f	WK 3	WK 4	WK 5	WK 6	WK 7	WK 8	WK 9	WK 10	WK 11	WK 12	WK 13	WK 14
Forecast		50	45	55	60	45	50	50	55	50	55	55	40
Supplier Capacity (PO)		50	50	55	55	55	50	50	50	50	50	55	55
Inventory (PI)	10	10	15	15	10	20	20	20	15	15	10	10	20

To think about

If you consider this planning approach, what would make this process easier, more automatic? As it stands, it relies too much on you thinking through the decision processes.

The complexity of inventory management within business systems

Introduction

Business systems, no matter how good, only manage inventory for a business according to the instructions given to them by people. The instructions given to the systems are based on the decisions of those managing the organization. This chapter looks at:

- complexity: how businesses regularly have to deal with hundreds of thousands of decisions to manage their inventory;
- results-driven inventory management;
- volumes of data to manage;
- how MRP calculates and executes this data;
- parameter management;
- KPIs, including compliance/non-compliance and exception management; and
- the cost of control.

We will start by looking at inventory planning at its simplest.

Inventory planning at its simplest

At its simplest, inventory management has four straightforward steps:

- Understand the current inventory position: how much stock do I have on hand?

- Identify the business targets for inventory: what inventory do I need?

- Create an inventory plan: what do I have to do to achieve the business targets and how difficult will it be?

- Implement the plan: what actions must I take to achieve the plan?

The simple stock record that Brown (1982) used to demonstrate the re-order process shown in Figure 3.1 is still in use in small businesses today, and forms the basis of simple accounting-based stock control systems. It starts from the same position as the four straightforward steps for inventory management: how much inventory do I have on hand? Figure 3.2 shows the flow of these four steps from this initial position.

Inventory management can be very straightforward in simple and usually very small organizations. And indeed when a simple inventory management

FIGURE 3.1   Simple stock record (Brown, 1982)

Transaction log

Source	J. B. BIGLEY 930 THIRD AVE. NYC 10020			Cost 3.07	Unit EACH	Package 200	
				Order up to 2800		Reorder point 2000	
Date	To/from reference	Compl date	Due date	Quantity IN	Quantity OUT	On Hand	Available stock
DEC 30, 78	Physical Inventory	12/30/78				2675	2675
JAN 3, 79	5-11279 JONES	1/3/79			600	2075	2075
JAN 4, 79	5- 11283 SMITH	1/4/79			319	1756	1756
JAN 5, 79	P-88357 BIGLEY	3/8/79	MAR	1000		1756	2756
FEB 11, 79	5-11306 HARRIS	2/11/79			350	1806	2406
FEB 13, 79	5-11511 JONES	2/18/79			350	1056	2056
MAR 8, 79	P-88357	3/8/79		1000		2056	2056
MAR 9, 79	5-11382 JACKSON	3/9/79			800	1656	1656
MAR 16, 79	P-88402 BIGLEY		MAY	1200		1656	2856
MAR 17, 79	5-11497 SMITH	3/17/79			373	1283	2483
Part No JCO61	Description WIDGET SPROCKETS					Buyer 20	Class A

FIGURE 3.2 Inventory management at its simplest

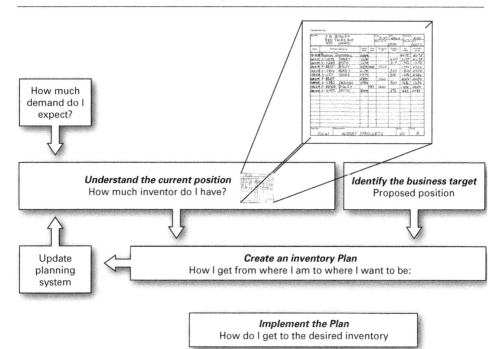

approach works, there is no need to overcomplicate the situation. However, in many organizations, and in the vast majority of manufacturing organizations, inventory will need careful management.

What is complexity?

Inventory decisions at strategic, tactical and operational levels

In Chapter 2 we looked at how organizations need to manage long-, medium- and short-term objectives and needs by operating at strategic, tactical and operational levels. Figure 3.3 gives a brief overview of factors that affect inventory management at these different levels.

Strategic decisions include:

- the number of production units required and where they should be located;
- high level product volumes to be produced by country and by factory;
- product strategy and portfolio;

FIGURE 3.3 Inventory management at strategic, tactical and operational levels in the organization

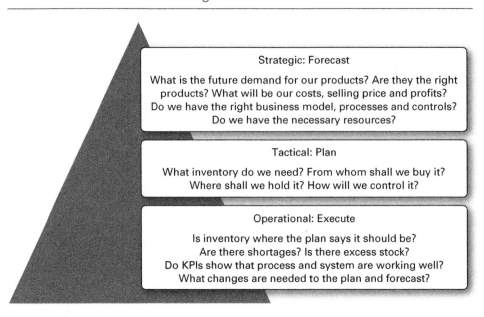

Strategic: Forecast

What is the future demand for our products? Are they the right products? What will be our costs, selling price and profits? Do we have the right business model, processes and controls? Do we have the necessary resources?

Tactical: Plan

What inventory do we need? From whom shall we buy it? Where shall we hold it? How will we control it?

Operational: Execute

Is inventory where the plan says it should be? Are there shortages? Is there excess stock? Do KPIs show that process and system are working well? What changes are needed to the plan and forecast?

- investment needed in production units, warehouses, large equipment, people (recruitment, skills, reduction);
- the correct production process for the product/market, for example:
  - whether to make to order, assemble to order, or make to stock;
  - how to include product customization as late as possible in the process.

Tactical decisions will be viewed on a shorter timeframe and may be made for a single production unit (or small number of units) or warehouse. They occur at the level of the MPS and are likely to include:

- production volumes at a more detailed level (eg how to make best use of production capacity where there is uneven demand);
- deployment of people (holiday plans, flexibility and skills, suitability, training and development);
- supplier relationships;
- investment of capital for projects; and
- protection against unexpected changes in demand and in supply (eg safety stock decisions).

Operational decisions are made at a detailed level on a short timeframe. In manufacturing this deals with shop floor scheduling and control, to direct and track production in as near to real time as possible. Decisions include:

- production schedules for the day, week and/or month;
- material availability information – shortages, overstock, supplier performance;
- production status – schedule performance, backlog, machinery performance and breakdown; and
- staff status – availability, holiday cover.

A simple financial decision driving a complex operational process

In Chapter 1, we also looked at how the decisions made at a strategic level are made in financial terms (eg reduce inventory by 25 per cent, or reduce by a financial amount). These then need to be translated into product information at a tactical level before the effect of the impact to the business (eg availability of products for production or to customers) can be understood. This is shown in Figure 3.4.

FIGURE 3.4 Translating financial saving to detailed items in the inventory management pyramid

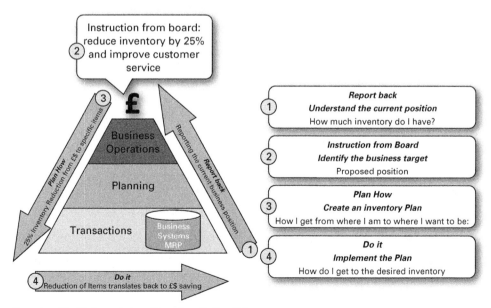

Reproduced by kind permission of Inventory Matters Ltd

In most MRP systems, whether MRPI or MRPII, it can be a lengthy process to test out how and where to reduce inventory in order to meet a business directive to cut costs. This is because what MRP asks the planner to do is to make many decisions in an attempt to achieve the desired outcome (ie in this case to reduce the inventory), for example:

- Which products will be changed and which ones will be left unchanged?
- Will batch sizes be reduced? If so, is there the capability in the business to manage the additional number of batches?
  - If we decrease the batch sizes in production this might increase the number of product changeovers, reducing capacity utilization and increasing unit costs.
  - If we decrease the batch sizes in purchase orders, do we have the capacity to process the increased number of deliveries received? What is the cost implication?
- If products are to be moved between different inventory management categories, which ones are to be moved or how will we move the boundaries?
- Do we know our true inventory management costs? Can we reduce them? Can we change our processes?

Once a planner has made many decisions and made the necessary changes to the relevant parameters for the chosen products in MRP, then MRP will process these decisions (preferably in a what-if planning environment).

FIGURE 3.5   Inventory complexity: the operations view of inventory in MRP

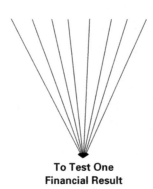

MRP

To Test One
Financial Result

The result from MRP then needs to be tested to see if it meets the business objective of a reduction in costs. It may then be necessary to change the decisions made, change different parameters or different products, run MRP again, test against the desired result, and repeat until the desired answer is found, as shown in Figure 3.5.

In this situation the planner has to rely on experience and to be able to make many changes as well as to run many what-if scenarios. This starts to explain one reason why inventory is complicated to manage within the wider context of the business.

Businesses obviously vary tremendously, with the number of parts varying greatly too. As can be seen from the examples in Figure 3.6, the number of parts being handled in a business can easily run into the tens of thousands and even the hundreds of thousands.

The operations view of inventory in MRP is one that considers what parts are needed to meet demand, and all the items that need to be planned and managed as a result. Whether this is considering the parts at aggregate level (ie by group) or individually, ultimately the decisions will always have to be made at the individual level, part by part.

This is a different view point from the financial view which is looking to make one financial decision, and using that to drive the many parameter decisions, whether these changes are made to many hundreds or many thousands of parts, as shown in Figure 3.7.

Simplifying the operational process

Financial management may give a single constraint or target for the cost of inventory management or a reduction in inventory costs. This then needs to drive the number of decisions made, allowing you to then verify the decisions and remain in control. In Chapter 5 we look at this problem again and show how to drive the changes in MRP through making a small number of decisions and simplifying the decision-making process that needs to be made in operations.

Volumes of data to manage

The volumes of data that need managing in the planning system tend to be either large or very large. We considered the different parameters that need to be managed for each part in Chapter 2. Table 3.1 gives an indication of the size of the data control challenge in inventory management, and shows how simple individual decisions carried out 100,000 times creates huge results.

FIGURE 3.6 How many parts on a product?

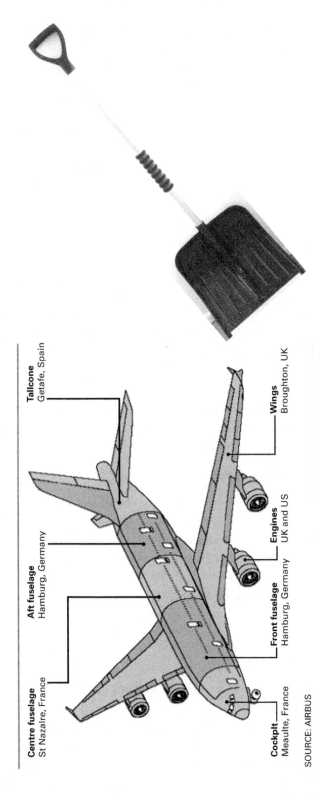

Centre fuselage
St Nazaire, France

Aft fuselage
Hamburg, Germany

Tailcone
Getafe, Spain

Front fuselage
Hamburg, Germany

Engines
UK and US

Wings
Broughton, UK

Cockpit
Meaulte, France

SOURCE: AIRBUS

- Number of parts on an aircraft: the Airbus A380 has approximately 4 million individual components with 2.5 million part numbers (Airbus, 2014)
- Number of parts on a car: Toyota estimate there are around 30,000 parts on a car, including every part down to the nuts and bolts (Toyota, nd)
- The number of parts stocked in a supermarket can be huge – a large Sainsbury's store will have around 30,000 products on the shelves in a supermarket at any one time (Sainsburys, nd) – although approximately half the sales revenue will come from the thousand top selling products. (Sharp, 2012)
- Number of parts on a mobile phone: even a mobile phone has many parts, including: the top and bottom halves of the case, a circuit board (which has many parts soldered on it, eg semiconductors, connectors, sim-card holder, memory, radio frequency converters), antenna, a liquid crystal display (LCD), a keyboard, a microphone, a speaker, and a battery (Brain, nd)
- Number of parts to make a single snow shovel: 15 plus packaging

FIGURE 3.7 Inventory complexity driven by a simple financial view of inventory

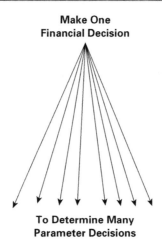

**Make One
Financial Decision**

**To Determine Many
Parameter Decisions**

TABLE 3.1 The number of parameters that typically need to be managed in a business

# parts / #SKUs	10,000
# parameters	Minimum of 10 to manage
# decisions	# parts x # parameters = 100,000 decisions to be made which govern the executed result or number of recommendations

It would be inefficient in most businesses to set all parameters individually by part – making one hundred thousand decisions in the case in Table 3.1 would not make good business sense in the vast majority of cases.

It's good inventory management practice to group parts by similar inventory characteristics (for example, frequency of demand: for more details of this grouping by inventory characteristic please see Chapter 4) and to then create rules that can be applied to the different groups (ie specify the parameters that will apply across the parts in that group, for example one group might have purchase orders raised to cover demand for the next five days).

It is essential to complete parameter information for all parts (for example, lead time, purchasing batch sizes, manufacturing batch sizes, safety stock, etc). Once the parameters are filled in and demand predicted, it will be possible to automate planning decisions in MRP. MRP is then able to calculate the decisions resulting from the parameter information, the bills of materials (discussed in Chapter 2) and the predicted demand, and tells the planner:

- purchase order receipts;
- works order receipts; and
- order changes – moving orders closer or pushing them out, or cancelling orders.

Inventory management still has the four basic steps as was shown in Figure 3.2. These simple steps are still true but can now be considered in the context where many thousands of parts need to be managed by a business system.

- Understand the current inventory position: how much stock have I currently got?
  - What stock is there and what stock will result from current orders? What is the status of the current stock – are we overstocked? Are there shortages?
- Identify the business targets for inventory: what do I have to achieve?
  - What are the inventory management targets set by the business? How do I achieve these while satisfying the production and sales requirements?
- Create an inventory plan: what do I have to do to achieve the business targets and how difficult will it be?
  - What is the proposed position from my analysis rules? Is my current analysis working?
- Implement the plan: what actions must I take to achieve the plan?
  - Is the plan working? Is demand being met?
  - What problems are there? Have the necessary corrections been made?

Figure 3.8 shows a more detailed flow around these four steps.

CASE STUDY   Airbus inventory management challenges in a complex business

Airbus, one of the world's leading aircraft manufacturers, is a global company with manufacturing and design facilities in France, the UK, Germany, and Spain, and subsidiaries in China, the US, Japan, and the Middle East. Their largest passenger aircraft is the A380.

FIGURE 3.8 Inventory planning within the business system

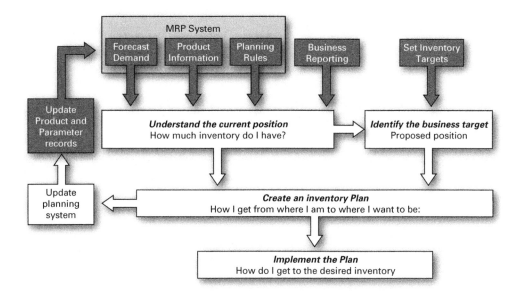

Airbus press centre information shows the size of the inventory management challenge:

> *An A380 consists of around 4 million individual components with 2.5 million part numbers produced by 1,500 companies from 30 countries around the world. It takes 13,000 rivets to join the 3 sections of the fuselage and 4,000 rivets are used for the junction of the wings and the fuselage.*

Final European assembly of the A380 takes place in Toulouse, France, as shown in Figure 3.9. Figure 3.10 shows where the production of the major structures takes place.

The wings are assembled in Broughton in the UK, as shown in Figure 3.11. Each wing is built of around 32,000 major parts, plus 750,000 bolts and rivets. The origin of every part and fastener is recorded: the supplier of each is documented along with the batch of base metal and the time and date of manufacture.

In addition to the major structure assembly locations, there are many suppliers of components and key parts, 800 of whom are in the USA. The largest four suppliers are Rolls Royce, Safran, United Technologies and General Electric.

Airbus uses the SAP ERP system throughout its design and manufacturing locations in Europe. Production planning, including inventory and capacity management, is handled within its SAP system. Sources: (Airbus, 2014) (Edemariam, 2006) (HP, 2009)

FIGURE 3.9   Airbus A380 assembly in Toulouse, France (© Airbus permission granted)

FIGURE 3.10   Airbus A380 major structure assembly locations in Europe (© Airbus permission granted)

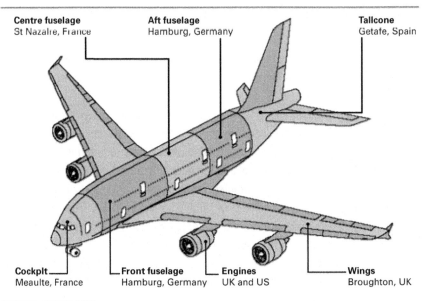

SOURCE: AIRBUS A380

FIGURE 3.11   Airbus A380 wing assembly locations in the UK
(©Airbus permission granted)

Complexity in managing inventory in MRPI *and* MRPII

Calculations within the MRP system

Master production schedule

The creation of the production plan is the first major planning task. This is the Master Production Schedule (MPS) and has a large input from the sales and operations plan (S&OP), as shown in Figure 3.12. It works at the

FIGURE 3.12   Creation of the Master Production Schedule
(MPS) for independent demand (simplified from
Vollmann *et al*, 2005, p 8)

finished good level and records demand and production, ie wherever there is independent demand. This will take into account any policy decisions, forecasts of demand, known customer orders and finished goods stock on hand.

The MPS may smooth the production plan, as shown in Table 3.2. This will relate to the calculation of batch size information; for example, there may exist a maximum capacity of 20 and production batch size may be: for a minimum of 1 and with a multiple of 1; or for a minimum of 10 with a multiple of 10 as shown in Table 3.2.

The MPS will also consider minimum stock or safety stock requirements and the current and predicted inventory/stock on hand (SOH). In Table 3.3 these factors now show why the MPS has planned additional production in weeks 3 and 5.

The master production schedule then drives the manufacturing resource planning.

TABLE 3.2   The MPS determines production of finished good stock (FGS) for which there is independent demand

	Week 1	Week 2	Week 3	Week 4	Week 5	Week 6
Forecast demand	5	10	15	15	25	15
MPS	10	10	20	10	30	10

TABLE 3.3   MPS considers predicted stock on hand (SOH) for each time period and safety stock

	Week 1	Week 2	Week 3	Week 4	Week 5	Week 6
Opening SOH	5	10	10	15	10	15
Forecast demand	5	10	15	15	25	15
MPS	10	10	20	10	30	10
Closing finish good SOH	10	10	15	10	15	10
Safety Stock	10	10	10	10	10	10

Executing the manufacturing resource planning

Figure 3.13 shows how MRP is fed by the master production schedule (MPS).

FIGURE 3.13 MRP is fed by the MPS to enable it to consider material and capacity in its creation of detailed production plans (simplified from Vollmann *et al*, 2005, p 8)

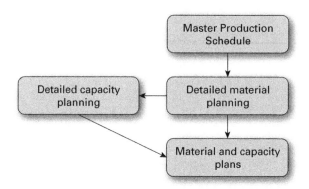

If we now consider the snow shovel which we looked at in Chapter 2, we can look at some MRP calculations that would result from the above MPS. Figure 3.14 shows that one of the subassemblies needed to produce the snow shovel is the scoop assembly.

MRP (explosion) process

When the planning processes are all run in the system and all the changes and new orders created, this is sometimes described as an MRP explosion. This process is described either as a regenerative or net change process.

Regenerative and net change processing

Businesses expect and in many cases need to operate with data that is as up to date as possible. MRP systems originally were unable to achieve this because the computer power needed to regenerate all computer records was unavailable while the business was operating. This processing of all part records in a single computer run meant that there was a regeneration of the records overnight (or perhaps only at the weekend). The regenerative process would completely recalculate the whole MRP: it calculated the existing and new orders and changes to existing orders for every item for every order from the top level. Later net change processing became possible where only those records affected by new or changed information were reconstructed.

FIGURE 3.14 Bill of materials for the snow shovel

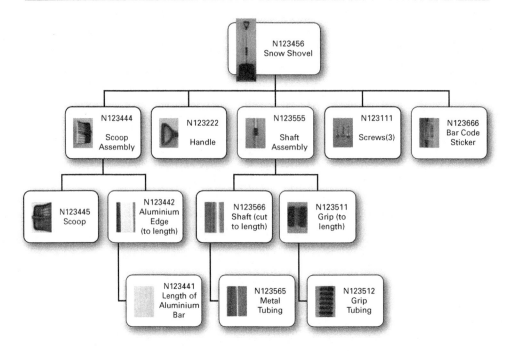

In large companies even today it may be that not all data is able to be accurate with up-to-the-minute changes because of the amount of processing that has to be carried out. There are advantages to both regenerative and net change processing, and both are still in use.

Parameters

In Chapter 2 we introduced the importance of parameters. If parameters are not well managed then the results from the planning system will need many changes. Here we will consider the importance of a few of those: lead time, cycle stock and safety stock parameters.

Lead time

If the lead time in MRP to produce the scoop assembly is one week, then the scoop assembly must be available one week before the final assembly of the snow shovel. MRP must therefore raise the works order for the assembly of the works order one week earlier than the week the finished snow shovel is to be assembled, as shown in Table 3.4.

Once the time-phased MRP calculations are complete for all the dependent demand of all products the instructions (eg works orders, purchase orders) are then executed.

TABLE 3.4 MRP scheduling of scoop assembly production with one week lead time to meet independent demand for the snow shovel

	Week 1	Week 2	Week 3	Week 4	Week 5	Week 6
MPS for the snow shovel	10	10	20	10	30	10
Opening SOH scoop assembly	10	10	30			
Assemble scoop works order	10	20	10	30	10	10
Closing SOH scoop assembly	10	30				
Min / safety stock	10	10	10	10	10	10

MRP needs to record both forecast orders and actual orders placed by customers, and to be able to differentiate between them. If there is then a conflict in resource utilization, operations can give priority to the customer order.

This can be relevant where there is late customization of products (for example in the automotive industry). In these industries sub-assemblies are often built as modules, which may be fitted on any final product. An example would be that all cars are built with seats in them, but only some of them will have seat heaters; the seats are likely to be interchangeable and can be fitted near the end of the build depending on actual customer orders.

Management of product lead time is essential in all planning systems. There will always be a lead time within which changes cannot, or perhaps should not, be made. Within a given lead time production planning systems will not make changes to the production plan automatically – hence the benefit of late customization. Outside of the lead time the system can continue to adjust the production plans, according to the parameters that it has been given to work with.

Planning systems for purchasing similarly will work to a lead time, within which the system cannot automatically make changes (for example to the purchase orders and the scheduled deliveries), but outside the lead time the system will be able to continue to make changes.

A typical schedule for the net demand of the snow shovel is shown in Table 3.5.

In simple terms the calculations are as follows:

- Net demand inside the lead time is the orders plus any backlog.
  In week 1, net demand is: Orders + Backlog = 950 + 200 = 1150, which is higher than the original forecast of 1000.

TABLE 3.5 Snow shovel net demand calculations inside lead time and outside the lead time

	Week 1	Week 2	Week 3	Week 4	Week 5	Week 6	Week 7	Week 8
	Within lead-time			Outside lead-time				
Forecast	1000	1000	1000	1000	1000	1000	1000	1000
Orders (start with backlog of 200)	950	980	1050	750	400	20	0	0
Net Demand	1150	980	1050	1000	1000	1000	1000	1000
MPS	1000	1000	1000	1000	1000	1000	1000	1000
FGS closing stock (starting SOH = 300)	150	170	120	120	120	120	120	120

- Net demand inside the lead time is generally the higher of the forecast or orders, so for week 4, net demand is: = 1000, thus the order book would be described as 75 per cent complete.
- Predicted closing stock (SOH) in week 1 is: Opening SOH – net demand + planned production (MPS) = 300 – 1150 + 1000 = 150.
- Predicted closing stock (SOH) in week 2 is: Opening SOH – net demand + planned production (MPS) = 150 – 980 + 1000 = 170.

FIGURE 3.15 Material and capacity plans drive the shop floor and purchasing systems (simplified from (Vollmann, 2005))

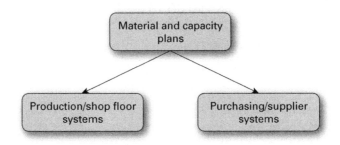

Managing cycle stock and safety stock

Cycle stock is the stock that is replenished for routine use or sale, and was included in Chapter 2 when the standardized saw tooth diagram was considered. One of the decisions that needs to be made when implementing an MRP system is whether cycle stock should be replenished by a fixed quantity or at a fixed interval.

Fixed quantity ordering is when the system is set to reorder a fixed quantity each time an order is placed, which means that the frequency of ordering may vary, as shown in Figure 3.16.

The opposite of fixed quantity ordering is fixed interval ordering. This is where we keep the time between ordering the same and vary the quantity ordered. For example, a supplier gets an order every Monday but the quantity ordered varies slightly, as shown in Figure 3.17.

The benefit of fixed interval ordering isn't necessarily immediately obvious. Figure 3.18 shows a product where demand has reduced significantly over time. If fixed quantity ordering were being used then the MRP system would continue, until told otherwise, to place an order for the same number of items every time an order were placed, although the frequency of the order would be less often. The inventory would then take longer and longer to be consumed, tying money up in unnecessary inventory.

FIGURE 3.16   Fixed quantity ordering

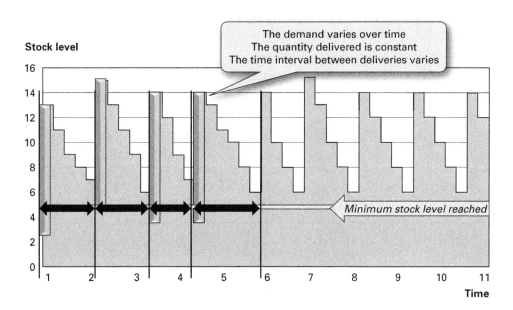

FIGURE 3.17   Fixed interval ordering

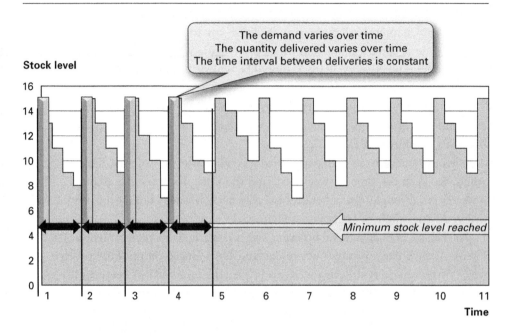

FIGURE 3.18   The advantage of fixed interval ordering

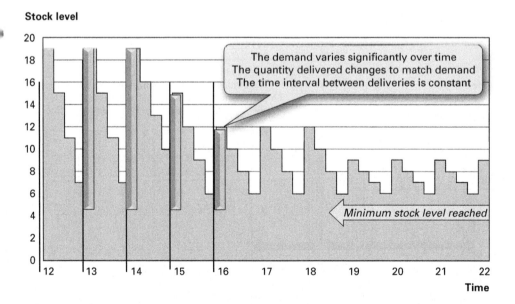

MRP can respond to this problem, without any intervention, if fixed interval ordering is used. When the product demand varies significantly over time, the time interval between deliveries remains constant, and the quantity delivered automatically changes to match demand, as shown in Figure 3.18. Because the system is set up to order the quantity needed to meet demand in the next time period (which has been specified), the quantity ordered adjusts automatically.

Businesses that have many thousands of parts can prevent excess inventory building up by choosing to have cycle stock replenishment rules set to fixed interval ordering, as well as it taking less maintenance and input from the planner.

There are other ways of managing cycle stock that should be considered for some products. For example, vendor managed inventory (VMI) is used to good effect in many industries for replenishment of low value, high volume products such as nuts and bolts.

Safety stock settings may also be set to safety time or safety quantity replenishment in MRP and planning systems. Safety time should be chosen for the same reasons as for cycle stock. However, as we shall see in Chapter 6, there are other considerations when safety stock rules are created for products (for example if a product has volatile and low demand then a minimum stock or hybrid rule may be implemented).

Managing inventory control data

Inventory: parts, audit trail and value

Parts are recorded and tracked together with their inventory management data through the planning system. Current information on part number, item description, location and cost are all needed. The cost of an item increases through the process as it moves from raw material, via work in progress and on to final product. This is a useful piece of information, and needs to be updated through the process so that people from the whole organization can access valid information, whether they are from sales, finance, purchasing or production.

Many organizations also need to retain quality information and records to ensure that there is an audit trail that can be followed. The Airbus case study earlier in this chapter is a good example of this. It is clear that the quality of the parts and assemblies is critical to the product; this has seen the rise of six sigma as a quality philosophy. What is less obvious is that data accuracy within MRP systems is equally important and vital to the efficiency of the business.

Consider the question: is 99 per cent accuracy acceptable for MRP data?

MRP will make many thousand decisions based on the data that is in its databases. If, for example, our stock information was 99 per cent accurate, we had 10,000 parts in which MRP needs to plan for a planning period of 104 weeks (two years). Based on the above there would be in the order of $1\% \times 10,000 \times 104 = 104,000$ time-phased demand records that were potentially incorrect. This type of failure rate would not be accepted in the build of an aircraft or a car, and should not be accepted in the data. ***Data accuracy is vital to the effectiveness of MRP systems.***

We started this chapter talking about the four easy steps to inventory planning, which become more challenging as the complexity of the business increases. The four steps are still valid, and Figure 3.19 expands the earlier Figure 3.8 by adding the top line of data, targets, parameters and inventory management methods. This then allows the inventory planning process to work within the system as well as being focused on the business needs.

FIGURE 3.19   Inventory planning within the business system and focused on business needs

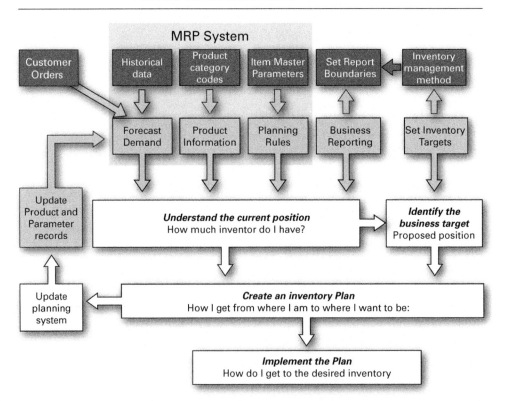

Measuring success

Key performance indicators (KPIs)

There's an old saying: 'what gets measured gets done'. It is also true that if different parts of an organization are being judged on measures that conflict with those elsewhere in the business then they are likely to be pulling against each other.

KPIs are essential for an organization and ERP systems give businesses a great deal of data to choose to report from. Measurements are very important but should be not be contradictory or overly onerous to produce.

Table 3.6 shows some typical KPIs used for operations and inventory management; it is important that the KPIs should tie into the critical success factors (CSFs) in an organization, which should be set to tie into the business's strategy.

Compliance/non-compliance

Non-compliance is a key measure of how well a planning system is working. It is one that many companies overlook, and as a consequence it is hard for them to judge how well their system is being managed and how effective it is.

Non-compliance measures the number of system-generated transactions (eg works and purchase orders) that have to be changed by a person. Conversely, compliance is the number of system-generated transactions that do not need to be changed.

When a new system is first implemented it is likely that there will be a high level of non-compliance. Figure 3.20 shows how, when a non-compliance to a system transaction is necessary, there are two actions that need to be taken:

- The transaction needs to be corrected and executed. This is the first step and this corrective action is almost always taken.

- The underlying reason why the transaction was incorrect needs to be corrected if at all possible. This is the second step, and if it is not taken and the root cause corrected then incorrect transactions are likely to continue to be generated.

This starts to show the importance of measuring non-compliance. It will focus on parameter management and encourage people to make the system as effective and efficient as possible. It is a good indicator of how well the system is being managed and how well it is able to calculate information so that it is able to create the correct transactions.

TABLE 3.6 Some typical inventory management KPIs

Measure	Description	Reason
Inventory turns/stock turn	The number of times the inventory in a business turns or is consumed in a year	Gives a comparison between similar businesses and helps external benchmarking. Also monitors inventory holding costs
On time delivery in full (OTIF)	The percentage of times customer orders were completed and delivered complete and on time	Monitors customer service and delivery performance
Finished goods stock (FGS) in inventory	Amount of FGS held in days, quantity and cost	Inventory holding costs, over stock indicators, inventory control implications
Raw material/component inventory	Amount of non-FGS held in days, quantity and cost	Inventory holding costs, over stock indicators, inventory control implications
Total work in progress (WIP)	Amount of WIP held in days, quantity and cost	Inventory balancing and control
Total lead time/cycle time	Total time for an order to be processed/time taken from start to end of process	Monitors efficiency and WIP increases or decreases accordingly
Non-compliance	The number of system generated transactions (eg works and purchase orders) that have to be changed by a person	Measures the effectiveness of the system. The more changes that are necessary the less effectively the system is working

FIGURE 3.20   Non-compliance is a key measure of how well the planning system is working

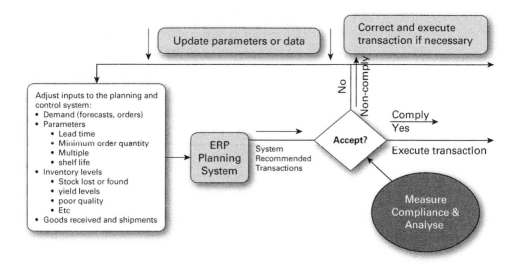

Exception management

We have looked at the magnitude of the inventory planning challenge in some businesses in this chapter. Realistically, it is not possible to manage all parts equally. In Chapter 4 we look at some traditional ways of analysing parts so that the ones that should have the most attention can be given it. However, one aspect of ERP and planning systems is that exception management reports can be produced and put to great use.

For example, overstock of high value items, unless of exceptional strategic importance, is more important in inventory management than overstock of nuts and bolts.

Traditionally decisions were made individually, and were normally left to the planners to make them. Exception reporting can be generated from some simple rules-based systems, and a much better overview achieved of the individual parts as well as the whole business.

Is the cost of control too high?

The benefit of business systems is the increased planning and control over what happens within the organization and the improved business insight provided. These benefits come at a cost, however, and the trade-off between the cost and the value of the increased control needs to be understood.

A company does not have to be very complex before it can benefit from an effective planning and control system to help manage the delivery of good service to its customers. The mantra is well-known: right product, right place, right quality, right time and right cost.

The planning and control system itself though does not add to the value of the product in the eyes of the customer. So what is its value to the company itself? And does this outweigh the cost?

The costs of the system itself come from several sources, including:

- the initial implementation, for example: company disruption, planning and control system costs (eg licence), implementation services (eg integration, data migration, training), hardware and infrastructure;

- the ongoing management and maintenance of the system (eg maintenance and support fees, updates and retraining);

- adapting to changes that may be required to meet the changing needs of the business without being a drain on valuable resources; and

- the capability to manage the transactions required to make the system work and the frustrations that these may not be seen as optimal by the people who have to interact with the system routinely.

There are, however, costs of not having an ERP system. An estimation of the cost of losing control is not easy to estimate. Many factors would need to be taken into account, including:

- the cost of poor service and late delivery: contracts often carry penalty clauses, lack of availability can cause customers to take their business elsewhere, poor performance may well lose business and create a bad reputation;

- a greater manual effort in planning the business – what purchase orders need to be placed and when (unit price, amount of stock on hand predicted at the point in the future when the order will be delivered, quantity, delivery date), scheduling and placing production orders to meet future needs, etc;

- many islands of un-joined-up and possibly conflicting data;

- lack of efficiency increasing costs and threatening competitiveness; and

- lack of business insight.

This book is not about whether or not a company should implement an ERP system. It is about the management of a company's inventory within a planning and control system such as ERP. However, it is our experience with companies that often there can be a tangible level of frustration with the system and the way it works. Some of this may be due to a lack of understanding about the system or a lack of training, or it may be that the business has developed over the years since implementation and the system is unable to accommodate some of the changes, or it may be that the level of customization or integration with legacy systems has been more costly or difficult to manage than anticipated. Whatever the frustrations or problems with an existing system it is always important to understand the costs to the business of being completely without a planning and control system (eg ERP). The frustrations and problems can then be managed within whatever 'big picture solution' is right for the business.

Summary

The four simple steps to inventory planning are clear and in this chapter we have looked at how, although simple when applied even to a simple product, there is a rapid increase in complexity. MRP is now, in effect, the de facto standard method of planning for batch manufacturing and it is important to understand how to manage the complexity. By considering the way that MRP calculates requirements at all the different levels of the bills of materials, this chapter has shown how accurate data and well-managed parameters are key to an effective and efficient ERP and planning systems. KPIs are essential, and the measure of non-compliance shows how well the system is being used.

In Chapter 4 we will look in more detail at how the different traditional methods of inventory analysis can help a business to improve their inventory planning.

Notes

Airbus (2014, Oct) www.airbus.com/presscentre/presskits/. Retrieved 2 November 2014

Brain, M (nd) http://electronics.howstuffworks.com/inside-cell-phone.htm. Retrieved 2 November 2014

Brown, R (1982) *Advanced Service Inventory Parts Control* (2nd edn), Material Management Science Inc, Norwich

Edemariam, A (2006, 23 February). www.theguardian.com/business/2006/feb/23/theairlineindustry.travelnews. Retrieved 2 November 2014 from www.theguardian.com: www.theguardian.com/business/2006/feb/23/theairlineindustry.travelnews

HP (2009, Dec) http://h20195.www2.hp.com/v2/GetPDF.aspx/4AA3-0569EEW.pdf. Retrieved 2 November 2014 from http://h20195.www2.hp.com/v2/GetPDF.aspx/4AA3-0569EEW.pdf

Sainsburys (nd) www.j-sainsbury.co.uk/extras/faqs/media/how-many-products-does-sainsburys-supermarkets-sell/. Retrieved 2 November 2014

Sharp, B (2012, Aug 16) http://byronsharp.wordpress.com/2012/08/16/shopping_long_tail/. Retrieved 2 November 2014

Toyota (nd) www.toyota.co.jp/en/kids/faq/d/01/04/. Retrieved 2 November 2014 from www.toyota.co.jp/en/kids/faq/d/01/04/

Vollmann, B W (2005) *Manufacturing Planning and Control Systems*, Irwin McGraw-Hill, New York

You do the maths

FIGURE 3.21

CB-87484-1 Control Box 2I-9O

CB-87496-1 Control Box 4I-5O

CB-87495-1 Control Box 4I-9O

CB-87483-1 Control Box 2I-5O

Control Box UK PLC manufacture control boxes. They have a control box which takes two or four inputs and splits into two or four (positive and negative) outputs with a grounding output.

The MPS for the four products has been recalculated. Unfortunately the MRP system has a headache and has stopped halfway through. The requirements for WR14259-2R urgently need to be calculated.

Tasks

The projected on hand and net requirements for RC-67896-8 have been calculated as an example.

Calculate the projected on hand and net requirements for:
OL-26877-150
OL-26877-190

Assuming the above three parts are the only parts that use WR14259-2R calculate the projected on hand and net requirements based on their planned order release.

What effect if the off-set net requirements is used rather than the planned order release to create the gross requirement?

TABLE 3.7

Worked example

RC-67896-8	Week No	1	2	3	4	5	6	7	8	9	10	11	12
Gross Requirements		10	25	20	30	15	45	50	10	20	30	25	35
Scheduled Receipts					90								
Projected on Hand	60	50	25	5	65	50	5	45	35	15	75	50	15
Net Requirements								45	10	20	30	25	35
Planned Order Receipts	Qty 90							90				90	
Planned Order Releases	6 weeks	90				90							

OL-26877-15O	Week No	1	2	3	4	5	6	7	8	9	10	11	12
Gross Requirements		3	8	7	10	5	15	17	3	7	10	8	12
Scheduled Receipts					35								
Projected on Hand	30												
Net Requirements													
Planned Order Receipts	Qty 35												
Planned Order Releases	1 week												

OL-26877-19O	Week No	1	2	3	4	5	6	7	8	9	10	11	12
Gross Requirements		7	17	13	20	10	30	33	7	13	20	17	23
Scheduled Receipts				40									
Projected on Hand	25												
Net Requirements													
Planned Order Receipts	Qty 40												
Planned Order Releases	1 week												

TABLE 3.8

Case 1 - Requirements based on Planned Order Release

Planned Order Release	Week No	1	2	3	4	5	6	7	8	9	10	11	12
RC-67896-8		90	0	0	90	0	0	90	0	0	0	90	0
OL-26877-15O													
OL-26877-19O													

Gross Requirement	BOM Usage	1	2	3	4	5	6	7	8	9	10	11	12
RC-67896-8	6	540	0	0	540	0	0	540	0	0	0	540	0
OL-26877-15O	2												
OL-26877-19O	4												
Total Gross Requirement													

WR-14259-2R	Week No	1	2	3	4	5	6	7	8	9	10	11	12
Gross Requirements													
Scheduled Receipts					900								
Projected on Hand	900												
Net Requirements													
Planned Order Receipts	Qty 900												
Planned Order Releases	1 week												

TABLE 3.9

Case 2 – Requirements based on Offset Net Requirements

Offset Net Requirement	Offset	1	2	3	4	5	6	7	8	9	10	11	12
RC-67896-8	6 weeks	45	10	20	30	25	35	20	10	45	20	20	15[1]
OL-26877-15O	1 week												7[2]
OL-26877-19O	1 week												13

Gross Requirement	BOM Usage	1	2	3	4	5	6	7	8	9	10	11	12
RC-67896-8	6	270	60	120	180	150	210	120	60	270	120	120	90
OL-26877-15O	2												
OL-26877-19O	4												
Total Gross Requirement													

WR-14259-2R	Week No	1	2	3	4	5	6	7	8	9	10	11	12
Gross Requirements													
Scheduled Receipts					900								
Projected on Hand	900												
Net Requirements													
Planned Order Receipts	Qty 900												
Planned Order Releases	1 week												

1 Offset net requirements for Weeks 7–12 are based on net requirements for Weeks 13–18 not shown in Table 3.7.

2 Offset net requirement for Week 12 is based on net requirement for Week 13 not shown in Table 3.7.

TABLE 3.10 — answers for Table 3.7

RC-67896-8	Week No	1	2	3	4	5	6	7	8	9	10	11	12
Gross Requirements		10	25	20	30	15	45	50	10	20	30	25	35
Scheduled Receipts					90								
Projected on Hand	60	50	25	5	65	50	5	45	35	15	75	50	15
Net Requirements								45			15		
Planned Order Receipts	Qty 90							90			90		
Planned Order Releases	6 weeks	90			90								0

OL-26877-15O	Week No	1	2	3	4	5	6	7	8	9	10	11	12
Gross Requirements		3	8	7	10	5	15	17	3	7	10	8	12
Scheduled Receipts					35								
Projected on Hand	30	27	19	12	37	32	17	0	32	25	15	7	30
Net Requirements									3				5
Planned Order Receipts	Qty 35								35				35
Planned Order Releases	1 week							35				35	0

OL-26877-19O	Week No	1	2	3	4	5	6	7	8	9	10	11	12
Gross Requirements		7	17	13	20	10	30	33	7	13	20	17	23
Scheduled Receipts				40									
Projected on Hand	25	18	1	28	8	38	8	15	8	35	15	38	15
Net Requirements						2		25		5		2	
Planned Order Receipts	Qty 40					40		40		40		40	
Planned Order Releases	1 week				40		40		40		40		0

TABLE 3.11   – answers for Table 3.8

Case 1 - Requirements based on Planned Order Release

Planned Order Release	Week No	1	2	3	4	5	6	7	8	9	10	11	12
RC-67896-8		90	0	0	90	0	0	90	0	0	0	90	0
OL-26877-15O		0	0	0	0	0	0	35	0	0	0	35	0
OL-26877-19O		0	0	0	40	0	40	0	40	0	40	0	0

Gross Requirement	BOM Usage	1	2	3	4	5	6	7	8	9	10	11	12
RC-67896-8	6	540	0	0	540	0	0	540	0	0	0	540	0
OL-26877-15O	2	0	0	0	0	0	0	70	0	0	0	70	0
OL-26877-19O	4	0	0	0	160	0	160	0	160	0	160	0	0
Total Gross Requirement		540	0	0	700	0	160	610	160	0	160	610	0

WR-14259-2R	Week No	1	2	3	4	5	6	7	8	9	10	11	12
Gross Requirements		540	0	0	700	0	160	610	160	0	160	610	0
Scheduled Receipts					900								
Projected on Hand	900	360	360	360	560	560	400	690	530	530	370	660	660
Net Requirements		0	0	0	0	0	0	210	0	0	0	240	0
Planned Order Receipts	Qty 900							900				900	
Planned Order Releases	1 week	0	0	0	0	0	900	0	0	0	900	0	0

TABLE 3.12 – answers for Table 3.9

Case 2 - Requirements based on Offset Net Requirements

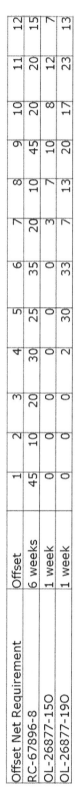

Offset Net Requirement	Offset	1	2	3	4	5	6	7	8	9	10	11	12
RC-67896-8	6 weeks	45	10	20	30	25	35	20	10	45	20	20	15
OL-26877-15O	1 week	0	0	0	0	0	0	3	7	10	8	12	7
OL-26877-19O	1 week	0	0	0	2	30	33	7	13	20	17	23	13

Gross Requirement	BOM Usage	1	2	3	4	5	6	7	8	9	10	11	12
RC-67896-8	6	270	60	120	180	150	210	120	60	270	120	120	90
OL-26877-15O	2	0	0	0	0	0	0	6	14	20	16	24	14
OL-26877-19O	4	0	0	0	8	120	132	28	52	80	68	92	52
Total Gross Requirement		270	60	120	188	270	342	154	126	370	204	236	156

WR-14259-2R	Week No	1	2	3	4	5	6	7	8	9	10	11	12
Gross Requirements		270	60	120	188	270	342	154	126	370	204	236	156
Scheduled Receipts					900								
Projected on Hand	900	630	570	450	1162	892	550	396	270	800	596	360	204
Net Requirements		0	0	0	0	0	0	0	0	100	0	0	0
Planned Order Receipts	Qty 900									900			
Planned Order Releases	1 week								900	0			

The key learning point is that the use of any batching rules brings forward the demand to earlier weeks. It also increases the lumpiness of the demand. Look at Weeks 2, 3, 5 and 7 in Table 3.11. They are zero. The variation in the demand in Table 3.11 is between 160 and 700, whereas in Table 3.12 the variation in demand is 60 to 270. The selection of batch size is critical to the stability and ease of management of the recommended orders.

Traditional thinking in inventory optimization

Introduction

The need to manage inventory is not new. Ever since the Industrial Revolution, when the manufacture of goods moved from cottage industry to mass production through the division of labour, we have been tied to batch manufacture. In order to achieve the 'right product, right place, right amount and right time', researchers have focused on the development of a variety of methods for planning, controlling and balancing inventory. The development of these inventory management techniques is driven by the need to minimize the investment in stock. A vast array of complex techniques have been developed from a relatively small base of principles. In this chapter we will examine the principles which we believe form the basis for most manufacture and retail inventory. This chapter looks at:

- inventory saw-tooth;
- EOQ/EOP;
- statistical safety stock;
- safety time;
- hybrid safety stock;
- Pareto ABC or 80/20 rule;
- Pareto exchange curve;
- runner repeater stranger;
- inventory matrix;
- overage;
- a diagnosis of the five levels which businesses reach as they progress through their inventory management operation.

FIGURE 4.1   Standard inventory saw-tooth model for ROP logic

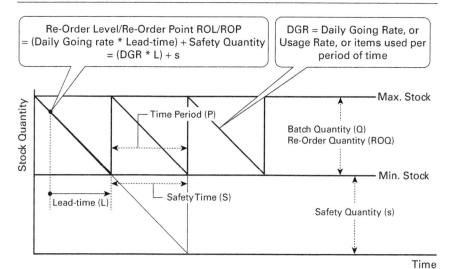

Re-Order Level/Re-Order Point ROL/ROP
= (Daily Going rate * Lead-time) + Safety Quantity
= (DGR * L) + s

DGR = Daily Going Rate, or
Usage Rate, or items used per
period of time

Stock Quantity

Max. Stock

Time Period (P)

Batch Quantity (Q)
Re-Order Quantity (ROQ)

Min. Stock

Lead-time (L)

Safety Time (S)

Safety Quantity (s)

Time

Inventory saw-tooth

The inventory saw-tooth easily defines the essential challenge for inventory management. For any item we use, we have a stock of the item, which we use over time, at some point in the future we will run out of the item. To make sure we are not inconvenienced by running out we attempt to predict when we will run out, then order new supplies to arrive at about the time we will run out. We need to decide how much to order, and how confident we are about our prediction of how many we use, and how reliable our supplier is at delivering on time. We may hold some stock in contingency in case we experience more demand or our supplier is late.

If we examine Figure 4.1 we can see each element of the above statement. The prediction of demand is the usage rate or DGR (daily going rate); to ensure the order arrives on time we calculate the ROL (re-order level) based on the predicted usage (DGR) and the time to get more stock, the lead-time (L). To determine the amount we buy, we specify a re-order quantity (ROQ) or make an estimate of quantity needed to last a known period (P), ie a week of usage. To protect against high demand and late deliveries we add safety quantity (s) or safety time (S). The figure is stylized as it shows the usage as straight line; we know that parts are not usually used in a uniform manner, however for simplicity it is usually shown as a straight line. In summary, to define the inventory plan we need to make two decisions:

- How much do we order or how often do we order?
- How much do we protect against supply and demand uncertainties?
- How long will it take to make/supply them?

As mentioned in Chapters 2 and 3 there are principally two approaches to answering the above questions. The first approach is to use ROP logic, which is a combination of the ROP which includes safety and ROQ for ordering; this approach works when the future demand is not known and the DGR is calculated based on usage history. The second approach is to use MRP logic which, as discussed in detail in Chapter 3, uses the future demand (independent or dependent) and order and safety parameters to project future stock and thus place orders to maintain stock levels. However, both approaches rely on the planner specifying the order quantity/time and the safety quantity/time. The next section covers the possible approaches available to the planner if they wish to apply science to the problem.

Determining the order size

Once we have understood that we need to determine how much we need to order and how much we might provision for higher than expected demand and late deliveries from our suppliers, we can divide the problem into two halves. What is important to note is that MRP systems, as discussed in Chapter 2, require these same decisions to be made and input into their item master data for the MRP system to manage the materials supply. Thus paying attention to determining the optimum value for the orders and safety will pay significant dividend in helping MRP to run efficiently. The first challenge is how much to order.

How much do I order?

In the absence of any guidance most planners/buyers will usually rely on the quantity specified by the supplier. In most cases the supplier has a preferred minimum order quantity, which can be based on their manufacturing process, packaging or transport considerations. For example, we may decide that as the supplier delivers once a week that we should buy a week's worth at a time; if we use 10 a day then we will order 50 at a time. If, however, when we talk to the supplier he advises that he will only supply in 100's then we will more usually accept his conditions and buy 100 at a time, every two weeks. Now this 'instinctive' approach takes no account of the consequences of the decision. It is worth considering the example of the two for one deal often used by retailers to encourage shoppers to buy larger quantities (batches). If the goods purchased are, say, dishwasher tablets, then all this will do is delay the time of the next purchase. However, if it is Seville Oranges, then there is a risk that they will deteriorate before they have all been consumed, leading to waste. The planner must therefore know that if larger quantities are purchased they will not deteriorate before they are required to be used. This is discussed again in the 'inventory matrix' section later in this chapter. The best-known method for determining the most economic order quantity using the product's value was determined by Harris (1913) and popularized by Wilson in the early part of the 1920s.

EOQ (Economic Order Quantity)

To understand the principles of economic ordering first proposed by Harris (1913) let us consider the young entrepreneur Sam Cornish. Sam has spotted an opportunity to buy and sell footballs; he has found a supplier who will sell him footballs for a £1 each; and he can sell for £2 after applying the club badge. His supplier Clare's Sports Plc charges him £10 per order and £20 to deliver, irrespective of the quantity ordered. Sam estimates that he can sell 100 footballs each week. Sam needs to decide how many footballs to buy. If he buys 100 footballs they will last him a week, and it will cost him £30 pounds for ordering and delivery. If he does this each week it will cost him £30 × 52 weeks or £1,560. If, however, he buys enough for two weeks – 200 – he will need to order 26 times in a year which will cost him 26 × £30 or £780. Thus it appears to be cheaper to order more. To find the best order size Sam evaluates a number of options. The results are shown in Table 4.1. What is clear from the table is that the lowest cost would be to order the entire year's worth in one go.

If Sam went ahead he would now have a storage problem. So Sam goes and talks to his brother Ollie who works for Warehouses Unlimited Ltd to arrange for some storage space. Ollie can provide space but will charge based on the average number of footballs in stock each day. The charge is £1 per 100 footballs per week. The cost of storing the footballs can be calculated as follows. If one week's worth of footballs were purchased at the beginning of the week there would be 100 footballs in stock and all being well by the end of the week there would be none left. Thus if we wanted to know the average number we could take the stock at the beginning and the stock at the end and divide by two. So the average stock is 50. The charge is £1 per 100 per week or 1p per football per week, so to store an average stock of 50 footballs for one year it would cost 1p × 50 footballs × 52 weeks or £26. Extending this logic in the same way as for the cost of ordering Sam constructed a table showing the cost of holding stock, shown in Table 4.2.

TABLE 4.1   Evaluation of ordering costs from suppliers

- We have set up a small business selling Footballs
- I can buy for £1 and sell for £2
- The supplier will charge £10 per order and £20 to deliver
- Our expected demand is 100 units per week
- How many should I order?
- I need to consider the cost of ordering
- Evaluate the cost over a year
- Which is the best order quantity?

Order period	1 week	2 weeks	4 weeks	8 weeks	13 weeks	26 weeks	52 weeks
Quantity	100	200	400	800	1300	2600	5200
Cost	£100	£200	£400	£800	£1,300	£2,600	£5,200
Orders in a year	52	26	13	6.5	4	2	1
Order / Delivery Cost in year	£1,560	£780	£390	£195	£120	£60	£30

Now this presents an entirely different picture. The highest cost is when the entire year's stock is purchased. Sam goes to his Finance Director Emily for advice. She suggests that adding the two costs would be a simple way to see what the total costs are. This evaluation is shown in Table 4.3.

What is clear to Sam is that as one cost increases the other decreases. By adding up we can see that at some point there is a balance between increasing and decreasing costs. In this case it is around eight weeks, thus the best option would be to order from Clare Sports every eight weeks and store an eight-week order, an average of four weeks at Ollie's Warehouse. To get a better view of this we can view it as a graph, shown in Figure 4.2.

If we look at this graph it is clear that there is a balance between the cost of ordering and the cost of holding stock. What Harris noted, all those years ago, was that this balance point was when the order cost = the holding cost. What Harris did was to express the evaluation as an equation. Figure 4.3 shows the development of the economic formula used by Harris.

The result shows the calculated EOQ is in reality 774.59, which is usefully precise, but practically we would round up to 800/8 weeks supply.

TABLE 4.2 Evaluation of cost of holding stock

- If I buy a week's stock I need space to store
- I can rent space from a warehouse, at a cost of £1 per 100 footballs per week
- I only pay for space I use
- How many should I store?
- I need to consider the cost of buying the storage
- Evaluate the cost of holding over a year
- What is the best quantity to store?

Order period	1 week	2 weeks	4 weeks	8 weeks	13 weeks	26 weeks	52 weeks
Quantity to be stored	100	200	400	800	1,300	2,600	5,200
Average quantity in stock	50	100	200	400	650	1,300	2,600
Cost/football/year	£0.52						
Holding Cost per year	£26	£52	£104	£208	£338	£676	£1,352

FIGURE 4.2 Graph of inventory costs (ordering and holding)

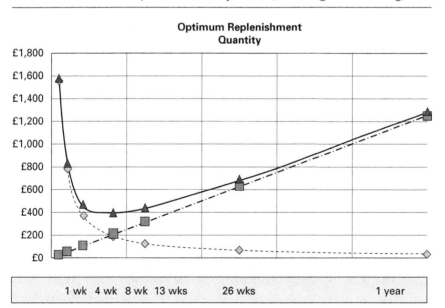

TABLE 4.3 Total inventory costs over the year

- Increasing the order size reduces the Order cost, but
  - Reducing the order quantity reduces the storage cost so is there a solution?
- Consider both, thus the total cost of storing and holding...

	1 week	2 weeks	4 weeks	8 weeks	13 weeks	26 weeks	52 weeks
Order Quantity	100	200	400	800	1300	2600	5200
Order/Delivery Cost in year	£1,560	£780	£390	£195	£120	£60	£30
Holding Cost per year	£26	£52	£104	£208	£338	£676	£1,352
Total Cost	£1,586	£832	£494	£403	£458	£736	£1,382

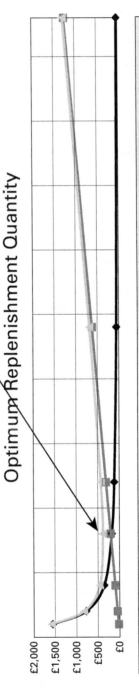

Optimum Replenishment Quantity

1wk 2wk 1month 2 months 3months 6 months 1 year

—◆— Order / Delivery Cost in year —■— Holding Cost per year —+— Total Cost

FIGURE 4.3 The classic economic order quantity formula (Harris, 1913)

Based on Sam's footballs

D = Demand C = Cost of Ordering/Set-up P = Unit Cost i = inventory holding rate as %	5,200 £30.00 £1.00 52%	
Annual Ordering Costs = $\dfrac{\text{Annual Demand * Ordering Cost}}{\text{Quantity}}$	$OC = \dfrac{D * C}{Q}$	$\dfrac{5,200 * £30.00}{Q}$
Annual Holding Costs = $\dfrac{\text{Quantity Ordered * Inventory Holding Cost}}{2}$ Inventory Holding Costs = holding cost % * the cost per item	$HC = \dfrac{Q * i * P}{2}$	$\dfrac{Q * 52\% * £1.00}{2}$
Balance is achieved when OC = HC	$\dfrac{D * C}{Q} = Q * i * P$	$\dfrac{£156,000}{Q} = £52.00 * Q$
Economic Order Quantity	$\sqrt{Q} = \dfrac{2 * D * C}{P * i}$	$Q = \sqrt{\dfrac{2 * 5,200 * £30.00}{£1.00 * 52\%}}$ 774.60

In our example we took a very simplistic view of the order and holding costs. If we consider these more carefully we would come up with the following:

- Ordering cost:
  - cost of placing an order, ie administrations costs – staff, paperwork;
  - cost of transporting goods;
  - costs for receiving/issuing materials to manufacture batches; and
  - cost of transit packaging/pallets.
- Holding cost
  - storage costs, ie renting, heating, lighting, insurance, personnel, containers;
  - capital costs, ie interest on loans (working capital costs), land, building, equipment;
  - risk costs, ie obsolescence, deterioration, shrinkage or evaporation; and
  - opportunity costs, ie lost opportunity to invest elsewhere, opportunity to reduce purchase price.

EXCEL 4.1   Simple EOQ calculator

	A	B	C
1	Annual Demand Quantity	D	£5,200.00
2	Order Cost	C	£30.00
3	Cost per Part	P	£1.00
4	Inventory Holding Cost	i	£0.52
5			
6			
7	Economic Order Quantity		£774.60

Enter this formula

Cell C7   = SQRT((2*C*D)/(P*i))   = SQRT((2*C2*C1)/(C3*C4))

The costs indicated above are the more obvious; later academics expanded this to include the cost of shortage. There are issues with this formula in that while it is logical and important to find the balance between conflicting costs of inventory, the key elements of the EOQ formula are difficult to calculate accurately, ie the cost of holding inventory and the cost of placing an order. If we are able to get an estimate at the costs the approach is beneficial because it is common to all parts being managed and is equally applicable to all. It also assumes that the demand is constant, which is not always true. This is easily overcome by frequent re-validation. The formula can easily be expressed as a handy calculator in Excel, as seen in Excel 4.1.

EOP: extending EOQ to represent days of supply

In our example, once we had calculated the EOQ we mentally converted to a time period. If we think how we normally relate to our suppliers we tend to use regular deliveries, daily, weekly, usually a specific day in the week, monthly etc. Thus it would be useful to express the EOQ as a time period. Figure 4.4 shows the extension of the formula which, when calculated, gives 37.23 days or approximately two months based on 4 weeks a month.

FIGURE 4.4   EOQ extended to calculate the economic order period

Based on Sam's footballs

D = Demand C = Cost of Ordering / Set-up P = Unit Cost i = inventory holding rate as % £0.52 per year or 52% of the unit cost W = working days in a year		5,200 £30.00 £1.0 52% 250	
Economic Order Quantity	$Q = \sqrt{\dfrac{2*D*C}{P*i}}$	$Q = \sqrt{\dfrac{2*5,200*30.0}{£1.0*52\%}}$	774.60
Economic Order Period (EOP)	EOQ / D		774.60 / 5,200 0.148 years
	(EOQ / D) * W	0.148 * 250	37.24 days
Economic Order Period (EOP)	$\left\{\dfrac{\sqrt{\dfrac{2*D*C}{P*i}}}{D}\right\} * W$	$EOP = \left\{\dfrac{\sqrt{\dfrac{2*5,200*30.0}{£1.0*52\%}}}{5,200}\right\} * 250$	774.60 / 5,200 0.148 years 37.24 days

This is easily converted to a simple Excel sheet to provide a handy calculator shown in Excel 4.2.

EXCEL 4.2

	A	B	C	D
1	Annual Demand Quantity	D	5200	
2	Order Cost	C	£30.00	
3	Cost per Part	p	£1.00	
4	Inventory Holding Cost	i	52%	
5	Working Days a year	W	250	
6				
7	Economic Order Quantity		774.597	Units
8	Economic Order Period in Days		37.240	Days
9	Economic Order Period in Days		37.240	Days
10				

Enter these formulae

Cell C7 = SQRT((2*C*D)/(p*i))   = SQRT((2*C2*C1)/(C3*C4))
Cell C8 = (EOQ / D) * W   = (C7/C1)*C5
Cell C9 = (SQRT((2*C*D)/(p*i))/D)*W = (SQRT((2*C2*C1)/(C3*C4))/C1)*C5

EOQ and price breaks

The last twist in the tale is the possibility that the supplier, in an effort to induce you to buy larger quantities, will offer a price reduction, say if you buy 1,000 footballs I will let you have them for £0.95p and if you buy 2,000 then you can have them for £0.90p. In simple terms we would calculate the EOQ and EOP for the two price breaks; a simple modification to the Excel 4.2 would create an easily used ready reckoner, as shown in Excel 4.3.

EXCEL 4.3

	A	B	C	D
1	Annual Demand Quantity	D	5,200	
2	Order Cost	C	£30.00	
3	Cost per Part	P	£75.00	
4	Inventory Holding Cost	i	52%	
5	Working days	W	250	
6	Economic Order Quantity	= SQRT((2*C*D)/(P*i))		
7				
8	Supplier Order Quantity	Cost per Part	EOQ	EOP Days
9	up to 1000	£1.00	774.597	37.240
10	> 1000	£0.95	794.719	38.208
11	> 2000	£0.90	816.497	39.255

Enter these formulae

Cell C9, *then copy down*   – SQRT((2*$C$2*$C$1)/(B9*$C$4))
Cell D9, *then copy down*   = (C9/$C$1)*$C$5

By looking at the result we can easily see that on this occasion we should resist the temptations of our supplier to buy more. The initial rounding to 40 days is not exceeded by even the most generous discounts.

Economic ordering summary

We have looked at a number of ways we can use the principles of economic ordering and a couple of formulas. The debate still continues nearly 100 years after Wilson and Harris first proposed the EOQ formula. Many other academics have extended and modified the formula, but at its heart it is seeking to balance the conflicting costs of ordering and costs of holding stock. The issues of how to determine the costs will be addressed in Chapter 5, but the simple conclusion is that there is a balance point between a small number of big orders and a large number of small orders.

Protecting against supply and demand issues

We know that all the best laid plans can go awry, in the case of operations planning and MRP systems we make a forecast of what we think our customers want and we plan, based on a given lead-time deliveries to arrive 'just' before the stock we have runs out. There are four possible outcomes:

- Supplier delivers late.
- Supplier delivers early.
- Demand is higher than expected.
- Demand is lower than expected.

These four possibilities are shown in Figure 4.5: if the supplier delivers late then we will likely run out of stock; conversely, if the supplier is early then we will have still have some left. If the demand is higher then again we will run out before the next delivery from the supplier, and if the demand is

FIGURE 4.5 Supply demand variations effect on the inventory saw-tooth

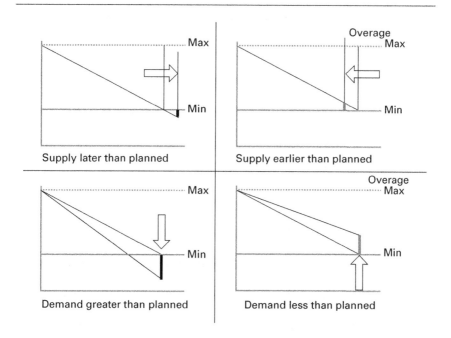

lower we will have some in hand when the next delivery arrives. Thus we only need to focus on two scenarios: late deliveries and higher than expected demand.

Forecast error

In Chapter 2 we mentioned the importance of forecasting in the management of demand; it was also made clear that the forecast would likely be wrong. This not a failure of an individual, weak business processes or poor quality software, it is merely a fact of life. Predicting the future is impossible; we can often get close but there will always be an event on the horizon which will not be expected. Forecast and inventory planning systems have come a long way and utilize statistics to help protect against a predictable amount for forecast error. Most forecast error and statistical safety stock systems utilize the Normal and Poisson distributions.

Normal distribution/Poisson distribution

If we measure the accuracy of a forecast, we will find that in most cases it behaves like a 'normal' distribution, that is to say that there are a lot of occasions where the forecast is only slightly above or below the prediction, there are a few occasions where the demand is significantly higher or lower and on rare occasions the demand is very significantly higher or lower. A typical Normal distribution curve is shown in Figure 4.6. The Normal distribution holds true for all but the very low levels of demand, when the distribution is said to be a Poisson distribution, shown in Figure 4.6. The key is that both are used to provide a link between customer service level and the determination of safety stock. The similarity between the two types of distributions is not really a surprise as we are looking to determine the probability of an event. These distributions are used by all disciplines when estimating the probability of an event. In the case of safety stock we use these distributions to determine a customer service level, thus if we want to ensure that we are able to cope with 90 per cent of the possible forecast error we need to use the appropriate service factor from the normal distribution.

Statistical safety stock

The simplest way to protect against higher than expected demand would be to keep an additional quantity in stock as a reserve against unexpected demand. However, academics have utilized this 'normal' relationship that

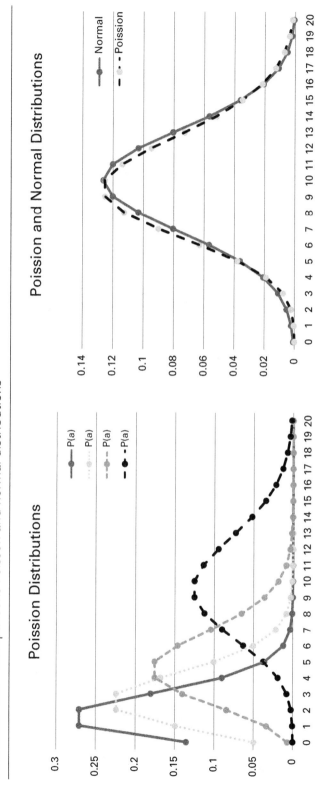

FIGURE 4.6 Comparisons Poisson and normal distributions

FIGURE 4.7 Safety stock to protect against demand variation (Waters, 2003: 174)

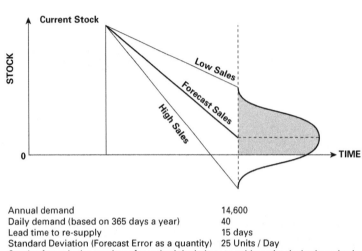

Normal Distribution Table	
Service Level	Standard Deviations
50.000%	0.0000
60.000%	0.2533
70.000%	0.5244
80.000%	0.8416
85.000%	1.0364
90.000%	1.2816
95.000%	1.6449
96.000%	1.7507
97.000%	1.8808
98.000%	2.0537
99.000%	2.3263
99.500%	2.5758
99.900%	3.0902
99.950%	3.2905
99.990%	3.7190
99.997%	4.0128

Annual demand	14,600
Daily demand (based on 365 days a year)	40
Lead time to re-supply	15 days
Standard Deviation (Forecast Error as a quantity)	25 Units / Day

Service factor is the number of standard deviations to achieve the desired service level
Thus to deliver a Service Level (to the customer) of 98% the Service Factor from the Table is 2.054

Safety stock = Service Factor x Standard Deviation x SqRt of Lead-time = 2.054 * 25 *$\sqrt{15}$
= 199

naturally results from forecasting/demand to develop formula that help us to calculate safety stock. There is a wide range of formulas which will attempt to cover a wide range of eventualities. We have focused on the three most commonly used when applying statistics to demand safety, demand and supply safety and demand considering the batch size safety.

Demand safety

If we are only concerned with demand variability and assume that it behaves 'normally' then we can use the simple formula shown in Figure 4.7 above.

Safety stock to protect against demand variation has three elements:

1 Desired service level.

2 Demand variation per day.

3 Square root of time to re-supply in days.

The three elements are explained in detail below.

- Service factor – this is the conversion of the desired service level into a 'factor' that represents the number of standard deviations from the average demand. If you look at the table in Figure 4.6 you will see that to achieve a service level of 85 per cent you will need a service factor of 1.0364; this would result in disappointing 15 per cent of your customers. To achieve 98 per cent will require a service factor of 2.0537; here only 2 per cent of your customers will be disappointed. High volume business would need to aim for a much higher level, say 99.9 per cent service on 0.1 per cent or 1 in a 1,000 customers. To achieve this a service factor of 3.0902 would be needed.

- Demand variation – this is the variability of the demand, either by looking at the demand history over time or by comparing the forecast with the actual demand and calculating the error. Either way it is expressed as a variation per (day) unit time. For example, we have an average sales of 40 units per day ± 25 units, that is the demand could be as low as 15 or as high as 65.

- Lead-time (of the replenishment order) – this is needed as we state the demand variation per unit time, so if we have to wait a long time for the next order the risk are much higher. The lead-time sits on the base of the saw-tooth triangle and the variation occurs on the hypotenuse, thus the increase is based on the square root of the lead-time and not a direct relationship.

Looking at the results we can see we need to have 199 units of safety stock; to understand this we can convert to time based on the daily demand, thus the safety stock represents 199/40 = 4.75 days or approximately five days. If you also express the demand variation as days 0.625, just over half a day. From this we can see that our demand is very variable; when we place an order for a product it will be 15 days before it will arrive. On this basis this amount of safety stock begins to seem reasonable. This can be easily expressed as an excel formula as shown in Excel 4.4.

The excel model makes it very easy to see the effect of varying the service level. The next problem is to consider the value for money against the protection provided. Let us say that we can buy this product for £10 and sell it for £15. As we said earlier, if we achieve a 98 per cent service level we will disappoint 2 per cent of our customers. This would potentially result in lost sales. If we are selling 14,600 units a year and we lose 2 per cent of sales we will miss the opportunity to sell:

$$14,600 \times 2\% = 292 \text{ @ £15 each} = £4,300 \text{ of lost sales}$$

If we compare this to our investment of 199 units of safety stock @ £10 = £1,990 it begins to look like a good deal. We need to be careful to make sure

EXCEL 4.4

	A	B	C	D	E	F	G
1	Annual Demand	14,600	Units			Service Level	Standard Deviations
2	Daily Demand	40	Units			50.000%	0.0000
3	Leadtime to re-supply	15	Days			60.000%	0.2533
4	Standard Deviation	25	Units			70.000%	0.5244
5						80.000%	0.8416
6						85.000%	1.0364
7						90.000%	1.2816
8						95.000%	1.6449
9						96.000%	1.7507
10	Safety Stock for	98%	=	198.853		97.000%	1.8808
11						98.000%	2.0537
12	Safety stock as days of demand			4.971		99.000%	2.3263
13						99.500%	2.5758
14						99.900%	3.0902
15						99.950%	3.2905
16						99.990%	3.7190
17						99.997%	4.0128

Enter these formulae

Cell D10	= NORMSINV(B10)*B4*SQRT(B3)
Cell D12	= +D10/B2
Cell G2 *then copy down to* G17	= NORMSINV(F2)

we do not get carried away and evaluate the lost sales with the investment in safety stock. By comparing the investment with the service level we can quickly come to a decision on the most appropriate safety stock level. An evaluation table can be easily be built in excel as shown in Excel 4.5.

A quick examination of the table will show that a service level of 95 per cent and the investment in safety is too low when compared to the lost sales; by increasing the service level to 98 per cent a small increase in investment of £395.91 potentially prevents £6,570 in lost sales. However, investing the next £263.95 would reduce the lost sales by £2,190, a much lower figure, a total investment of £2,252.48, a little more than the lost sales prevented. The argument is not quite so straightforward as the safety inventory investment is still available the following year and for no additional investment, however it does cost to hold the safety stock year on year. What is clear is that (in

EXCEL 4.5

	A	B	C	D
1	Annual Demand	14600	Units	
2	Daily Demand	40	Units	
3	Leadtime to re-supply	15	Days	
4	Standard Deviation	25	Units	
5	Unit Cost	£10.00	Each	
6	Selling Price	£15.00	Each	
7				
8	Service Level	Safety Quantity	Safety Value	Lost Sales
9	95.000%	159.26	£1,592.62	£10,950.00
10	98.000%	198.85	£1,988.53	£4,380.00
11	99.000%	225.25	£2,252.48	£2,190.00
12	99.900%	299.21	£2,992.10	£219.00
13	99.997%	388.54	£3,885.39	£6.57

Enter these formulae

Cell B9 *then copy down to* B13 = NORMSINV(A9)*$B$4*SQRT($B$3)
Cell C9 *then copy down to* C13 = B9*$B$5
Cell D9 *then copy down to* D13 = (1-A9)*$B$1*$B$6

this example) less than 98 per cent the losses are too high and much above 98 per cent the additional cost makes the ROI questionable.

Demand/supply safety

If we want to extend the safety to cover the performance of our supplier it would make sense to use a formula that covers both. Waters (2003: 180) extends his demand safety formula as shown in Figure 4.7. The additional variation used is the supplier lead-time variation, for example if we were to monitor our supplier we may find that on average his lead-time is 15 days, but that he could be five days early or five days late (when measuring one standard deviation).

There is quite a significant effect by adding supply variation, which will possibly affect what would be a cost-effective service level. This formula is simple enough to convert into an excel as shown in Excel 4.6.

By adding the supply safety the cost-effective service level has been lowered. It is now somewhere between 97 per cent and 98 per cent, rather than 98 per cent and 99 per cent.

EXCEL 4.6

	A	B	C	D
1	Annual Demand	14600	Units	
2	Daily Demand	40	Units	
3	Leadtime to re-supply	15	Days	
4	Standard Deviation Demand	25	Units	
5	Standard Deviation Supply	5	Days	
6	Unit Cost	£10.00	Each	
7	Selling Price	£15.00	Each	
8				
9	Demand Safety			96.825
10	Supply Safety			200.000
11	Total Safety for	98%	=	456.353
12				
13	Service Level	Safety Quantity	Safety Value	Lost Sales
14	95.000%	365.49	£3,654.94	£10,950.00
15	97.000%	417.92	£4,179.21	£6,570.00
16	98.000%	456.35	£4,563.53	£4,380.00
17	99.000%	516.93	£5,169.26	£2,190.00
18	99.500%	572.36	£5,723.62	£1,095.00

Enter these formulae

Cell D9	= B4*SQRT(B3)
Cell D10	= B2*B5
Cell D11	= NORMSINV(B11)*SQRT((D9*D9)+(D10*D10))
Cell B14 *then copy down to* B18	= NORMSINV(A14)*SQRT(($D$9*$D$9)+($D$10*$D$10))
Cell C14 *then copy down to* C18	= B14*$B$6
Cell D14 *then copy down to* D18	= (1–A14)*$B$1*$B$7

Safety stock including the effect of batch size

Having protected against supply and demand, we have focused on the point of time when the supply is just due to arrive. In reality, for most of the time there is a considerable amount of stock, which gives a natural protection. It is therefore no surprise to find that academics have considered the size of the incoming order as well as supply/demand. Figure 4.9 shows this graphically.

Looking at the left of Figure 4.9 we can see that for the larger order size would only reach a level where safety may be needed three times in a given

FIGURE 4.8   Safety stock to protect against demand and supply variation

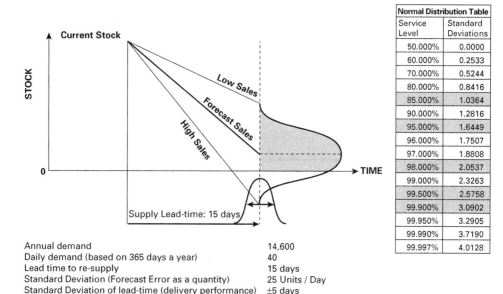

Normal Distribution Table	
Service Level	Standard Deviations
50.000%	0.0000
60.000%	0.2533
70.000%	0.5244
80.000%	0.8416
85.000%	1.0364
90.000%	1.2816
95.000%	1.6449
96.000%	1.7507
97.000%	1.8808
98.000%	2.0537
99.000%	2.3263
99.500%	2.5758
99.900%	3.0902
99.950%	3.2905
99.990%	3.7190
99.997%	4.0128

Annual demand	14,600
Daily demand (based on 365 days a year)	40
Lead time to re-supply	15 days
Standard Deviation (Forecast Error as a quantity)	25 Units / Day
Standard Deviation of lead-time (delivery performance)	±5 days

Service factor is the number of standard deviations to achieve the desired service level
Thus to deliver a Service Level (to the customer) of 98% the Service Factor from the Table is 2.054

Safety stock	$= \text{Service Factor} \times \sqrt{(\text{Demand Safety})^2 + (\text{Supply Safety})^2}$	
Demand Safety	$= \text{Standard Deviation of Demand} \times \sqrt{\text{lead-time}}$	$= 25 \times \sqrt{15}$
Supply Safety	$= \text{Standard Deviation of Supply} \times \text{Demand}$	$= 5 * 40$
Safety Stock	$= 2.054 * \sqrt{(25 \times \sqrt{15})^2 + (5 * 40)^2}$	$= 456$

FIGURE 4.9   Effect of order quantity on the need for safety stock

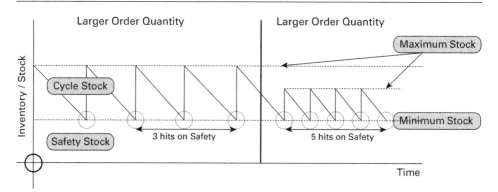

FIGURE 4.10   Supply demand safety considering order size and replenishment time

SL = Service Level		98%
SF = Service factor		2.0542
QRP = replenishment Quantity		900 units
TRP = replenishment time (lead-time)		15 days
D = Demand		14,600 / 40/day
σ_n = standard deviation of demand		±25 units
σ_{trp} = standard deviation of replenishment time		±5 units

Safety Stock =	$SF(1 - \frac{(1-SL)(QRP)}{(TRP)(D)})\left(\sqrt{(TRP)(\sigma_N^2) + (D^2)(\sigma_{TRP}^2)}\right)$	
	$(1 - \frac{(1-SL)(QRP)}{(TRP)(D)})$ * Safety Stock Supply & Demand	
	$(1 - \frac{(1-98\%)(900)}{(15)(40)}) \times 2.054 * (25 * 15)^2 + (5 * 40)^2$	= 0.9700 * 456 = 442.32

period, whereas as can be seen on the right the smaller order size will be in the 'zone' five times. Conversely, since we know that the demand safety is based on the time between orders, that small orders may require less safety, which is a bit of a contradiction. Schmidt, Hartmann and Nyhuis (2007) investigated this anomaly and derived a formula which attempts to take this into account. The formula is shown in Figure 4.10.

A closer look at the formula shows that it is essentially the same as the Supply Demand Safety formula with an additional factor to account for the effect of the batch size. The effect of this factor here is to reduce the safety stock by a small amount which recognizes that the size of the batch naturally protects for a period of time. Overall, the effect in simple terms is that the higher the order size the lower the safety stock, when compared with the supply demand safety. The caveat that Schmidt, Hartmann and Nyhuis (2007) apply to the formula is that it is only valid when the order size is greater than the quantity used during the lead time, that is to say where there is only one order being processed at any time. Where the lead-time is longer than the order cycle, ie there would more than one order being processed at any time, this is what happens in MRP systems. The time to replenishment (lead time) is, in reality, the time between batches which is in effect the order size, in which case the formula simplifies to: Safety Stock = Service Level Percentage × Supply Demand Safety Stock

This formula is a little more complex to convert into an excel and is shown in Excel 4.7.

EXCEL 4.7

	A	B	C	D
1	Annual Demand	14600	Units	D
2	Daily Demand	40	Units	d
3	Leadtime to re-supply	15	Days	TRP
4	Standard Deviation Demand	25	Units	σ_D
5	Standard Deviation Supply	5	Days	σ_{TRP}
6	Order Size	900	Units	QRP
7	Unit Cost	£10.00	Each	
8	Selling Price	£15.00	Each	
9				
10	Demand Safety			96.82
11	Supply Safety			200.00
12	SD Safety			222.20
13	QRP Function			0.9700
14	Total Safety for	98%	=	442.66

Enter these formulae

Cell D10   = B4*SQRT(B3)
Cell D11   = B2*B5
Cell D12   = SQRT((D10*D10)+(D11*D11))
Cell D13   = (1-((1-B14)*B6)/(B3*B2))
Cell D14   = NORMSINV(B14)*D13*SQRT((D10*D10)+(D11*D11))

Safety time

There is a simple alternative to the complex statistical based safety stock which simply adds time, to protect against supply and demand variations. It would be possible to convert any value determined as a quantity to time. As discussed in earlier chapters the advantage of using a time-based parameter is that it will require less maintenance. It is common to use in combination with Pareto, which is discussed in the next section, and specify a number of days per value class.

Hybrid safety stock

It is possible to combine safety quantity and time to create hybrid approaches which can resolve some of the issues. There are three options when using this approach:

- Calculate both, then take the least of the two values – this is useful if you are looking to minimize the safety stock holdings, and service level is not a significant issue. It will tend to under-protect the very high value items, which should already be focus items.

- Calculate both, then take the higher of the two values – this is useful if you want to focus on customer service level and inventory holding is not a specific issue. It will tend to over-protect the low value items.

- Use a combination of both, ie safety time of five days plus safety quantity of 100. This approach will give the advantages of adjusting as the demand varies up and down, but retain a minimum if the demand fall below a certain level. A common method of determining the values is to calculate a statistical safety stock and then allocate part of the safety quantity as safety time based on the daily going rate of the product.

Parts classification

When managing large numbers of items it is often useful to segregate into groups by:

- commodity;
- supplier;
- depot;
- buyer; and
- planner.

All these groupings do not consider the attributes of the item itself, they are focused on the management grouping. Parts/products have different attributes:

- value;
- volumes;
- volatility – variation of the demand of the product;
- physical size;
- shelf-life; and
- product lifecycle.

It is these attributes that will affect the way you want to manage the part, and thus if we can classify the product using these attributes we can divide our parts into useful sub-groups for inventory management. In this section we will look at a number of the most popular techniques and how they can be combined to define inventory policy to produce inventory plans.

ABC/Pareto classification

ABC or Pareto planning is a very common classification technique. It is based on the observation of the economist Vilfredo Pareto in 1906. Pareto identified that 80 per cent of the wealth was held by 20 per cent of the population. This observation was developed by Juran and others in the period after World War II as part of the drive to improve production efficiency. This work gave rise to the use of the Pareto Curve in operations management, in inventory planning, inventory control and quality and problem solving. The ABC classification for inventory planning will take a group of parts and divide into three groups, based on their annual usage value. That is to say the number of pieces used in 12 months times the unit cost. This group of parts is then ranked highest spend parts at the top and lowest at the bottom. They are then divided into three groups based on the following rule:

- A Class – the top 80 per cent of parts by value, normally about 20 per cent of the parts.
- B Class – the next 15 per cent (95 per cent of the total value), normally the next 30 per cent of parts.
- C Class – the last 5 per cent of parts by value which is the remaining 50 per cent of parts.

The benefit of this approach is that you can take a large number of parts that you are trying to manage and identify the parts that are the most financially important. To understand this a little better we can look as a sample group of parts. If we take a sample group of 27 parts as shown in Appendix A we can create a Pareto Curve and divide the parts into the three categories, by following the following steps:

- Calculate the annual usage spend.
- Sort annual spend highest at top.
- Cumulate the annual spend.
- Calculate the percentage of cumulative annual spend.
- Calculate percentage of items.

Once you have calculated the cumulative spends you will be able to divide the list into three parts by applying the Pareto rules above. An example of this process is shown in Excel 4.8.

EXCEL 4.8

Count	Part Number	Annual Usage or Demand	Cost Per Part	Annual Spend Value £	Cumulative Annual Spend £	Cumulative percentage of Annual Spend	Cumulative percentage of Parts	ABC
1	B78811ZD	1324	£42.84	£56,720.16	£56,720.16	26.6%	3.7%	A
2	B78812ZF	987	£41.87	£41,325.69	£98,045.85	45.9%	7.4%	A
3	B78810741A	1012	£18.50	£18,722.00	£116,767.85	54.7%	11.1%	A
4	N6554004M0256	523	£35.08	£18,346.84	£135,114.69	63.3%	14.8%	A
5	SK98751	46	£316.19	£14,544.74	£149,659.43	70.1%	18.5%	A
6	LE763	781	£11.11	£8,676.91	£158,336.34	74.2%	22.2%	A
7	D0883030014C	267	£27.54	£7,353.18	£165,689.52	77.6%	25.9%	A
8	C78810742A	360	£16.87	£6,073.20	£171,762.72	80.4%	29.6%	B
9	D0862060018Y	163	£33.26	£5,421.38	£177,184.10	83.0%	33.3%	B
10	C78810761A	567	£8.43	£4,779.81	£181,963.91	85.2%	37.0%	B
11	LE02	396	£11.09	£4,391.64	£186,355.55	87.3%	40.7%	B
12	B78812001B	458	£7.10	£3,251.80	£189,607.35	88.8%	44.4%	B
13	KN552130	10	£319.98	£3,199.80	£192,807.15	90.3%	48.1%	B
14	A0906030015	18	£150.22	£2,703.96	£195,511.11	91.6%	51.9%	B
15	B78810721A	749	£3.44	£2,576.56	£198,087.67	92.8%	55.6%	B
16	D0991020012	164	£14.60	£2,394.40	£200,482.07	93.9%	59.3%	B
17	D0862070019Y	60	£35.25	£2,115.00	£202,597.07	94.9%	63.0%	B
18	D0978040014	35	£57.63	£2,017.05	£204,614.12	95.8%	66.7%	C
19	A78810601E	450	£4.20	£1,890.00	£206,504.12	96.7%	70.4%	C
20	B78818AE	35	£49.57	£1,734.95	£208,239.07	97.5%	74.1%	C
21	C78810762A	199	£7.44	£1,480.56	£209,719.63	98.2%	77.8%	C
22	D0753100033	75	£15.36	£1,152.00	£210,871.63	98.8%	81.5%	C
23	D1017040014	10	£95.36	£953.60	£211,825.23	99.2%	85.2%	C
24	KDB300600	8	£93.75	£750.00	£212,575.23	99.6%	88.9%	C
25	A0889030013	52	£9.59	£498.68	£213,073.91	99.8%	92.6%	C
26	B30880112C	700	£0.45	£315.00	£213,388.91	99.9%	96.3%	C
27	B30880113C	105	£1.18	£123.90	£213,512.81	100.0%	100.0%	C
Totals				£213,512.81				

Enter these formulae

Cell E2 *then copy down to* E28   = C2*D2
Cell F2 *then copy down to* F28   = SUM(E$2:E2)
Cell G2 *then copy down to* G28   = F2/MAX($F$2:$F$28)
Cell H2 *then copy down to* H28   = A2/MAX($A$2:$A$28)

If we look at the list we can see that if we were to simply look at the list in part number order the first part would have been A0889030013. However, this is the 25th in importance rank in our Pareto list, and the most important part B78811ZD is eighth, effectively buried somewhere in the middle. In this example we have one part that accounts for about one quarter of our annual spend. The likelihood is that this part already receives a lot of attention as it is probably a very important part of the range of products or a key part of the product we are making. We would tend to manage this part very closely and only bring into stock at the last minute. We would use JIT to manage the flow for either purchasing or manufacture. Once we have divided the parts into groups we would define a policy/approach to the management of the parts in the group based on the class the part falls into. Table 4.4 summarizes the key policy considerations.

TABLE 4.4 Action/focus for the three Pareto inventory classes

Class	Percentage of Spend	Cumulative Percentage of Spend	Percentage of Parts	Cumulative Percentage of Parts
A	80%	80%	20%	20%
B	15%	95%	30%	50%
C	5%	100%	50%	100%

Class	Percentage of Spend	Percentage of Parts	Action/Focus
A	80%	20%	A small number of very important and valuable items needing close management
B	15%	30%	A slightly larger number of parts which are considerable less valuable so need to be managed efficiently
C	5%	50%	A large number of parts of no monetary value that need to be managed in a way that they minimize the time to manage.

For the A Class we dealing with high value key components/products. We want to ensure that they arrive 'at the last possible moment' or JIT and in small quantities, which means very frequent deliveries often daily. For our C Class parts we have to manage a large range of products but they are in inventory value terms of no consequence, but do not forget that they are still capable of stopping production. To paraphrase the proverb:

> For the want of a nail, the horse was lost, for want of the horse the army was lost.

So although these are of no financial value they still have the potential to disrupt the business, thus we must ensure we have sufficient without spending time managing.

We can summarize into a simple inventory law:

> If I am going to manage inventory I want small amounts of high value inventory received frequently, and large amounts in low value inventory received infrequently.

Pareto is always represented as a Pareto Curve which is shown in Figure 4.11. This curve is achieved by plotting Columns H and G using the Excel XY chart type. In this case the curve of our 27 parts does not strictly confirm the 80/20 rule, although it clearly shows the important few and the trivial many.

FIGURE 4.11 Pareto

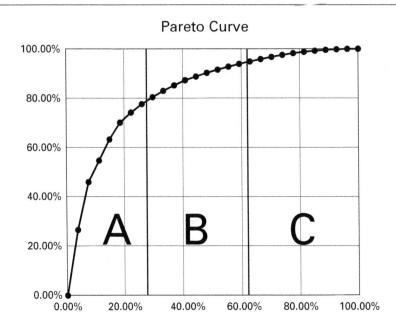

Using Pareto to plan inventory using cycle and safety stock

Pareto inventory policy and estimate

Once the principle is understood, the next important step is to look at how we can utilize this in the process of inventory planning, how to develop an inventory policy and use it to calculate inventory based on Pareto. As we are dealing with a group of parts we do not want to make individual decisions about how many to hold for each part, so we can use the order period as a representation of the order size. We could consider holding a week of stock, two weeks, one month etc.

It would be easy to guess at the appropriate days of supply, but by using a simple table, as shown in Table 4.5, we can put some logic behind the decision. First, we summarize the list of parts into the three Pareto classes ABC, next we take the cumulative value for each group, and the number of parts. If we assume that the working year is 250 days then we can calculate the daily going rate, the amount of value used in a working day. We can also list, for reference, the number of parts in each group. If we now create a table with an evaluation of 5, 10, 20 etc days of supply we can see how much inventory we would need to invest if we were to adopt a particular days of supply policy. Looking at Table 4.5, it now becomes clear that even at five days for Class A the investment is significant when compared to the other groups. However, for Class C we can easily afford to buy much larger quantities – the benefit of this is less frequent orders, for example if we bought weekly we would have to process 10 orders a week for 52 weeks in the year (a total of 520); if we bought 80 days supply we would only need to process 3–4 orders a year for the 10 parts (a total of 30–40), which is a considerable saving in time, which can then be spent focusing on the A class parts. Thus we are, in effect, exchanging a higher inventory level for less time and effort. Using this analysis we can see the logic behind the typical ABC policy shown below in Table 4.6.

Table 4.6 shows all the summarized information, along with the policy decisions, which will clearly define what needs to be done to implement the policy. Note the average inventory is half the days of supply, as for planning we assume the average inventory is half the order size. Having defined the plan we can communicate our decision to the planner. All the planner needs to do to implement it would be to look up their part in the Pareto list in Excel 4.8 and he would be able to determine what order policy he should apply. For example, Part C78810742A is a B Class product and should as a

TABLE 4.5   Determining inventory policy based on Pareto analysis

Class	Total Annual Spend	Daily Going Rate	No of parts	Days of Supply					
				5	10	20	40	80	160
A	£165,689.52	£662.76	7	£3,313.79	£6,627.58	£13,255.16	£26,50.32	£53,020.65	£106,041.29
B	£36,907.55	£147.63	10	£738.15	£1,476.30	£2,952.60	£5,905.21	£11,810.42	£23,620.83
C	£10,915.74	£43.66	10	£218.31	£436.63	£873.26	£1,746.53	£3,493.04	£6,986.07
	£213,512.81	£854.05	27						

TABLE 4.6   Inventory policy statement

Class	Annual Spend Value £	Daily Going Rate	No of Parts	Class Limits	Days of Supply	No of Orders	Average Inventory
A	£165,689.52	£662.76	7	80.0%	5	350	£1,656.90
B	£36,907.55	£14763	10	95.0%	20	125	£1,476.30
C	£10,915.74	£43.66	10		80	31.25	£1,746.52
Totals	£ 213,512.81	£854.05	27			506.25	£4,879.72

Note: Average Inventory is half Days of Supply

result be ordered every 20 days. The planner knows that 360 are used a year, so an order of 360 divided by 250 (working days in a year) multiplied by a 20 days order cycle will give 28.8 as a recommended order size, which would be rounded to 30 (a month's supply). In addition to making the decision about the order size we must also consider the safety stock. We can apply the same approach by looking at the value of safety based on time (Table 4.7).

The table is essentially the same as the days of supply, however the decision here is not the amount to be ordered but the amount of demand/supply protection, thus we would be saying that for Class A we can only afford five days, whereas for C Class having 20 days' extra stock to protect against late deliveries or higher than expected demand is more than sufficient. We can now add these decisions to our inventory plan/policy. The final results can be seen in Table 4.8.

The table now shows the days of supply and safety stock decisions we have made, so we now have a clearly defined policy for each Pareto inventory class which can be implemented by the planner. Thus for our example, part C78810742A, we have also indicated the amount of safety; either it can be set to 10 days safety time or a quantity of 14.4, rounded to 15.

Pareto exchange curve

It goes without saying that any business will focus on year on year improvements on all aspects of the business. As a result we can expect a request to reduce inventory each year. To achieve a reduction we will have to change one or more elements of the policy. The two options we have are:

1 Change the days of supply/safety stock for each Pareto Class.

2 Change the number of parts in each Pareto Class.

To understand which of these is better we can look at the effect on each policy to see which option is the most effective way to reduce inventory.

Change the days of supply/safety stock for each Pareto Class

For this we could consider first reducing the safety stock on the A class parts by one day – these are the most closely managed parts and we should be able to manage. The days of supply for C Class parts could be reduced from 80 days to, for example, 60 days. If we evaluate these changes the results would be as shown in Table 4.9.

By applying these changes we have reduced the inventory from £10,543.07 to £9,443.68, some £1,099.39 or about 10 per cent.

TABLE 4.7 Determining inventory policy based on Pareto analysis

Class	Total Annual Spend	Daily Going Rate	No of parts	Days of Safety					
				5	10	20	40	80	160
A	£165,689.52	£662.76	7	£3,313.79	£6,627.58	£13,255.16	£26,510.32	£53,020.65	£106,041.29
B	£36,907.55	£147.63	10	£738.15	£1,476.30	£2,952.60	£5,905.21	£11,810.42	£23,621.83
C	£10,915.74	£43.66	10	£218.31	£436.63	£873.26	£1,746.52	£3,493.04	£6,986.07
	£213,512.81	£854.05	27						

TABLE 4.8 Inventory policy statement including safety stock

Class	Annual Spend Value £	Daily Going Rate	Class Limits	No of Parts	Days of Supply	Safety Stock Days	No of Orders	Average Cycle Inventory	Safety Stock Value	Total Planned Inventory
A	£165,689.52	£662.76	80.0%	7	5	5	350	£1,656.90	£3,313.79	£4,970.69
B	£36,907.55	£147.63	95.0%	10	20	10	125	£1,476.30	£1,476.30	£2,952.60
C	£10,915.74	£43.66		10	80	20	31	£1,746.52	£873.26	£2,619.78
Totals	£ 213,512.81	£854.05		27			506	£4,879.88	£5,663.35	£10,543.07

Change the number of parts in each Pareto Class

If we decide to alter the class limit in order to reduce the inventory we will need to increase the number of parts in A Class and reduce the number in C Class, thus changing the limit from 80 per cent to 82 per cent and similarly shifting 95 to 97 per cent. We will move parts from B to A and from C to B. The results can be seen in Table 4.10.

We can see from the table that we have achieved a reduction from £10,543.07 to £9,614.28, or £928.79 or about 9 per cent. This is slightly less than the option of changing the parameters. If we take a close look at this approach we can see a distinct advantage. If we change the parameters we affect every part in the classes affected, thus to execute the first option we have to take more risk on our seven A class parts by reducing safety and need to discuss with all the suppliers/manufacturing affected by the changes to the days of supply for the 10 Class C parts. However, to execute the second option we only have to change one part from B Class to A Class and two parts from C Class to B Class. The parts can easily be identified by looking at the Pareto listing and marking of the new limits. In the example parts in Excel 4.8, we can see they are C78810742A, D0978040014 and A78810601E. It is a much easier task to look at three parts than 17. Thus we can see that the manipulation of the Class limits is the most effective method of reducing inventory within a Pareto model.

Runner repeater stranger

Dividing parts by their usage value is not the only way of splitting products; as we mentioned earlier in the chapter there are other attributes we can consider to split the parts into groups. Dividing into groups by volume of demand is another popular approach. By dividing products into their volume, the logic is that high volume parts will, assuming the demand is regular, need to be made often and low volume parts we may choose to make less often but in larger quantities. The most often cited example is Runner, Repeater and Stranger:

- *Runner.* A runner is typically defined as high volume products which are typically produced each day or week.

- *Repeater.* A repeater is typically defined as medium volume products, which are made on a regular basis, possibly fortnightly or monthly.

- *Stranger.* A stranger is the low volume residue, which are usually only made when sufficient demand is identified; the demand may also be

TABLE 4.9 The effect of changing days of supply and safety stock

Class	Annual Spend Value £	Daily Going Rate	Class Limits	No of Parts	Days of Supply	Safety Stock Days	No of Orders	Average Cycle Inventory	Safety Stock Value	Total Planned Inventory
A	£165,689.52	£662.76	80.0%	7	5	4	350	£1,656.90	£2,651.03	£4,307.93
B	£36,907.55	£147.63	95.0%	10	20	10	125	£1,476.30	£1,476.30	£2,952.60
C	£10,915.74	£43.66		10	60	20	42	£1,309.89	£873.26	£2,183.15
Totals	£ 213,512.81	£854.05		27			517	£4,443.09	£5,000.59	£9,443.68

TABLE 4.10 The effect of changing class limits in inventory plan

Class	Annual Spend Value £	Daily Going Rate	Class Limits	No of Parts	Days of Supply	Safety Stock Days	No of Orders	Average Cycle Inventory	Safety Stock Value	Total Planned Inventory
A	£171,762.72	£687.05	82.0%	8	5	5	400	£1,717.63	£3,435.25	£5,152.88
B	£34,741.40	£138.97	97.0%	11	20	10	137.5	£1,389.66	£1,389.66	£2,779.31
C	£7,008.69	£28.03		8	80	20	25	£1,121.39	£560.70	£1,682.09
Totals	£ 213,512.81	£854.05		27			562.5	£4,228.87	£5,385.61	£9,614.28

regular. Some people will add an additional category of Aliens, which, as the name implies, are even rarer than the strangers.

Dividing the products into the groups, there is little advice on how to determine these groups. The decision is largely driven by the range of volume in the parts being managed. For example, if we consider automotive manufacturing, Ford GB's output of 75,000 compared with Morgan's output of 1,000 per year. The number of parts to be managed may be similar, but magnitude of the volumes will be entirely different. Table 4.11 below shows possible split approaches using a boundary based on dividing the maximum by 10.

TABLE 4.11 Runner, repeater, stranger volume comparison

Category	Usage per vehicle	Ford	Morgan
Total Volume		75,000	1,000
Runner	1,000 to 100	75,000,000 to 7,500,000	1,000,000 to 100,000
Repeater	100 to 10	7,500,000 to 750,000	100,000 to 10,000
Stranger	10 to 0	750,000 to 0	10,000 to 0

A second alternative would be to divide the group of parts into three groups such that the middle group is 50 per cent of the total volume, in the middle of the distribution. The results for our sample groups of parts is shown in Table 4.12.

The first approach divides into >1,000, <1,000 but >100, whereas the second approach takes the total volume of 9,554 divided by 2, giving 4,777 and then starting from the middle spread up and down till half the volume is covered. The thresholds in the second case are >700, <700 but >35. The second approach produces a more balanced list, although is more complex to implement.

Where RRS is appropriate

The RRS approach may be more appropriate than Pareto where the parts values are similar, manufacture process have high setup time, or the key attribute in the supply chain is the volume throughput not the inventory

TABLE 4.12   Division of sample group into runner, repeater and stranger

	RRS × 10	RRS @ 50%
Runner	2	5
Repeater	15	18
Stranger	10	4
Total	27	27

Part Number	Annual Usage or Demand	Cumulative Volume	RRS × 10	RRS @ 50%	
B78811ZD	1324	1324	Runner	Runner	
B78810741A	1012	2336	Runner	Runner	
B78812ZF	987	3323	Repeat	Runner	
LE763	781	4104	Repeat	Runner	0
B78810721A	749	4853	Repeat	Runner	9
B30880112C	700	5553	Repeat	Repeat	8
C78810761A	567	6120	Repeat	Repeat	7
N6554004M0256	523	6643	Repeat	Repeat	6
B78812001B	458	7101	Repeat	Repeat	5
A78810601E	450	7551	Repeat	Repeat	4
LE02	396	7947	Repeat	Repeat	3
C78810742A	360	8307	Repeat	Repeat	2
D0883030014C	267	8574	Repeat	Repeat	1
C78810762A	199	8773	Repeat	Repeat	
D0991020012	164	8937	Repeat	Repeat	1
D0862060018Y	163	9100	Repeat	Repeat	2
B30880113C	105	9205	Repeat	Repeat	3
D0753100033	75	9280	Stranger	Repeat	4
D0862070019Y	60	9340	Stranger	Repeat	5
A0889030013	52	9392	Stranger	Repeat	6
SK98751	46	9438	Stranger	Repeat	7
B78818AE	35	9473	Stranger	Repeat	8
D0978040014	35	9508	Stranger	Repeat	9
A0906030015	18	9526	Stranger	Stranger	0
D1017040014	10	9536	Stranger	Stranger	
KN552130	10	9546	Stranger	Stranger	
KDB300600	8	9554	Stranger	Stranger	
	9554			4777	

value. It becomes very much a business judgement as to whether RRS or Pareto is favoured.

Inventory matrix

To overcome this an inventory matrix can be used, which combines these two approaches, thus dividing the parts into two simple three-way splits to create a nine-box matrix. This has the advantage of being able to differentiate between high value/high volume products and high value low volume products which may benefit from different planning rules.

Table 4.13 shows how we can use different techniques to provide a more sophisticated approach than the simple division into three groups.

Alternatives matrices

We began this section by talking about the different attributes of the parts and so far we have only focused on value and volume. The inventory matrix approach allows us to possibly consider, within our business operation, the most important attributes for the product. It may be that we are in the business of making products that have a variable shelf-life. Thus we can replace the runner, repeater and stranger with long, medium and short shelf life, which would allow us to alter our policies inline with the difficulty of managing shelf life.

TABLE 4.13   Inventory matrix of ABC Pareto and runner, repeater and stranger

	Runner	Repeater	Stranger
A	High Volume/High Value JIT style production	Medium Volume/High Value MRP Consider EOQ ordering	Low Volume/High Value MRP Lot for Lot orders
B	High Volume/Medium Value MRP Consider EOQ ordering	Medium Volume/Medium Value MRP Consider EOQ ordering	Low Volume/Medium Value
C	High Volume/Low Value Vendor Managed Inventory	Medium Volume/Low Value Re-order point Bulk Purchase	Low Volume/Low Value Make to Order

Developing a plan that will succeed

So far we have built an inventory plan/policy based on the sum of the average cycle stock and safety stock; this is also known as the average inventory. Average inventory is the level of inventory that our MRP system would attempt to achieve based on the specified parameters that define cycle stock (order quantity or order period) and safety stock (quantity or time). As we know, one of MRP's key assumptions is that what is planned to happen actually occur, now we know that this is never true, more importantly, as we discussed in the earlier chapter, the very purpose of safety stock is to protect against the unplanned increase in demand and/or the late arrival from our supplier.

What is underage and overage?

Thus our plans are built to protect against late orders and higher than expected demand. As we can see in Figure 4.12, there is almost as much chance that the order will be early or the demand lower than planned. If the demand is *less* than predicted or the supplier does deliver *early* then the

FIGURE 4.12   Supply and demand variations
(Relph and Barrar, 2001)

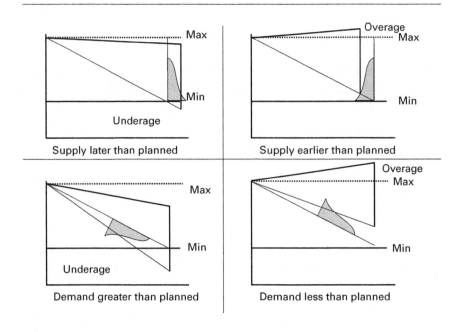

FIGURE 4.13   Definitions of overage, underage and optimum stock

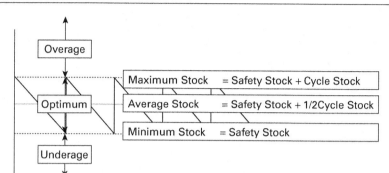

stock level would be higher than we would have planned. The overstock we shall call OVERAGE – which is defined as when the stock level is above the MAXIMUM stock. Conversely, if we have made use of the safety stock we are below the MINIMUM and we will define this as UNDERAGE. If we are between the MINIMUM and MAXIMUM stock we can define this as OPTIMUM. These definitions are shown pictorially in Figure 4.13. If parts are in overage MRP's logic will attempt to resolve the situation at the earliest opportunity, by recommending that orders are scheduled-out.

Why is overage important?

In the research conducted by Relph and Barrar (2001) to evaluate the amount of overage in companies, the report abstract summarizes the findings:

> The paper argues that overage is important because there is evidence that, even in well managed businesses a significant proportion of the inventory is in overage at any given time. Evaluations of twenty-inventory profiles from companies in different business sectors show between 10% and 98% of the inventory values were 'in overage'. For most businesses this will not be a trivial amount and any actions that can reduce it will bring significant benefit. The paper concludes that overage should be recognised in the same way as safety stock and thus, formally planned. Hence the effective control of overage will enhance the business's profitability by minimising the inventory investment.
>
> (Relph and Barrar, 2001)

The overage occurs for the same reason that shortage/underage occurs, in that people and systems are not perfect. As a result we get parts moving between shortage, underage, optimum and overage. In the main the MRP system will manage this movement by issuing re-scheduling actions, re-schedule-in for

Underage which if ignored will lead to Shortage, at which point the item is the focus of considerable attention. With overage MRP will recommend schedule out or cancel actions; the consequence of ignoring these is less dramatic, in that unlike shortage the immediate effect is not apparent. Assuming the part is current the Overage will eventually be used; the costs of Overage are associated with extra storage, cost of holding and risk of obsolesce. While it can be argued that some overage is inevitable and should be tolerated it is important to ensure that it remains a small amount. As the research showed, companies can operate with up to 90 per cent overage. The important step is to recognize the existence of the overage conditions and then agree upon the appropriate action. This is self-evident as, according to the renowned Management Consultant Peter Drucker, 'What gets measured gets managed'. It is worthwhile being a little more specific about overage to ensure that we do not focus on parts unnecessarily. The two questions related to overage are first how much, and second how long will it last. If we were to focus only on the highest value overages using a simple list in descending overage value order we would identify high value items but they will be consumed in a short period of time. This is what we call overage dissipation.

What is overage dissipation?

Dissipation is defined as 'how long before the item returns to within the optimum range'.

Figure 4.14 shows a typical stock level above maximum, ie 'in overage' as the part is consumed it falls below the maximum; when this happens the

FIGURE 4.14 Overage dissipation

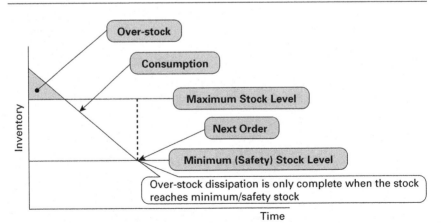

TABLE 4.14   Inventory condition definitions

Inventory Condition	Definition
Shortage	Stock is 0
Underage	Stock is below the minimum
Optimum	Stock is between the minimum and maximum
Overage	Stock is above the maximum
Severe Overage	Stock is twice the maximum
Excess	Stock is > 12 months demand
Surplus	Stock is > 24 months demand

item is no longer in overage. However, the overage dissipation is only complete when the stock reaches the minimum. This is because the next order due will take the item back up to maximum. We can express the overage dissipation as a length of time, ie overage days. The overage days are a simple expression of how long before the item returns to normal. This can provide a useful additional filter to the value, as a high value overage item whose dissipation is only five overage days is less of a worry than an item that has a dissipation of 50 days.

It is useful to provide generalized categories of overage. Table 4.14 shows a typical set of inventory conditions that could be used with inventory reporting.

The benefit of categorization is to be able to simply express the inventory performance and identify appropriate actions/level of management review against each inventory condition. For example, all surplus items should be reviewed by a senior manager, confirmation that all orders have been cancelled etc.

Importance of the next order

When defining overage we specified that it was not truly recovered until the stock level reaches the minimum stock, Figure 4.15 shows that if the order arrives before the stock reaches minimum the item is returned to over, albeit for a small period of time.

FIGURE 4.15   Incomplete overage dissipation

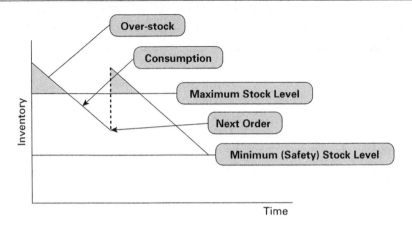

This serves to emphasize the importance of the next order in the management of overage.

It is possible to create a report which identifies items where the next order is due to be received before the overage has dissipated to the minimum stock level. In theory this will mirror the re-schedule out action report, however this list is usually presented in part number order so the 'needle is well hidden in the haystack'. Presenting an action report in inventory value order will ensure that if time is short the highest value items are actioned first.

Summary

In this chapter we have looked at the tools and techniques available for determining the optimum order size and safety stock. They are of their nature complex and need to be carefully considered before use when setting these two key parameters in MRP. However, just using judgement or blindly accepting the recommendations from suppliers will lead the planners to an inevitable cycle of increasing parameters followed by a purge where they are reduced by commands from high, only to creep back up as suppliers press for increased order sizes and delivery failure permit the adding of safety.

It is worth quickly summarizing the use of statistical safety stock, before considering alternatives. While statistical safety stock techniques can take account of the demand, supply variations and the order size the formulas do not include in the calculations the values of the part. Thus, if a safety stock calculation recommended 442 units, if the product was £10 it would only be £4,420 of inventory; if, however, the part was a £1,000 the safety stock value would be £442,000. The decision to accept this level of investment would be very different. It is therefore important when planning safety inventory always to extend the calculations to include the unit cost and keep an eye on the inventory investment.

Advantages of statistical-based safety stock

Statistical-based safety stock protects against the real world of variations of supply, demand and order size. There is significant research that continues to refine these formula as well as compare and contract their performance. The real challenge with any formula is the collection of the data required, as well as interpreting the results.

Disadvantages of statistical-based safety stock

The disadvantages of statistical-based safety stock are that it protects at any cost no check and balance against the unit cost. Complex formula require increasing amounts of data which may not be readily available.

Advantages of safety time

Safety time will require less maintenance as it will rise and fall as the demand increases and decreases.

Disadvantages of safety time

In its simplest form it has no recognition of the variations of supply, demand and order size, however safety quantity can simply be converted to time, overcoming this weakness.

Hybrid safety offer a way of mitigating the disadvantages and capitalizing on the advantages.

In the second half of the chapter we have focused on understanding the importance of correctly identifying the correct attributes and then using them to drive the categorization of the parts into groups which can be managed based on their importance. This led naturally on to the development of a plan utilizing techniques like Pareto to help create plans that can be easily manipulated to both determine an initial plan and then evaluate options for improving the plan year on year. Finally we looked at the importance at looking into overage to ensure that we cover all four possibilities for supply and demand variation. Thus we can be confident that an inventory plan has considered all the components needed to ensure that the plan is realistic and achievable. The next chapter will look at some of the weaknesses in the traditional inventory management methods and techniques that have been developed to overcome them.

Notes

Brown, R (1982) *Advanced Service Inventory Parts Control* (2nd edn), Material Managemant Science Inc, Norwich

Harris, F W (1913) How many parts to make at once, *Factory, The Magazine of Management*, **10**(2), pp 135–36, 152

Relph, G and Barrar, P (2001) Overage inventory – How does it occur and why it is important? *International Journal of Production Economics*, ISIR Proceedings (81–82), pp 163–71

Schmidt, M, Hartmann, W and Nyhuis, P (2007) Simulation based comparison of safety stock calculation methods, *CIRP Annals – Manufacturing Technology*, **61**(1), pp 403–06

Schwarz, M (2000) *Multi-Item Inventory Control: The k-curve Methodology*, PhD Thesis, Hamburg University

Shah, S (1992) Setting Parameters in MRP for the Effective management of bought-out inventory in a JIT assembly environment, PhD Thesis, Aston University

Silver, E A, Pyke, D F and Peterson, R (1998) *Inventory Management and Production Planning and Scheduling* (3rd edn), John Wiley and Sons, New York

Vollmann, T E, Berry, W L and Whybark, D C (1998) *Manufacturing Planning and Control Systems* (4th edn), Irwin/McGraw-Hill, Bolton

Waters (2003) *Inventory Control and Management* (2nd edn), John Wiley & Sons, Chichester

Wild (2002) *Best Practice in Inventory Management*, Routledge, London

You do the maths

Using the formulae for EOQ and EOP from Excel 4.2 extend the Pareto Table in Excel 4.8 and calculate for each part the EOQ and EOP, assuming the cost of ordering is £5.00 and cost of holding 30 per cent.

1 Now look at the EOP values and compare their values as they change down the Pareto list?

2 In Table 4.6 we divided the list in three, and allocated, the days of supply based on Class. How good is that decision compared with EOQ?

Copy of Table 4.6 form page 138 for reference

Class	Annual Spend Value £	Daily Going Rate	Class Limits	No of Parts	Days of Supply	No of Orders	Average Inventory
A	£165,689.52	£662.76	80.0%	7	5	350	£1,656.90
B	£36,907.55	£147.63	95.0%	10	20	125	£1,476.30
C	£10,915.74	£43.66		10	80	31.25	£1,746.52
Totals	£ 213,512.81	£854.05		27		506.25	£4,879.72

Note: Average Inventory is half Days of Supply

3 Now divide the list into six groups. Try a) using per cent limits, b) using the EOP as a guide and rounding to the nearest number of days or weeks.
Which do you think is the best approach?

4 What happens if you alter the cost of ordering or cost of holding inventory?

EXCEL 4.9

	A	B	C	D	E	F	G	H	I	J	K
1	Purchase Order Cost	£5.00			£4.50						
2	Carrying Rate	30%			34%						
3	Working Days	250									
4											
5	Count	Part Number	Annual Usage or Demand	Cost Per Part	Annual Spend Value £	ABC	EOQ	EOP	Rounded EOP	No of Orders	Average Inventory
6	1	B78811ZD	1324	£42.84	£56,720.16	A	£32.10	£6.06	£5.00	£50.00	£567.20
7	2	B78812ZF	987	£41.87	£41,325.69	A	£28.03	£7.10	£5.00	£50.00	£413.26
8	3	B78810741A	1012	£18.50	£18,722.00	A	£42.70	£10.55	£10.00	£25.00	£374.44
9	4	N6554004M0256	523	£35.08	£18,346.84	A	£22.29	£10.66	£10.00	£25.00	£366.94
10	5	SK98751	46	£316.19	£14,544.74	A	£2.20	£11.97	£10.00	£25.00	£290.89
11	6	LE763	781	£11.11	£8,676.91	A	£48.41	£15.50	£15.00	£17.00	£260.31
12	7	D0883030014C	267	£27.54	£7,353.18	A	£17.98	£16.83	£15.00	£17.00	£220.60
13	8	C78810742A	360	£16.87	£6,073.20	B	£26.67	£18.52	£20.00	£13.00	£242.93
14	9	D0862060018Y	163	£33.26	£5,421.38	B	£12.78	£19.60	£20.00	£13.00	£216.86
15	10	C78810761A	567	£8.43	£4,779.81	B	£47.35	£20.88	£20.00	£13.00	£191.19
16	11	LE02	396	£11.09	£4,391.64	B	£34.50	£21.78	£20.00	£13.00	£175.67
17	12	B78812001B	458	£7.10	£3,251.80	B	£46.37	£25.31	£25.00	£10.00	£162.59
18	13	KN552130	10	£319.98	£3,199.80	B	£1.02	£25.52	£25.00	£10.00	£159.99
19	14	A0906030015	18	£150.22	£2,703.96	B	£2.00	£27.76	£30.00	£9.00	£162.24
20	15	B78810721A	749	£3.44	£2,576.56	B	£85.19	£28.44	£30.00	£9.00	£154.59
21	16	D0991020012	164	£14.60	£2,394.40	B	£19.35	£29.50	£30.00	£9.00	£143.66
22	17	D0862070019Y	60	£35.25	£2,115.00	B	£7.53	£31.39	£30.00	£9.00	£126.90
23	18	D0978040014	35	£57.63	£2,017.05	C	£4.50	£32.14	£30.00	£9.00	£121.02
24	19	A78810601E	450	£4.20	£1,890.00	C	£59.76	£33.20	£35.00	£8.00	£132.30
25	20	B78818AE	35	£49.57	£1,734.95	C	£4.85	£34.65	£35.00	£8.00	£121.45
26	21	C78810762A	199	£7.44	£1,480.56	C	£29.86	£37.51	£40.00	£7.00	£118.44
27	22	D0753100033	75	£15.36	£1,152.00	C	£12.76	£42.53	£45.00	£6.00	£103.68
28	23	D1017040014	10	£95.36	£953.60	C	£1.87	£46.74	£45.00	£6.00	£85.82
29	24	KDB300600	8	£93.75	£750.00	C	£1.69	£52.70	£55.00	£5.00	£82.50
30	25	A0889030013	52	£9.59	£498.68	C	£13.44	£64.64	£65.00	£4.00	£64.83
31	26	B30880112C	700	£0.45	£315.00	C	£227.71	£81.33	£80.00	£4.00	£50.40
32	27	B30880113C	105	£1.18	£123.90	C	£54.46	£129.67	£130.00	£2.00	£32.21
33		Totals			£213,512.81					£376.00	£5,142.91

Enter these formulae

Cell G6 *and copy down to* G32 $= SQRT((2*C6*\$B\$1)/(D6*\$B\$2))$

Cell H6 *and copy down to* H32 $= (G6/C6)*\$B\$3$

Cell I6 *and copy down to* I32 $= ROUND(H6/5,0)*5$

Cell J6 *and copy down to* J32 $= ROUNDUP(\$B\$3/I6,0)$

Cell K6 *and copy down to* K32 $= (E6/\$B\$3)*(I6/2)$

Notes for Excel 4.9 You do the maths exercise

1 The EOQs do not have any direct relation to their position in the Pareto list, but the EOPs increase as they move further down the list. This is similar to the approach taken in Tables 4.5 and 4.6.

2 The rounded EOPs for Class A range from 5 to 15 days, compared with the chosen value of 5 days. Similarly for Class B the EOPs range from 20 to 30 days, compared with 20 days. And finally for Class C the EOP range is 30 to 130 days, compared with 80 days. The average inventory is £5,142.91, £264.03 higher, but there are 130.5 fewer orders.

3 Dividing into 6 groups using percentage limits is pure guesswork. Using EOP as a guide is significantly easier.

4 Decreasing the cost of ordering will decrease inventory and increase the numbers of orders. The opposite is true if you decrease the cost of holding inventory by setting the order cost to £4.50 and inventory holding to 34%. The inventory is roughly equal to Pareto, but the number of orders is only 395 compared with 506.5 – a 20% reduction.

k-curve methodology

5

Introduction

This chapter will describe the *k*-curve methodology (KCM) developed in the late 1980s/early 1990s and how it improves upon the strengths of Pareto and EOQ and addresses the weaknesses. First, we will look at the strengths and weaknesses of EOQ, Pareto and exchange curve. Second, a brief history of the development of *k*-curve. Third, how the '*k*-curve' is created and how it resolves the weaknesses of EOQ and Pareto and the chapter concludes with the creation of a composite curve that becomes the basis for planning inventory in MRP systems.

In the previous chapter we looked at the ways in which we can determine the cycle stock and safety stocks for individual items and how using Pareto or the Inventory Matrix we can begin to consider all the parts that we are trying to manage. The key problem facing any operations manager is how to determine the optimum inventory level. The tools described in the previous chapter all, in their own way, help determine the optimum. However, they all have their strengths and weaknesses. It is the weaknesses that remain the key barrier to their effective application in an operations management. So what are these weaknesses?

- EOQ – it needs to know the cost of ordering and the cost of holding inventory; both these values can quickly be shown to be very difficult to determine. I once asked a finance manager for the cost of ordering and after 12 months his considered reply was 'you can have any value from £1 to £100 depending on what resources you wish to consider are part of the cost of ordering'.

- EOQ – it also relies on the assumption that the demand (which is usually based on 12 months) is constant. This is rarely the case, although this is easily overcome by more frequent calculations.

- Safety stock – the main statistical formulae typically do not use the unit cost of the item, so they in effect will 'protect the parts at any cost', which is OK if you have an unlimited budget, which is rarely the case.

- Pareto – this ascribes a rank/importance of the part based on their annual spends, and divided the whole population of parts into three groups. In many businesses simply dividing into three groups is not sufficiently detailed. Dividing into three groups by percentage only required two decisions 80/20 and 95/50. Now consider how you might divide into six groups? It is clear very quickly that this is not really practical.
- Pareto – the fundamental principle is correct: the important *few* have to be closely managed, and the low value *many* are infrequently replenished with long inventory coverage, *but* this leads to too many unconnected decisions, *and* it's too simple for anything other than a simple business.
- Pareto forces a predetermined per cent into each class regardless of what's appropriate for each item.
- Pareto – like the EOQ – makes the assumption that demand is constant over 12 months. The effect of this is more serious than its effect on EOQ; the effect can be seen in Table 5.1. As the demand changes by quarter the classification based on the quarter and the Pareto classification based on the annual average is different.

TABLE 5.1 Comparison of Pareto classification for different demand patterns during the annual period

Groups	Q1	Q2	Q3	Q4	Annual Demand
Flat	100	100	100	100	400
Seasonal	50	125	150	75	400
End of Life	175	100	75	50	400
New Product	25	75	100	200	400
Pareto rank					
Demand	**Q1**	**Q2**	**Q3**	**Q4**	**Annual Demand**
Flat	B	B	B	B	B
Seasonal	B/C	A	A	B/C	B
End of Life	A	B	C	C	B
New Product	C	C	B	A	B

It is always easy to criticize, but what is needed is a solution to the problem.

History of *k*-curve

The *k*-curve methodology (KCM) is not new; it has been used since the early 1990s. It has a strong academic and operational pedigree and there are a number of software products based on the principles. The original KCM approach was developed as part of a PhD by Shah (1992) in collaboration with the planning staff at IBM's Havant manufacturing plant. It was this project which set out to resolve the question of what does it cost to place an order? The finance manager's response to the question 'What does it cost to place an order?' was, after some considerable thought, 'You can have any value from £1 to £100 depending on what resources you wish to consider are part of the cost of ordering.' This response set off a train of thought that concluded that we were trying to solve the wrong problem. It was already known that you could treat the 2C/i in the EOQ equation as a constant (Brown, 1982) so why not simply vary the constant *k* between 1 and 100 and look at the result. Thus the *k*-curve was created and the methodology was born. The methodology was used to set the MRP parameters for IBM's Havant Plant in the 1990s and won awards within IBM for its innovation. IBM sponsored further research (Dupernex, 1993) to examine the optimum number of classes and the effect of different datasets. Following on, Dupernex (1997) went on to extend the optimization to cover batch manufacturing environments where capacity was constrained. In the late 1990s IBM extended the use of the methodology into their consultancy work; it was used during projects with large multinationals like Heidelberg Druken Machin, Wartsila and Mann+Hummell. It was published in academic journals by Burcher, Dupernex and Relph (1996) focusing on theory and Handley (1999) who reviewed the benefits of implementation. IBM developed software AIM (Advanced Inventory Manager) which finally became DIOS (Dynamic Inventory Optimization Solution). Schwarz (2000) extended the methodology looking at more sophisticated approaches to determining the cycle stock using heuristic optimization. Relph (2006) researched the use of optimization tools that were already built into MRP systems and the potential for implementation of *k*-curve. The research conducted four six-month case studies looking at the current practice and then the effect of using *k*-curve on the planning process. The methodology is still used by IBM consultants for their clients. We continue to champion the methodology when working with our own clients to help them optimize their MRP systems and business operations.

Pareto exchange curve

In Chapter 4 we looked at how by entering the percentages we reduced inventory. We also observed in the exercise that a reduction causes an increase in orders. Thus we exchange inventory for orders. The weaknesses of using Pareto to determine this exchange is:

- With only three groups the granularity is quite coarse.
- The decisions between the Class A/B boundary and the Class B/C boundary are arbitrary.
- The days of supply for all the Classes is arbitrary, with the first 20 per cent irrespective of what they are getting the lowest days of cover.

The next sections will cover the development and generation of an alternative approach, the *k*-curve, which will show how the *k*-curve brings together the strengths of both Pareto and EOQ to eliminate their weaknesses.

Generating a *k*-curve

There are three key stages to the creation of the *k*-curve: stage 1 expressing the EOQ as an economic period; stage 2 building a bridge between Pareto and Economic Order Period (EOP); stage 3 the variation of *k* to create an exchange curve. As we saw in the creation of the Pareto exchange curve in the previous chapter, if we express the order policy in terms of days of supply (DOS) we can calculate the average inventory and the number of deliveries per year. These two values stand for the axis of the exchange curve.

Stage 1: Expressing the EOQ as the economic order period (EOP)

Figure 5.1 show the steps for expressing the EOQ as EOP; the first step is to substitute *k* for 2C/i in the EOQ formula (1), which give us the simplified EQO (2). You can create using Excel 5.1 and try out different parts from the '27 parts' list in Appendix A to see the variations for different part numbers.

The next step is to convert the EOQ to an order period by dividing by the annual demand quantity (D) which gives the EOP in years (3). Expressing this using the EOQ formula (4) gives a long-winded formula, however with a little algebra the formula can be simplified to (5). This can be further simplified if we substitute Annual Spend for Demand × Unit Cost; remember that a Pareto curve is created using Annual Spend. Also expressing the EOP in years is

FIGURE 5.1 Classical EOQ and simplification (Brown, 1980: 131 with examples)

	D = Demand Quantity C = Cost of Ordering / Set-up P = Unit Cost I = inventory holding rate as %		1000 £4.50 £75.00 30%	
1	Economic Order Quantity	$Q = \sqrt{\dfrac{2*D*C}{P*i}}$	$Q = \sqrt{\dfrac{2*1000*4.50}{£75.00*30\%}}$	20
	Common Factor (k)	$2C/i = k$	2 * £4.50 / 30%	30
2	Simplified EOQ	$\sqrt{kD/P}$	$\sqrt{30*1000/£75.00}$	20
3	Economic Order Period (EOP)	EOQ / D	20 / 1000	0.02 years
4	Economic Order Period (EOP)	$\left(\sqrt{\dfrac{2*D*C}{P*i}}\right)/D$		
5		$\sqrt{k/D*p}$	$\sqrt{30/1000*£75.00}$	0.02 years
	But Dp is Annual Spend = A and rather than express the EOP in years express in days, using W (working days) = 250			
6	Economic Order Period (EOP)	$W*\sqrt{k/A}$	$250*\sqrt{30/£75,000}$	5 days
7	Average Inventory	0.5 * EOP * A/W	$\dfrac{0.5*5*£75,000}{250}$	£750.00
8	No of deliveries	Working days / EOP	250 / 5	50

EXCEL 5.1 Economic order quantity

	A	B	C	D	E
1	Annual Demand Quantity	D	1000		
2	Constant 2C/i	k	£30.00		
3	Cost per Part	P	£75.00		
4					
5					
6	Economic Order Quantity		20.00		

Enter this formula

Cell C6 = SQRT((K*D)/P) = SQRT((C2*C1)/C3)

EXCEL 5.2 Calculating EOP in days based on EOQ

	A	B	C	D
1	Annual Demand Quantity	D	1000	
2	Constant 2C/i	k	30	
3	Cost per Part	p	£75.00	
4	Annual Spend	A	£75,000.00	
5	Working Days a year	W	250	
6				
7	Economic Order Period	EOP in Years	0.02	
8		EOP Simplified	0.02	
9	Economic Order Period in Days	EOP in Days = E	5.00	
10				
11	Average Inventory		£750.00	
12	No of deliveries		50	

Enter these formulae

Cell C7	= SQRT((K*D)/P))/D	= (SQRT((C2*C1)/C3))/C1
Cell C8	= SQRT(k/A)	= SQRT(C2/C4)
Cell C9	= W*(SQRT(k/A))	= C5*(SQRT(C2/C4))
Cell C11	= 0.5*E*A/W	= 0.5*C9*C4/C5
Cell C12	= W/E	= C5/C9

cumbersome, it would be better to work in days. Typically we use 250 working days (W) in a year, based on five days in a week. This final substitution leaves us with a very simple formula for the EOP in days (6). From this simple formula we can determine the average inventory (7) held. If we know the order period we also know how may deliveries we will get a year (8); you can create an excel model using the formulae shown in Excel 5.2.

You can experiment using the parts detailed from Appendix A.

Stage 2: Building a bridge between Pareto and EOP

This next step now applies the EOP calculation to all the parts in the group being managed; in our case the 27 parts from Appendix A, we calculate the EOP for each of items. Using the formula derived in Excel 5.2, the results can be seen in Excel 5.3 below.

EXCEL 5.3 Calculation of EOQ and EOP values on 27 sample parts

	A	B	C	D	E	F	G
1	Constant *k*	30					
2	Working Days	250					
3							
4							
5	Count	Part Number	Annual Usage or Demand	Cost Per Part	Annual Spend Value	EOQ	EOP Days
6	1	B78811ZD	1324	£42.84	£56,720.16	30	5.75
7	2	B78812ZF	987	£41.87	£41,325.69	27	6.74
8	3	B78810741A	1012	£18.50	£18,722.00	41	10.01
9	4	N6554004M0256	523	£35.08	£18,346.84	21	10.11
10	5	SK98751	46	£316.19	£14,544.74	2	11.35
11	6	LE763	781	£11.11	£8,676.91	46	14.70
12	7	D0883030014C	267	£27.54	£7,353.18	17	15.97
13	8	C78810742A	360	£16.87	£6,073.20	25	17.57
14	9	D0862060018Y	163	£33.26	£5,421.38	12	18.60
15	10	C78810761A	567	£8.43	£4,779.81	45	19.81
16	11	LE02	396	£11.09	£4,391.64	33	20.66
17	12	B78812001B	458	£7.10	£3,251.80	44	24.01
18	13	KN552130	10	£319.98	£3,199.80	1	24.21
19	14	A0906030015	18	£150.22	£2,703.96	2	26.33
20	15	B78810721A	749	£3.44	£2,576.56	81	26.98
21	16	D0991020012	164	£14.60	£2,394.40	18	27.98
22	17	D0862070019Y	60	£35.25	£2,115.00	7	29.77
23	18	D0978040014	35	£57.63	£2,017.05	4	30.49
24	19	A78810601E	450	£4.20	£1,890.00	57	31.50
25	20	B78818AE	35	£49.57	£1,734.95	5	32.87
26	21	C78810762A	199	£7.44	£1,480.56	28	35.59
27	22	D0753100033	75	£15.36	£1,152.00	12	40.34
28	23	D1017040014	10	£95.36	£953.60	2	44.34
29	24	KDB300600	8	£93.75	£750.00	2	50.00
30	25	A0889030013	52	£9.59	£498.68	13	61.32
31	26	B30880112C	700	£0.45	£315.00	216	77.15
32	27	B30880113C	105	£1.18	£123.90	52	123.02
33		Totals			£213,512.81		

Enter these formulae

Cell F6 *and copy down to* F32   = SQRT($B$1*C6/D6)
Cell G6 *and copy down to* G32   = $B$2*SQRT($B$1/E6)

If you examine the calculated values of EOP and EOP you will see that while the EOQ appear somewhat random the EOP's relationship with the Annual Spend for the items is such that as the Annual Spend Value decreases the EOP increases. This conforms to the logic used when applying the 'estimated' cycle stock for traditional Pareto Planning. Thus we now have a mechanism that will vary the size of the order (in days) in direct relation with the annual spend of the part. As with the original Pareto approach of using five days for Class A, 20 days for Class B and 125 days for Class C, we are keeping the order size small for the high value parts. However, it is obvious that setting an order size to 5.75 days or 27.99 days makes little sense as no system or supplier will deliver to that level of accuracy. It would be far more logical to use order sizes that reflected what would happen in practice, so order sizes of 5, 10, 20, 40, 80, 160 and so on would be a good place to start. If we plot the Annual Spend vs EOP on a Log/Log scale and draw gridlines at 5, 10, 20 etc we get an interesting result, as seen in Figure 5.2 below.

The points represent each of the individual parts from our list of 27 parts; the horizontal lines represent the order sizes of 5, 10, 20 days etc. It would be logical to round our exact EOP calculations to the nearest practical value, as with rounding the most logical place is halfway between each of these values, these points are shown as the vertical dash lines, we can see that the first two parts would be in the five days group, the next few would be in the 10 day grouping. The halfway point between the two EOP values on the log can be used as the switching point from one EOP value to the next. The derivation of the calculation is shown in Figure 5.3 below.

FIGURE 5.2 Annual spend vs economic order point

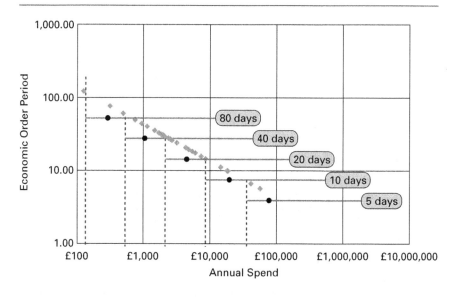

FIGURE 5.3 Calculation of the midpoint class boundary

A = Annual Demand Value	75,000	
k= constant	30	
W = working days	250	
EOP = E	$W * \sqrt{k/A}$	5 days
First we need to change the formula to give the Annual Spend for a given value of EOP -> E		
Annual Demand = A_1, where EOP = 5	$W^2 * k / E_1^2$	$250 * 250 * 30 / 5 * 5$	£75,000
Annual Demand = A_2, where EOP = 10	$W^2 * k / E_2^2$	$250 * 250 * 30 / 10 * 10$	£18,750
Next we want to find the Class Limit at the midpoint between A1 and A2 in Figure 5.2, but because it is on the log scale we need to use the Log of A		
Midpoint Demand $Log(A_m)$	$[Log(A_1) + Log(A_2)]/2$	This needs simplifying using Logarithm Algebra
	$[Log(W^2 * k / E_1^2) + Log(W^2 * k / E_2^2)]/2 \Rightarrow [Log(W^2 * k / E_1^2 * E_2^2)]/2 \Rightarrow [Log(W^2 * k / E_1 * E_2)]$	
Midpoint Demand A_m	$W^2 * k / E_1 * E_2$	$250 * 250 * 30/5 * 10$	£37,500

Thus we have now divided the list of parts into classes, similar to the Pareto exercise in Chapter 4. However, this approach has two distinct advantages: first, there are more boundaries, which provides better granularity when dealing with large populations of parts. Second, the order sizes chosen in each group are logical and the parts are selected based on an economic principle, unlike the Pareto approach where the order size is a matter of judgement, with the lowest order size being applied to the first 20 per cent irrespective of their annual spend.

For this to be practical we need to be able to express the information in the Figure 5.3 in a simple tabular form. This will enable the division of the group of parts into 'value classes' as opposed to ABC Class or Pareto Class. This can be done as seen in Excel 5.4; the Class Limit represents the point at which it would be most economical to switch from Class 1 and an order cycle of five days to Class 2 and an order cycle of 10 days.

If we applied these Class Limits to the parts in Excel 5.3, we can see how it compares with the original EOP values. This can be seen in Excel 5.5 below. What you will observe is that some items' actual EOP are less than the selected Cycle days and some are greater, which is as you would expect when using the midpoint to determine the switching point.

EXCEL 5.4   Value class tables for EOP

	A	B	C	D	E	F
1	Constant *k*	30				
2	Working Days	250				
3						
4						
5	Value Class	Cycle Days	Class Limit			
6	1	5	£37,500			
7	2	10	£9,375			
8	3	20	£2,344			
9	4	40	£586			
10	5	80	£146			
11	6	160	£0			
12	7		£0			
13	8		£0			
14	9		£0			

Enter this formula

Cell C6 *and copy down to* C14   = IF($B$7=0,0,+$B$2*$B$2*$B$1/($B6*$B7))
If there are no values in C12 to C14 formula returns a 0

EXCEL 5.5   Value class and limits applied to list of parts

	A	B	C	D	E	F	G	H
1	Constant *k*	30						
2	Working Days	250						
3								
4								
5	Value Class	Cycle Days	Class Limit					
6	1	5	£37,500					
7	2	10	£9,375					
8	3	20	£2,344					
9	4	40	£586					
10	5	80	£146					
11	6	160	£0					
12	7		£0					
13	8		£0					
14	9		£0					
15								
16								
17	Count	Part Number	Annual Usage or Demand	Cost Per Part	Annual Spend Value £	EOP Days	Value Class	Cycle Days
18	1	B78811ZD	1324	£42.84	£56,720.16	5.75	1	5
19	2	B78812ZF	987	£41.87	£41,325.69	6.74	1	5
20	3	B78810741A	1012	£18.50	£18,722.00	10.01	2	10
21	4	N6554004M0256	523	£35.08	£18,346.84	10.11	2	10
22	5	SK98751	46	£316.19	£14,544.74	11.35	2	10
23	6	LE763	781	£11.11	£8,676.91	14.70	3	20
24	7	D0883030014C	267	£27.54	£7,353.18	15.97	3	20
25	8	C78810742A	360	£16.87	£6,073.20	17.57	3	20
26	9	D0862060018Y	163	£33.26	£5,421.38	18.60	3	20
27	10	C78810761A	567	£8.43	£4,779.81	19.81	3	20
28	11	LE02	396	£11.09	£4,391.64	20.66	3	20
29	12	B78812001B	458	£7.10	£3,251.80	24.01	3	20
30	13	KN552130	10	£319.98	£3,199.80	24.21	3	20
31	14	A0906030015	18	£150.22	£2,703.96	26.33	3	20
32	15	B78810721A	749	£3.44	£2,576.56	26.98	3	20
33	16	D0991020012	164	£14.60	£2,394.40	27.98	3	20
34	17	D0862070019Y	60	£35.25	£2,115.00	29.77	4	40
35	18	D0978040014	35	£57.63	£2,017.05	30.49	4	40
36	19	A78810601E	450	£4.20	£1,890.00	31.50	4	40
37	20	B78818AE	35	£49.57	£1,734.95	32.87	4	40
38	21	C78810762A	199	£7.44	£1,480.56	35.59	4	40
39	22	D0753100033	75	£15.36	£1,152.00	40.34	4	40
40	23	D1017040014	10	£95.36	£953.60	44.34	4	40
41	24	KDB300600	8	£93.75	£750.00	50.00	4	40
42	25	A0889030013	52	£9.59	£498.68	61.32	5	80
43	26	B30880112C	700	£0.45	£315.00	77.15	5	80
44	27	B30880113C	105	£1.18	£123.90	123.02	6	160
45		Totals			£213,512.81			

Enter these formulae

Combine Excel 5.3 and 5.4 by adding 12 rows after row 4

Cell F18 *and copy down to* F44 = $B$2*SQRT($B$1/E18)

Cell G18 *and copy down to* G44 = IF(E18>$C$6,1,IF(E18>C$7,2,IF(E18>$C$8,3,IF(E18>$C$9,4,IF(E18>$C$10,5,IF(E18>$C$11,6,IF(E18>$C$12,7,IF(E18>$C$13,8,9))))))))

Cell H18 *and copy down to* H44 = CHOOSE(G18,$B$6,$B$7,$B$8,$B$9,$B$10,$B$11,$B$12,$B$13,$B$14,)

FIGURE 5.4   Calculation of average inventory and number of deliveries

	D = Demand Quality k = Common Factor P = Unit Cost A = Annual Spend W = Working Days		1,000 30 £75,000.00 £75,000.00 250	
1	Economic Order Period (EOP) = E	$W * \sqrt{k/A}$	$250 * \sqrt{30 / £7,500}$	5 days
2	Average Inventory	0.5 * E * A/W	0.5 * 5 * 75,000/250	£750.00
3	No of deliveries	Working days / EOP	250 / 5	50

So far so good, but as with the original EOQ we have known what the value of *k* is. If we cannot determine *k* we are no further on.

Stage 3: The creation of the k curve

The next step came from the comment from the finance director: 'You can have any value from £1 to £100.' So what if we were to vary the values of *k* from 1 to 100?

To evaluate this we can use the same technique that was used to create the exchange curve for the Pareto, by calculating the total cycle stock and the number of orders, using the formulae described in Figure 5.4, (2) Average Inventory and (3) No of deliveries, we can then sum the average inventory and total the number of expected deliveries as shown in Excel 5.6.

We now have totals for the number of orders and the average inventory. We can now vary the value of *k* for 30 to higher and lower values from 1–100; these can then be plotted on a scatter chart as seen in Figure 5.5 and Table 5.2. The results in Figure 5.5 show, as with the Pareto Exchange curve which is also shown for reference, how the number of deliveries increases as the inventory decreases, thereby exchanging increased deliveries for a lower level of inventory.

It would be much easier to visualize the data in Table 5.2 if it was presented as a chart. This can be easily done in Excel by using the chart option XY and plotting the data in the columns; number of orders and average inventory, the chart produced is shown in Figure 5.5.

EXCEL 5.6 Number of orders and average inventory calculations

	A	B	C	D	E	F	G	H	I
1	Constant k	30							
2	Working Days	250							
3									
4									
5	Value Class	Cycle Days	Class Limit						
6	1	5	£37,500						
7	2	10	£9,375						
8	3	20	£2,344						
9	4	40	£586						
10	5	80	£146						
11	6	160	£0						
12	7		£0						
13	8		£0						
14	9		£0						
15									
16									
17	Count	Part Number	Annual Usage or Demand	Cost Per Part	Annual Spend Value £	Value Class	Cycle Days	No of Orders	Average Inventory
18	1	B78811ZD	1324	£42.84	£56,720.16	1	5	50	£567.20
19	2	B78812ZF	987	£41.87	£41,325.69	1	5	50	£413.26
20	3	B78810741A	1012	£18.50	£18,722.00	2	10	25	£374.44
21	4	N6554004M0256	523	£35.08	£18,346.84	2	10	25	£366.94
22	5	SK98751	46	£316.19	£14,544.74	2	10	25	£290.89
23	6	LE763	781	£11.11	£8,676.91	3	20	12.5	£347.08
24	7	D0883030014C	267	£27.54	£7,353.18	3	20	12.5	£294.13
25	8	C78810742A	360	£16.87	£6,073.20	3	20	12.5	£242.93
26	9	D0862060018Y	163	£33.26	£5,421.38	3	20	12.5	£216.86
27	10	C78810761A	567	£8.43	£4,779.81	3	20	12.5	£191.19
28	11	LE02	396	£11.09	£4,391.64	3	20	12.5	£175.67
29	12	B78812001B	458	£7.10	£3,251.80	3	20	12.5	£130.07
30	13	KN552130	10	£319.98	£3,199.80	3	20	12.5	£127.99
31	14	A0906030015	18	£150.22	£2,703.96	3	20	12.5	£108.16
32	15	B78810721A	749	£3.44	£2,576.56	3	20	12.5	£103.06
33	16	D0991020012	164	£14.60	£2,394.40	3	20	12.5	£95.78
34	17	D0862070019Y	60	£35.25	£2,115.00	4	40	6.25	£169.20
35	18	D0978040014	35	£57.63	£2,017.05	4	40	6.25	£161.36
36	19	A78810601E	450	£4.20	£1,890.00	4	40	6.25	£151.20
37	20	B78818AE	35	£49.57	£1,734.95	4	40	6.25	£138.80
38	21	C78810762A	199	£7.44	£1,480.56	4	40	6.25	£118.44
39	22	D0753100033	75	£15.36	£1,152.00	4	40	6.25	£92.16
40	23	D1017040014	10	£95.36	£953.60	4	40	6.25	£76.29
41	24	KDB300600	8	£93.75	£750.00	4	40	6.25	£60.00
42	25	A0889030013	52	£9.59	£498.68	5	80	3.125	£79.79
43	26	B30880112C	700	£0.45	£315.00	5	80	3.125	£50.40
44	27	B30880113C	105	£1.18	£123.90	6	160	1.5625	£39.65
45		Totals			£213,512.81			370.31	£5,182.93

Enter these formulae

Using Excel 5.5 delete Column F and add Column H and G

Cell H18 and copy down to H44	= $B$2/G18
Cell G18 and copy down to G45	= 0.5*G18*E18/$B$2

FIGURE 5.5 *k*-curve plot of Table 5.2

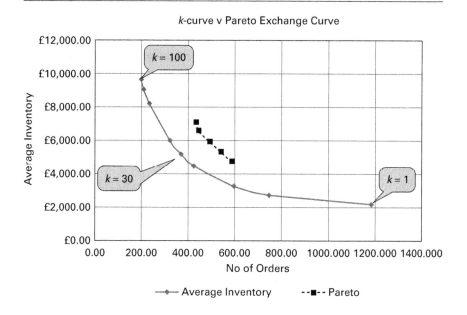

TABLE 5.2 Comparison of inventory and orders for different values of *k*

k	No of Orders	Average Inventory
1	1187.50	£2,175.54
5	750.00	£2,736.39
10	596.88	£3,265.19
20	425.00	£4,492.33
30	370.31	£5,182.93
40	323.44	£5,963.18
60	235.94	£8,164.83
80	212.50	£8,984.65
100	200.00	£9,568.77

Interpretation of the curve

This is where we finally break the deadlock on our inventory management problem. If we look at this curve in Figure 5.5 and consider the question of which value of k do we use, we are now presented with a question statement, which can be expressed 'How many deliveries can I cope with?' This is in reality a far easier question to answer than 'what does it cost to place an order?' If the parts we are concerned with are purchased, the number of orders generated directly equate to the number of deliveries received by the goods-in department. If they are manufactured they will directly relate to the number of changeovers we can perform on the work area. For a machine shop this will be the number of tool changes, for a moulding shop it will be the number of mould changes, etc. In summary, the number of orders can be said to be the 'capability' of the business to process orders in the work area in question. Thus we can look at this as an inventory capability exchange curve. If we are able to confirm a decision with respect to the number of deliveries that we can cope with we can then simply draw a vertical line and intersect the curve; this will give us the 'optimum' inventory for our capability (to process orders).

So let us imagine that we have spoken to our goods inward supervisor and that he has confirmed that at present they are receiving 400 receipts a year. If we then read of the curve 400 deliveries per year we get an average inventory of £4,784.60 when $k = 25$.

Once this decision is taken then we can use the list to identify the appropriate batch size for each part. The reverse process is also true, as if the management wanted to achieve an inventory target of say £4,000.00 then again reading of the k-curve we can see that we will need to be able to process 471 receipts to achieve an inventory of £4,082, with k set to 15. It should be an easy question to ask the goods inwards supervisor if he can increase his department's receipt rate from 400 to 471 per year. If this is possible then it is simply a matter of adjusting the k value in Excel 5.6 and the setting for all the parts will be given.

Why is it so useful?

The nirvana for all advocates of the EOQ is to solve the 2C/i question. By using this approach we have turned the question on its head and created a mechanism that allows us to make a rational decision that will 'fix' the EOQ at an 'optimum' value for the business. k-curve solves the EOQ weaknesses; instead of needing to find the cost of ordering and cost of holding, we now need to determine the number of batches and/or a target inventory level. It also solves the Pareto weaknesses as the Value Class Table created in Excel 5.4 allows more subdivisions and allocates the order size on an 'economic' order principle, rather than just allowing the lowest order size to the first 20 per cent. The proof that the *k*-curve is more effective is seen if we compare the results of the *k*-curve with the results of the Pareto Exchange Curve the dotted line shown in Figure 5.5. For the same number of orders a much lower level of inventory can be achieved using the *k*-curve. If we examine the two scenarios it is obvious as Pareto goes from five-day ordering to 20-day ordering, whereas *k*-curve goes from 5 days to 10 days to 20 days – a much more granular approach.

What is also of significance is that, as seen in Excel 5.7, if the value of *k* is varied the population in each group will alter. For example, with *k* set to 50 there are no Class 1 parts, which says that when *k* = 50 it is appropriate for your business not to order any parts on a weekly basis. This differs from Pareto approach which advises that the first 20 per cent will always be on the lowest order cycle, typically five days ordering, or whatever policy is chosen for the Class A parts.

k-curve for business case analysis

Usually, when asking to spend money, a business case has to be prepared to answer the question 'If I spend X how much benefit will I get?' It is not often that the reverse is tested. Inventory reduction is assumed to cost nothing to achieve, just hard work. If we now consider that capability to process receipts or that capability to increase the number of tool changes is directly related to the inventory reduction, as we have demonstrated with the *k*-curve. Thus we can now compare the cost of increasing the business's capability to meet the proposed inventory benefit. We can use the model created in Excel 5.6 and can vary *k* until we get the required inventory levels. Say we wish to reduce the inventory level from £5,000 to £4,000 then £3,000, the results are shown in Figure 5.6, and we see the need to increase the number of orders from 383 to 472 for the first £1,000 and from 472 to 641 for the second £1,000. Consider the two scenarios of goods in and a machine shop.

Goods *in*

In this case we can ask the goods in supervisor to increase the number of receipts by 22 per cent in the first case; his response may be 'more overtime' – this can then be costed, let's say £500, the business case is then passed easily. The second tranche is 35 per cent an increase in receipts but overall nearly

EXCEL 5.7 Top 7 sample parts show with cycle days when *k* is set to 50

	A	B	C	D	E	F	G	H	I
1	Constant *k*	50							
2	Working Days	250							
3									
4									
5	Value Class	Cycle Days	Class Limit						
6	1	5	£62,500						
7	2	10	£15,625						
8	3	20	£3,906						
9	4	40	£977						
10	5	80	£244						
11	6	160	£0						
12	7		£0						
13	8		£0						
14	9		£0						
15									
16									
17	Count	Part Number	Annual Usage or Demand	Cost Per Part	Annual Spend Value £	Value Class	Cycle Days	No of Orders	Average Inventory
18	1	B78811ZD	1324	£42.84	£56,720.16	2	10	25	£1,134.40
19	2	B78812ZF	987	£41.87	£41,325.69	2	10	25	£826.51
20	3	B78810741A	1012	£18.50	£18,722.00	2	10	25	£374.44
21	4	N6554004M0256	523	£35.08	£18,346.84	2	10	25	£366.94
22	5	SK98751	46	£316.19	£14,544.74	3	20	12.5	£581.79
23	6	LE763	781	£11.11	£8,676.91	3	20	12.5	£347.08
24	7	D0883030014C	267	£27.54	£7,353.18	3	20	12.5	£294.13

Enter these formulae

Cell C6 *and copy down to* C14	= IF($B7=0,0,+$B$2*$B$2*$B$1/($B6*$B7))
Cell E18 *and copy down to* E24	= C18*D18
Cell F18 *and copy down to* F24	= IF(E18>$C$6,1,IF(E18>C$7,2,IF(E18>$C$8,3,IF(E18 >$C$9,4,IF(E18>$C$10,5,IF(E18>$C$11,6,IF(E18> $C$12,7,IF(E18>$C$13,8,9))))))))
Cell G18 *and copy down to* G24	= +CHOOSE(F18,$B$6,$B$7,$B$8,$B$9,$B$10,$B$11, $B$12,$B$13,$B$14,)
Cell H18 *and copy down to* H24	= $B$2/G18
Cell I18 *and copy down to* I24	= 0.5*G18*E18/$B$2

FIGURE 5.6 using *k*-curve for business case analysis

k-Curve Exchange Curve

K	Inventory	Orders	Increased orders
27.5	£5,009	383	
15	£4,083	472	89 or 22%
7	£3,081	641	169 or 35%

Average Inventory (y-axis): £0.00 – £12,000.00

No of Orders (x-axis): 0.00 – 1400.00

k = 27.5, k = 15, k = 7

—◆— Average Inventory

67 per cent, at which point there may be a request for additional labour or new equipment. Again this can be costed, so the options are say £13,000 for labour or £6,000 for new equipment; in this case it is clear that there is no basic case for inventory reduction as the costs outweigh the benefits.

Machine shop

The machine shop scenario is interesting as the likely response is that in order to achieve more changeovers it would be perceived that all the tooling would need to be improved. The *k*-curve analysis would show which parts are to change from fortnightly processing to weekly processing. In Table 5.3 we can see the lists of parts, their classes for each of the *k* values and the recommended cycle days.

What can be seen is that to get the first £1,000, moving from *k* = 27.5 to *k* = 15 as shown in Figure 5.6, only four parts need to move from monthly to fortnightly tool-changeover, and one from bi-monthly to monthly. Whereas to get the next £1,000, three parts need to move to weekly, six need to change to fortnightly, leaving only one at monthly. The business case for the inventory reduction can be built on some very specific costs for the improvement to tooling, which can be identified at an item level.

In summary, the *k*-curve analysis tool use extends beyond a simple inventory ready reckoner as it can deliver detailed information at part level.

TABLE 5.3 Effect of changing k on value class population

| | | | | | k = 27.5 | | k = 15 | | k = 7 | |
Count	Part Number	Annual Usage or Demand	Cost Per Part	Annual Spend Value £	Value Class	Cycle Days	Value Class	Cycle Days	Value Class	Cycle Days
1	B78811ZD	1324	£42.84	£56,726.63	1	5	1	5	1	5
2	B77812ZF	987	£41.87	£41,325.69	1	5	1	5	1	5
3	B78810741A	1012	£18.50	£18,722.00	2	10	2	10	1	5
4	N6554004M0256	523	£35.08	£18,346.42	2	10	2	10	1	5
5	SK98751	46	£316.19	£14,544.64	2	10	2	10	1	5
6	LE763	781	£11.11	£8,679.28	2	10	2	10	2	10
7	D0883030014C	267	£27.54	£7,354.28	3	20	2	10	2	10
8	C78810742A	36C	£16.87	£6,071.97	3	20	2	10	2	10
9	D0862060018Y	163	£33.26	£5,420.88	3	20	2	10	2	10
10	C78810761A	567	£8.43	£4,780.58	3	20	2	10	2	10
11	LE02	396	£11.09	£4,393.19	3	20	3	20	2	10
12	B78812001B	458	£7.10	£3,250.36	3	20	3	20	2	10
13	KN552130	10	£319.98	£3,199.83	3	20	3	20	2	10
14	A0906030015	18	£150.22	£2,703.97	3	20	3	20	2	10
15	B78810721A	749	£3.44	£2,579.83	3	20	3	20	2	10
16	D0991020012	164	£14.60	£2,393.59	3	20	3	20	2	10
17	D0862070019Y	60	£35.25	£2,115.00	4	40	3	20	3	20

In simple terms, by using a *k*-cure you can establish the true cost/benefit of the inventory reduction, by understanding the costs of increasing the 'capability' prior to going ahead with an inventory reduction. This is likely to be better than having an irate goods inwards supervisor complaining bitterly that his people are overworked and the processing of goods is delayed causing problems on the shop floor. Similarly, discussing which tools need to be upgraded is better than being berated by a machine shop foreman complaining that the increase in tool changeovers has consumed valuable machine shop capacity.

Creating a composite curve

Adding safety stock

The use of basic formulae and the concept of using variable service level rates for each class

Having established the basic inventory capability exchange curve, the next logical step is to consider the addition of safety stock. We saw in Chapter 4 a wide range of safety stock options, from simple to complex statistical formula which are essentially based on the customer service levels desired, second the more straightforward safety time and finally the more sophisticated hybrid safety stock which combine both time and quantity. All require a 'parameter' to be decided which will affect the amount of safety held. These decision points are shown in Table 5.4.

TABLE 5.4 Safety stock parameter decision focus

Safety Stock Formula	Decision parameter	Focus	Ignores
Demand Variation	Service Level %	Service level to customer	Costs
Supply & Demand Variation	Service Level %	Service level to customer and from supplier	Costs
Batch, Supply & Demand Variation	Service Level% and Batch Size	Relationship between batch size and service levels	Costs
Time	No of Days	Inventory cost	Customer service
Hybrid	Greater or lesser of the Time / Quantity	Forces decision between cost or customer service	
Combination	Service Level % and No of Days	Elements of cost and customer service	

Typically, there is one parameter that drives each of the safety calculations. The result of the decision, as seen in Chapter 4, will increase or decrease the amount of safety. When used in the Pareto calculation the key decision was for the top value class to have the least value of safety stock, either by keeping the number of days to a minimum or lowering the expected service level. We can apply the same logic to the *k*-curve and assign different levels of safety for different classes. Once this decision is made it is relatively simple to add this to the inventory calculation. The results in our excel example can be seen in Excel 5.8. For simplicity we have chosen to use safety days. If we had demand variation data we could easily use statistical safety stock calculations in the same column, with the variation being the service level.

The choice of the number of days of safety is essentially judgement, starting from the lower values for the higher spend items, of which there are fewer. Now that we are making more detailed decisions what is becoming apparent that it would be useful to display the subtotals for each column. This will mean that we can rather than examine the 'fine detail' and can begin to consider the inventory by each value class. Excel 5.9 shows a class level inventory model; the columns have been rearranged into a logical flow that enables the use of DSUM and DCOUNT functions of Excel to work effectively. The formula have been designed to be copied easily.

This model now provides a clear summary picture of where the inventory is invested, and will enable easy examination of various scenarios, with differing cycle days and safety days, as well as easily allowing you to vary *k* to produce a curve which represents the sum of average inventory and safety. Figure 5.7 shows the *k*-curve generated showing the Average Cycle Inventory and Average Cycle Inventory + Safety Inventory.

We are now beginning to develop a clearer picture of the inventory and the key decisions that will enable us to manage the inventory at an aggregated level. The top line represents the optimum curve for a given set of parts. This can then be tested against the budget and capabilities of the department managing these parts.

Adding overage to the k-curve

Why include overage in the composite curve

In Chapter 4 we discussed the existence of overage and how it can be managed; we saw the importance of overage as part of overall inventory evaluation. Therefore it is worthy of consideration when developing a realistic inventory plan. Including overage takes account of the 'real world environment' in order to make a realistic commitment.

EXCEL 5.8 Safety stock added to inventory calculation mode

	A	B	C	D	E	F	G	H	I	J	K
1	Constant *k*	30									
2	Working Days	250									
3											
4											
5	Value Class	Cycle Days	Class Limit	Safety Days							
6	1	5	£37,500	5							
7	2	10	£9,375	5							
8	3	20	£2,344	10							
9	4	40	£586	15							
10	5	80	£146	20							
11	6	160	£0	25							
12	7		£0								
13	8		£0								
14	9		£0								
15											
16											
17	Count	Part Number	Annual Usage or Demand	Cost Per Part	Annual Spend Value £	Value Class	Cycle Days	Safety Days	No of Orders	Average Cycle Inventory	Safety Inventory
18	1	B78811ZD	1324	£42.84	£56,720.16	1	5	5	50	£567.20	£1,134.40
19	2	B78812ZF	987	£41.87	£41,325.69	1	5	5	50	£413.26	£826.51
20	3	B78810741A	1012	£18.50	£18,722.00	2	10	5	25	£374.44	£374.44
21	4	N6554004M0256	523	£35.08	£18,346.84	2	10	5	25	£366.94	£366.94
22	5	SK98751	46	£316.19	£14,544.74	2	10	5	25	£290.89	£290.89
23	6	LE763	781	£11.11	£8,676.91	3	20	10	12.5	£347.08	£347.08
24	7	D0883030014C	267	£27.54	£7,353.18	3	20	10	12.5	£294.13	£294.13
25	8	C78810742A	360	£16.87	£6,073.20	3	20	10	12.5	£242.93	£242.93
26	9	D0862060018Y	163	£33.26	£5,421.38	3	20	10	12.5	£216.86	£216.86
27	10	C78810761A	567	£8.43	£4,779.81	3	20	10	12.5	£191.19	£191.19
28	11	LE02	396	£11.09	£4,391.64	3	20	10	12.5	£175.67	£175.67
29	12	B78812001B	458	£7.10	£3,251.80	3	20	10	12.5	£130.07	£130.07
30	13	KN552130	10	£319.98	£3,199.80	3	20	10	12.5	£127.99	£127.99
31	14	A0906030015	18	£150.22	£2,703.96	3	20	10	12.5	£108.16	£108.16
32	15	B78810721A	749	£3.44	£2,576.56	3	20	10	12.5	£103.06	£103.06
33	16	D0991020012	164	£14.60	£2,394.40	3	20	10	12.5	£95.78	£95.78
34	17	D0862070019Y	60	£35.25	£2,115.00	4	40	15	6.25	£169.20	£126.90
35	18	D0978040014	35	£57.63	£2,017.05	4	40	15	6.25	£161.36	£121.02
36	19	A78810601E	450	£4.20	£1,890.00	4	40	15	6.25	£151.20	£113.40
37	20	B78818AE	35	£49.57	£1,734.95	4	40	15	6.25	£138.80	£104.10
38	21	C78810762A	199	£7.44	£1,480.56	4	40	15	6.25	£118.44	£88.83
39	22	D0753100033	75	£15.36	£1,152.00	4	40	15	6.25	£92.16	£69.12
40	23	D1017040014	10	£95.36	£953.60	4	40	15	6.25	£76.29	£57.22
41	24	KDB300600	8	£93.75	£750.00	4	40	15	6.25	£60.00	£45.00
42	25	A0889030013	52	£9.59	£498.68	5	80	20	3.125	£79.79	£39.89
43	26	B30880112C	700	£0.45	£315.00	5	80	20	3.125	£50.40	£25.20
44	27	B30880113C	105	£1.18	£123.90	6	160	25	1.5625	£39.65	£12.39
45		Totals			£213,512.81				370.31	£5,182.93	£5,829.17

Enter these formulae

Using Excel 5.6 insert column between G and H

Cell H18 *and copy down to* H44 = CHOOSE(F18,$D$6,$D$7,$D$8,$D$9,$D$10,$D$11,$D$12,$D$13,$D$14,)

Cell K18 *and copy down to* K45 = H18*E18/$B$2

EXCEL 5.9 Top 7 sample parts show with cycle days when *k* is set to 50

	A	B	C	D	E	F	G	H	I	J	K
1	Constant *k*	30									
2	Working Days	250									
3											
4											
5	Value Class		Class Limit		No of Parts in Class	Annual Spend Value £	Cycle Days	Safety Days	No of Orders	Average Cycle Inventory	Safety Inventory
6	1		£37,500		2	£98,045.85	5	5	100	£980.46	£1,960.92
7	2		£9,375		3	£51,613.58	10	5	75	£1,032.27	£1,032.27
8	3		£2,344		2	£16,030.09	20	10	25	£641.20	£641.20
9	4		£586		0	£0.00	40	15	0	£0.00	£0.00
10	5		£146		0	£0.00	80	20	0	£0.00	£0.00
11	6		£0		0	£0.00	160	25	0	£0.00	£0.00
12	7		£0		0	£0.00			0	£0.00	£0.00
13	8		£0		0	£0.00			0	£0.00	£0.00
14	9		£0		0	£0.00			0	£0.00	£0.00
15				Total	7	£165,689.52			200	£2,653.93	£3,634.39
16											
17	Count	Part Number	Annual Usage or Demand	Cost Per Part	Value Class	Annual Spend Value £	Cycle Days	Safety Days	No of Orders	Average Cycle Inventory	Safety Inventory
18	1	B78811ZD	1324	£42.84	1	£56,720.16	5	5	50	£567.20	£1,134.40
19	2	B78812ZF	987	£41.87	1	£41,325.69	5	5	50	£413.26	£826.51
20	3	B78810741A	1012	£18.50	2	£18,722.00	10	5	25	£374.44	£374.44
21	4	N6554004M0256	523	£35.08	2	£18,346.84	10	5	25	£366.94	£366.94
22	5	SK98751	46	£316.19	2	£14,544.74	10	5	25	£290.89	£290.89
23	6	LE763	781	£11.11	3	£8,676.91	20	10	12.5	£347.08	£347.08
24	7	D0883030014C	267	£27.54	3	£7,353.18	20	10	12.5	£294.13	£294.13

Enter these formulae

NOTE: Only Rows 1–24 are shown in this extract. All 27 parts are still used in Excel 5.9. Using Excel 5.8, first move Column E to F, and F to E. Next move B5–B14 to G5–G14, and D5–D14 to H5–H14.

Cell E6 *and copy down to* E14 = DCOUNT($E$17:$K$44,$E$17,$A$5:A6)-SUM(E$5:E5)

Cell F6 *and copy down to* F14 = DSUM($E$17:$K$44,F$17,$A$5:A6)-SUM(F$5:F5)

Cell I6 *and copy down and across to* K14 = DSUM($E$17:$K$44,I$17,$A$5:$A6)-SUM(I$5:I5)

Therefore the addition of overage into the inventory plan is important as what we are trying to do is prepare a plan that we intend to achieve. In the words of Benjamin Franklin: 'By failing to prepare, you are preparing to fail.'

If we do not include overage in the plan calculations then, as we have shown in Chapter 4, we are guaranteeing that we will exceed the plan. We know overage will occur, and ignoring it will not make it go away. As any experienced manager knows, the result of missing a plan is a lot of management attention in explaining why we are over plan.

FIGURE 5.7   *k*-curve of cycle and safety stock

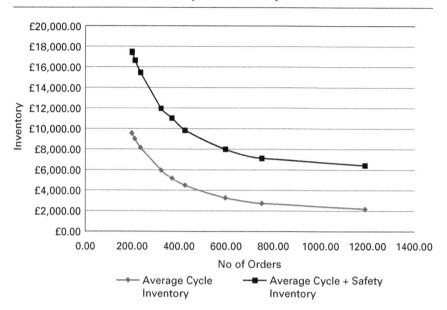

Overage logic

It would be easy to create a clever and complicated algorithm for the adding overage to the plan, but the research by Relph (2006) showed that adding a percentage to the maximum stock is as accurate as any more complex method. The formula is shown on the left-hand side of Figure 5.8; this may look counterintuitive as it would be more straightforward to simply add a percentage to the maximum stock. However, when you consider measuring the actual overage, the known values are the actual inventory and the maximum stock, thus the overage would be Actual – Maximum, shown on the right-hand side of Figure 5.8, which is more straightforward and can be used when analysing the actual inventory performance, which is covered in the next chapter.

This can be applied to the summary data; there is no real benefit in applying this to the part number level of the data.

Overage can be refined by adding a different percentage for each value class as you would expect to manage the parts in the higher value classes more closely. Excel 5.10 shows our sample parts with Overage built into the plan; you can see the two parts in Value Class 1 have significantly more overage than the two parts in Value Class 5. We can now create a *k*-curve to include safety and overage; as a result we can be confident that it is a good

FIGURE 5.8 Overage formula to determine the planned level of overage

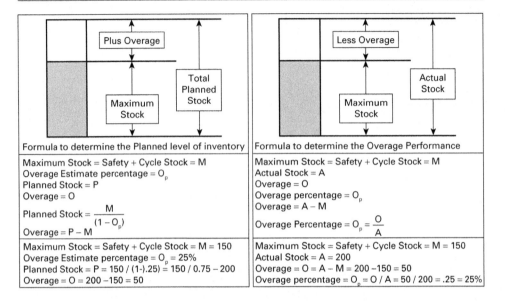

Formula to determine the Planned level of inventory	Formula to determine the Overage Performance
Maximum Stock = Safety + Cycle Stock = M Overage Estimate percentage = O_p Planned Stock = P Overage = O Planned Stock = $\dfrac{M}{(1 - O_p)}$ Overage = P – M	Maximum Stock = Safety + Cycle Stock = M Actual Stock = A Overage = O Overage percentage = O_p Overage = A – M Overage Percentage = $O_p = \dfrac{O}{A}$
Maximum Stock = Safety + Cycle Stock = M = 150 Overage Estimate percentage = O_p = 25% Planned Stock = P = 150 / (1-).25) = 150 / 0.75 – 200 Overage = O = 200 –150 = 50	Maximum Stock = Safety + Cycle Stock = M = 150 Actual Stock = A = 200 Overage = O = A – M = 200 –150 = 50 Overage percentage = O_p = O / A = 50 / 200 = .25 = 25%

representation of the optimum inventory envelope that could be achieved. Since the k-curve is based on a set of cycle days, a safety policy (in this case safety days) and an estimation of the expected overage it completely defines for the group of parts being managed the range of possible inventory levels. These rules are, in effect, a statement of the inventory plan in a set of policy rules, which can be documented as an inventory plan. Figure 5.9 shows the complete composite curve for the sample 27 parts. The only remaining decision is to identify the target inventory level, which is usually a given based on the business needs.

To be able to create Figure 5.9, using the Excel XY Chart function we need to create a table, shown in Table 5.5, where the three columns are cumulative rather than the specific values. Thus the three lines to be plotted are based on the values in Excel 5.10.

- Average Inventory = J15 / 2
- Average Cycle + Safety = J15/2 + K15
- Planned Inventory = Average Cycle + Safety + Overage = J15/2 + K15 + L15

Because we do not show k on the chart, it is not easy to see the relation between k and the inventory level.

EXCEL 5.10 Inventory model including overage

	A	B	C	D	E	F	G	H	I	J	K	L	M
1	Constant *k*	30											
2	Working Days	250											
3													
4													
5	Value Class		Class Limit	Overge Percentage	No of Parts in Class	Annual Spend Value £	Cycle Days	Safety Days	No of Orders	Average Cycle Inventory	Safety Inventory	Planned Overage	Total Inventory
6	1		£37,500	20%	2	£98,045.85	5	5	100	£980.46	£1,960.92	£735.34	£3,676.72
7	2		£9,375	25%	3	£51,613.58	10	5	75	£1,032.27	£1,032.27	£688.18	£2,752.72
8	3		£2,344	30%	2	£16,030.09	20	10	25	£641.20	£641.20	£549.60	£1,832.01
9	4		£586	35%	0	£0.00	40	15	0	£0.00	£0.00	£0.00	£0.00
10	5		£146	40%	0	£0.00	80	20	0	£0.00	£0.00	£0.00	£0.00
11	6		£0	50%	0	£0.00	160	25	0	£0.00	£0.00	£0.00	£0.00
12	7		£0		0	£0.00			0	£0.00	£0.00	£0.00	£0.00
13	8		£0		0	£0.00			0	£0.00	£0.00	£0.00	£0.00
14	9		£0		0	£0.00			0	£0.00	£0.00	£0.00	£0.00
15				Total	7	£165,689.52			200	£2,653.93	£3,634.39	£1,973.13	£8,261.45
16													
17	Count	Part Number	Annual Usage or Demand	Cost Per Part	Value Class	Annual Spend Value £	Cycle Days	Safety Days	No of Orders	Average Cycle Inventory	Safety Inventory		
18	1	B78811ZD	1324	£42.84	1	£56,720.16	5	5	50	£567.20	£1,134.40		
19	2	B78812ZF	987	£41.87	1	£41,325.69	5	5	50	£413.26	£826.51		
20	3	B78810741A	1012	£18.50	2	£18,722.00	10	5	25	£374.44	£374.44		
21	4	N6554004M0256	523	£35.08	2	£18,346.84	10	5	25	£366.94	£366.94		
22	5	SK98751	46	£316.19	2	£14,544.74	10	5	25	£290.89	£290.89		
23	6	LE763	781	£11.11	3	£8,676.91	20	10	12.5	£347.08	£347.08		
24	7	D0883030014C	267	£27.54	3	£7,353.18	20	10	12.5	£294.13	£294.13		

Enter these formulae

NOTE: Only Rows 17–24 are shown are in this extract. All 27 parts are still used in Excel 5.10 as shown in Excel 5.8.
Using Excel 5.9, add overage values in Column D
Cell M6 and copy down to M13   = (J6+K6)/(1–D6)
Cell L6 and copy down to L13   = M5–J5–K5

In Table 5.5 we can see the *k* value for each in relation to the total inventory, thus if we were given a target to achieve £15,000 we would select a *k* value very close to 30; if the target was further reduced to £10,000 we can easily see we need to reduce the *k* value to 10. From the discussion earlier in the chapter we know that to confirm our ability to achieve the inventory we simply need to confirm our ability to process 370 orders, for £15,000 and 596 orders for £10,000.

FIGURE 5.9   Complete inventory *k*-curve

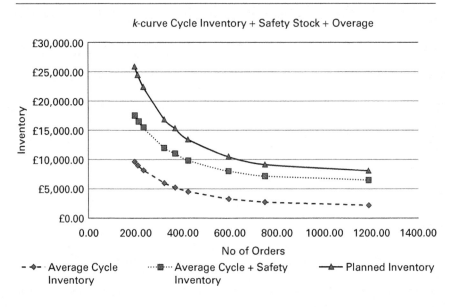

k-curve Cycle Inventory + Safety Stock + Overage

- ◆ - Average Cycle Inventory   ···■··· Average Cycle + Safety Inventory   ▲ Planned Inventory

TABLE 5.5   Table of *k* values and the resultant inventory

k	No of Orders	Average Cycle Inventory	Average Cycle + Safety Inventory	Planned Inventory
1	1187.50	£2,175	£6,449	£8,075
5	750.00	£2,736	£7,121	£9,130
10	596.88	£3,265	£7,986	£10,474
20	425.00	£4,492	£9,834	£13,365
30	370.31	£5,183	£11,013	£15,273
40	323.44	£5,963	£11,962	£16,842
60	235.94	£8,165	£15,455	£22,371
80	212.50	£8,985	£16,636	£24,428
100	200.00	£9,569	£17,439	£25,841

Testing the different options for inventory classes

In this chapter we have made some default assumptions about Pareto and *k*-curve. For Pareto we assumed three value classes and for *k*-curve we assumed six. The default position for Pareto is to use three classes, however Wild (2002) and other authors identify that it may be logical/appropriate to extend to four or even five as the granularity is not sufficient when managing larger group of parts. Similarly, Dupernex (1993) investigated which was the optimum number of class when using *k*-curve. The conclusion typically was that 'it depends' on the group of parts being examined. We know from our discussion in this chapter that Pareto becomes more difficult as we increase the number of classes to be managed. We also know that *k*-curve, unlike Pareto, will populate/de-populate classes dependant on the parts annual spend, thus if we specified too many classes they may well not be used. If we look at our sample parts in Excel 5.10 and look at the population in each class for the *k* values used in Table 5.5 we would clearly see this de-population of the value classes. The population of each class as the value of *k* is varied as shown in Table 5.6; we can see that as the value of *k* increases so the population of parts in the higher value classes decreases and the parts migrate to the lower value classes. We know from looking at Table 5.5 that as the value of *k* increases the inventory increases and the number of orders decreases; the increase in inventory is the result of

TABLE 5.6 Inventory class population

Value Class	No of Parts in Class								
	$k=1$	$k=5$	$k=10$	$k=20$	$k=30$	$k=40$	$k=60$	$k=80$	$k=100$
1	21	7	5	2	2	1	0	0	0
2	5	13	8	5	3	4	2	2	2
3	1	5	10	13	11	8	8	5	4
4	0	2	3	5	8	10	11	13	12
5	0	0	1	2	2	3	5	5	7
6	0	0	0	0	1	1	1	2	2

fewer parts in the higher classes where the order cycle is lower, ie fewer parts being ordered weekly, more ordered monthly.

It is possible to use to utilize this phenomenon to help decide which number of classes is the best option.

We can test a number of possible scenarios to see which may be the best. For example, we could look at the result of the classic Pareto, *k*-curve using 4, 6 and 8 classes. Table 6.3 below shows a number of possible scenarios we could test.

Note 1: There are two differences between the 3 class and 4 class scenarios, one the addition of a 40 days of supply class and that Pareto uses the percentage split, whereas *k*-curve uses the class limit to define the class boundaries.

Note 2: The 6 Class, 6 Class – Lean and 8 Class have similar sequences of days of supply, but in different classes.

We can use the Excel 5.10 model to conduct the test but for simplicity we will only examine the effect on the cycle stock and no of batches. The results are best displayed as *k*-curves as it is easier to see which result is better. These results are shown in Figure 5.10.

The key to interpreting the curve is that the best position is where we can achieve the lowest inventory for the least number of batches. This is because, as we saw in the exchange curve, to lower inventory we need to process more batches, thus by selecting a position that delivers the lowest inventory

FIGURE 5.10   Comparison of cycle stock scenarios using *k*-curves

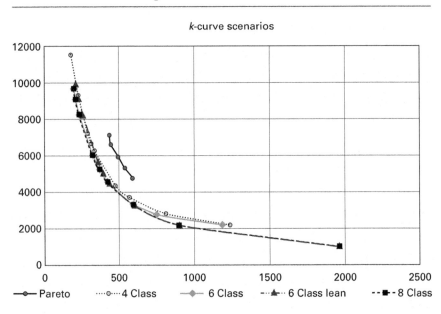

FIGURE 5.11   Close up of *k*-curve Figure 5.10

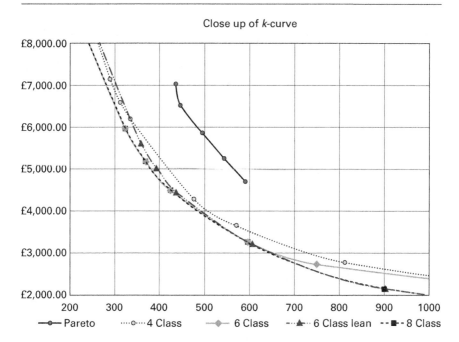

for the lowest number of batches we are making the most effective use of our batching rules. What is clear is that the Pareto is significantly less effective than the 4 Class scenario, which is a combination of the addition of an extra class with 40-day cycle between the 20-day and 125-day B and C classes and the effect of using percentage split vs value class boundaries. Looking more generally at the remaining scenarios, the difference is much less significant. We need to get a closer view of the centre of the curve. Figure 5.11 shows the centre of the curve.

Looking at the centre we can see that in the top right of the curve the 6 Class and 8 Class scenario are on the same line. This is because there is no parts in the 8 scenario Classes 1 and 2 and thus it will behave like the 6 Class. At the bottom right of the curve the 8 Class and 6 Class Lean are on the same curve, again this is because the parts are migrating from the lower classes to the higher classes. By looking at these three scenarios in Table 5.7 it can be seen that they are similar based on the populations of the higher and lower classes. Thus the correct interpretation is that for this group, the best course of action is that Pareto and 4 Class are not effective. First, while the inventory is in the £7,000 region with the batch processing capability circa 300 batches per year the best scenario is to use 6 class. Second, as we target

TABLE 5.7 Possible scenarios for number of classes and order cycles

| Classes | Scenarios | | | | |
	Pareto 80/20	4 Class	6 Class	6 Class – Lean	8 Class
1	5	5	5	1	1
2	20	20	10	2	2
3	125	40	20	5	5
4		125	40	10	10
5			80	20	20
6			160	80	40
7					80
8					160

inventory levels lower than £3,000 with a batch capability of 700 then using 8 Class, or 6 Class Lean becomes the most effective scenario. Thus by creating scenarios and plotting them we can visually identify which is the most effective for the group of parts. While in this above analysis we have focused only on the cycle stock, once this is done it is easy to add the safety stock and overage to create a complete k-curve policy for a given group of parts. The analysis of the exchange curve using only the cycle stock is recommended as there are a wide range of combinations of safety and overage values and they can mask the correct interpretation of the basic k-curve.

Create a plan group inventory plan

In Chapter 5 we identified that a weakness of Pareto was that because it uses percentage, the first 20 per cent will always be given the lowest cycle stock irrespective of the annual spend for the items. What we have seen in Table 5.6 is that k-curve will de-populate the highest inventory class if it is not appropriate to the annual spend of the parts. We can therefore be confident, even if we are overly optimistic about reducing our batch sizes the k-curve approach will adjust and balance our optimism, thus *k*-curve provides a robust and self-correcting technique. As it does not sub-optimize it means that you can with confidence plan different groups using different settings by specifying different numbers of classes, cycle stock ranges, safety stock techniques and levels of overage. For example, for new products you may specify higher levels of safety and overage as the demand is not yet fully understood. Similarly, for end of life you would be keen to keep overage and safety to a minimum.

In Chapter 5 we discussed that the key difference between purchased and manufacturing was their ability to process batches, thus we may not have the same *k* values for each group.

Once we have made the decisions, we are able to model the inventory plan and compare to the business targets. It is useful to express the plan in sufficient detail to be able to replicate or recalculate if the source data, typically the demand data, were to change. Table 5.8 shows a typical plan statement which would summarize the outcome of the planning analysis.

TABLE 5.8   Typical plan statement for a plan group

		Plan				
Classes	Parts in Class	No of Batches	Cycle Stock	Safety Stock	Overage	Inventory
1	1	50	5	5	10%	£1,891
2	4	100	10	5	20%	£4,647
3	6	75	20	10	25%	£1,710
4	12	75	40	15	30%	£5,831
5	3	9	80	20	40%	£2,754
6	1	2	160	25	50%	£104
k = 45	27	311	£6,221	£6,126	£3,927	£16,275
Inventory Target						£17,500
Capability it has been confirmed that the machine shop can process eight batches per week						400pa

Summary

In this chapter we set out to show how by combining parts of the Pareto curve approach with the modifications to EOQ proposed by Brown (1982) and Shah (1992) we can create an inventory plan that can be expressed simply and tested for viability before the plan is accepted. The base curve then has safety and overage to create a composite curve that is able to identify an envelope for an optimum inventory for a defined group of parts. This envelope can then be used to test any proposed plan for viability. Moreover, it can test any proposed inventory reduction for the required improvements in supporting process by showing the effective ROI (Return on Investment).

The key learning point in this chapter is that while the underlying theory may appear complex the use of the simplified EOP formula and resultant classification of each part into value classes based on EOP boundaries provides a very easy to manage analysis tool. The simplest exchange curve based only on cycle stock can easily be used to evaluate differing scenarios to find the most effective set of cycle day. The addition of safety and a guide as to the acceptable level of overage complete the generation of an exchange curve that is a good representation of the possible inventory for any group of parts. The chapter concluded by showing how we can use the k-curve to determine setting to meet a given target inventory. The next chapter will look at how this approach can be developed and used to create a credible inventory plan for a typical organization.

Notes

Brown, R (1982) *Advanced Service Inventory Parts Control* (2nd edn), Material Managemant Science Inc, Norwich

Burcher, P, Dupernex, S and Relph, G (1996) The road to lean repetitive batch manufacture: modelling planning system performance, *International Journal of Operations and Production Management*, **16**(2), pp 210–19

Dupernex (1993) Improving Inventory Performance using k-curve Methodology, Masters, Sunderland University

Dupernex (1997) Inventory Parameter Management and Focused Continuous Improvement for Repetitive Batch Manufacture, Ph Thesis, Aston University

Handley, R (1999) Inventory Management, *Control*, pp 24–26

Relph (2006) Inventory Management in Business Systems, PhD Thesis, Manchester University

Relph, G and Barrar, P (2001) Overage inventory – how does it occur and why it is important? *International Journal of Production Economics*, ISIR Proceedings (81–82), 163–71

Schwarz, M (2000) Multi-Item Inventory Control: The *k*-curve Methodology, PhD Thesis, Hamburg University

Shah, S (1992) Setting Parameters in MRP for the Effective management of bought-out inventory in a JIT assembly environment, PhD Thesis, Aston University

Wild, T (2002) *Best Practice in Inventory Management* (2nd edn), John Wiley, Oxford

You do the maths

If we add the actual stock information to the demand information, can you determine the amount of stock that is overage, based on a standard 6 class inventory plan.

Add the overage calculation to the Excel 5.10.

TABLE 5.9

Value Class	Cycle Days	Safety Days	Overage %age
1	5	5	10%
2	10	5	20%
3	20	10	25%
4	20	15	30%
5	80	20	40%
6	160	25	50%

What would the overage be if we set *k* to 45 as per the agreed plan in Table 5.8?

By how much would the overage change if we set the target for £15,000?

How does it compare to the planned overage levels?

k = 33 gives an inventory of £14,582.

EXCEL 5.11

	A	B	C	D	E	F	G	H	I	J	K	L	M	N	O
1	Constant k	45													
2	Working Days	250													
3															
4															
5	Value Class		Class Limit	Overge Percentage	No of Parts in Class	Annual Spend Value £	Cycle Days	Safety Days	No of Orders	Average Cycle Inventory	Safety Inventory	Planned Overage	Total Inventory	Actual Overage	
6	1		£56,250	10%	1	£56,720.16	5	5	50	£567.20	£1,134.40	£189.07	£1,890.67	£214.20	
7	2		£14,063	20%	4	£92,939.27	10	5	100	£1,858.79	£1,858.79	£929.39	£4,646.96	£4,015.85	
8	3		£3,516	25%	6	£36,696.12	20	10	75	£1,467.84	£1,467.84	£978.56	£3,914.25	£5,836.31	
9	4		£879	30%	12	£25,469.68	40	15	75	£2,037.57	£1,528.18	£1,528.18	£5,093.94	£12,593.21	
10	5		£220	40%	3	£1,563.68	80	20	9	£250.19	£125.09	£250.19	£625.47	£409.95	
11	6		£0	50%	1	£123.90	160	25	2	£39.65	£12.39	£52.04	£104.08	£55.46	
12	7		£0		0	£0.00			0	£0.00	£0.00	£0.00	£0.00	£0.00	
13	8		£0		0	£0.00			0	£0.00	£0.00	£0.00	£0.00	£0.00	
14	9		£0		0	£0.00			0	£0.00	£0.00	£0.00	£0.00	£0.00	
15				Total	27	£213,512.81			311	£6,221.24	£6,126.70	£3,927.43	£16,275.37	£23,124.98	

	A	B	C	D	E	F	G	H	I	J	K	L	M	N	O
17	Count	Part Number	Annual Usage or Demand	Cost Per Part	Value Class	Annual Spend Value £	Cycle Days	Safety Days	No of Orders	Average Cycle Inventory	Safety Inventory	Actual Stock	Planned Maximum	Overage	Actual Overage Value
18	1	B78811ZD	1324	£42.84	1	£56,720.16	5	5	50	£567.20	£1,134.40	58	53	5	£214.20
19	2	B78812ZF	987	£41.87	2	£41,325.69	10	5	25	£826.51	£826.51	20	59	0	£0.00
20	3	B78810741A	1012	£18.50	2	£18,722.00	10	5	25	£374.44	£374.44	75	61	14	£259.00
21	4	N6554004M0256	523	£35.08	2	£18,346.84	10	5	25	£366.94	£366.94	75	31	44	£1,543.52
22	5	SK98751	46	£316.19	2	£14,544.74	10	5	25	£290.89	£290.89	10	3	7	£2,213.33
23	6	LE763	781	£11.11	3	£8,676.91	20	10	12.5	£347.08	£347.08	321	94	227	£2,521.97
24	7	D0883030014C	267	£27.54	3	£7,353.18	20	10	12.5	£294.13	£294.13	98	32	66	£1,817.64
25	8	C78810742A	360	£16.87	3	£6,073.20	20	10	12.5	£242.93	£242.93	7	43	0	£0.00
26	9	D0862060018Y	163	£33.26	3	£5,421.38	20	10	12.5	£216.86	£216.86	65	20	45	£1,496.70
27	10	C78810761A	567	£8.43	3	£4,779.81	20	10	12.5	£191.19	£191.19	3	68	0	£0.00
28	11	LE02	396	£11.09	3	£4,391.64	20	10	12.5	£175.67	£175.67	0	48	0	£0.00
29	12	B78812001B	458	£7.10	4	£3,251.80	40	15	6.25	£260.14	£195.11	15	101	0	£0.00
30	13	KN552130	10	£319.98	4	£3,199.80	40	15	6.25	£255.98	£191.99	2	2	0	£0.00
31	14	A0906030015	18	£150.22	4	£2,703.96	40	15	6.25	£216.32	£162.24	8	4	4	£600.88
32	15	B78810721A	749	£3.44	4	£2,576.56	40	15	6.25	£206.12	£154.59	251	165	86	£295.84
33	16	D0991020012	164	£14.60	4	£2,394.40	40	15	6.25	£191.55	£143.66	104	36	68	£992.80
34	17	D0862070019Y	60	£35.25	4	£2,115.00	40	15	6.25	£169.20	£126.90	39	13	26	£916.50
35	18	D0978040014	35	£57.63	4	£2,017.05	40	15	6.25	£161.36	£121.02	91	8	83	£4,783.29
36	19	A78810601E	450	£4.20	4	£1,890.00	40	15	6.25	£151.20	£113.40	1117	99	1018	£4,275.60
37	20	B78818AE	35	£49.57	4	£1,734.95	40	15	6.25	£138.80	£104.10	14	8	6	£297.42
38	21	C78810762A	199	£7.44	4	£1,480.56	40	15	6.25	£118.44	£88.83	54	44	10	£74.40
39	22	D0753100033	75	£15.36	4	£1,152.00	40	15	6.25	£92.16	£69.12	34	17	17	£261.12
40	23	D1017040014	10	£95.36	4	£953.60	40	15	6.25	£76.29	£57.22	3	2	1	£95.36
41	24	KDB300600	8	£93.75	5	£750.00	80	20	3.125	£120.00	£60.00	6	3	3	£281.25
42	25	A0889030013	52	£9.59	5	£498.68	80	20	3.125	£79.79	£39.89	1	21	0	£0.00
43	26	B30880112C	700	£0.45	5	£315.00	80	20	3.125	£50.40	£25.20	566	280	286	£128.70
44	27	B30880113C	105	£1.18	6	£123.90	160	25	1.5625	£39.65	£12.39	125	78	47	£55.46
45		Totals				£213,512.81			310.94	£6,221.24	£6,126.70				

Enter these formulae

Using Excel 5.6 insert column between G and H
Cell H18 *and copy down to* H44 = CHOOSE(F18,$D$6,$D$7,$D$8,$D$9,$D$10,$D$11,$D$12,$D$13,$D$14,)
Cell K18 *and copy down to* K45 = H18*E18/$B$2

Notes for Excel 4.11 You do the maths exercise

1 The actual overage is £323,124.

2 $k = 33$ gives an Inventory of £14,582. The overage would increase to £23,839.

3 When k is set to $k = 45$, the overage is concentrated in Classes 2, 3 and 4. The highest level is in Class 4. There are 7 items with no overage and 7 items with overage over £1,000. Two items account for £9,058 of overage.

EXCEL 5.12

	A	B	C	D	E	F	G	H	I	J	K	L	M	N	O
1	Constant k	45													
2	Working Days	250													
3															
4															
5	Value Class		Class Limit	Overge Percent-age	No of Parts in Class	Annual Spend Value £	Cycle Days	Safety Days	No of Orders	Average Cycle Inventory	Safety Inventory	Planned Overage	Total Inventory	Actual Overage	
6	1		£56,250	10%	1	£56,720.16	5	5	50	£567.20	£1,134.40	£189.07	£1,890.67	£214.20	
7	2		£14,063	20%	4	£92,939.27	10	5	100	£1,858.79	£1,858.79	£929.39	£4,646.96	£4,015.85	
8	3		£3,516	25%	6	£36,696.12	20	10	75	£1,467.84	£1,467.84	£978.56	£3,914.25	£5,836.31	
9	4		£879	30%	12	£25,469.68	40	15	75	£2,037.57	£1,528.18	£1,528.18	£5,093.94	£12,593.21	
10	5		£220	40%	3	£1,563.68	80	20	9	£250.19	£125.09	£250.19	£625.47	£409.95	
11	6		£0	50%	1	£123.90	160	25	2	£39.65	£12.39	£52.04	£104.08	£55.46	
12	7		£0		0	£0.00			0	£0.00	£0.00	£0.00	£0.00	£0.00	
13	8		£0		0	£0.00			0	£0.00	£0.00	£0.00	£0.00	£0.00	
14	9		£0		0	£0.00			0	£0.00	£0.00	£0.00	£0.00	£0.00	
15				Total	27	£213,512.81			311	£6,221.24	£6,126.70	£3,927.43	£16,275.37	£23,124.98	

	A	B	C	D	E	F	G	H	I	J	K	L	M	N	O
17	Count	Part Number	Annual Usage or Demand	Cost Per Part	Value Class	Annual Spend Value £	Cycle Days	Safety Days	No of Orders	Average Cycle Inventory	Safety Inventory	Actual Stock	Planned Maximum	Overage	Actual Overage Value
18	1	B78811ZD	1324	£42.84	1	£56,720.16	5	5	50	£567.20	£1,134.40	58	53	5	£214.20
19	2	B78812ZF	987	£41.87	2	£41,325.69	10	5	25	£826.51	£826.51	20	59	0	£0.00
20	3	B78810741A	1012	£18.50	2	£18,722.00	10	5	25	£374.44	£374.44	75	61	14	£259.00
21	4	N6554004M0256	523	£35.08	2	£18,346.84	10	5	25	£366.94	£366.94	75	31	44	£1,543.52
22	5	SK98751	46	£316.19	2	£14,544.74	10	5	25	£290.89	£290.89	10	3	7	£2,213.33
23	6	LE763	781	£11.11	3	£8,676.91	20	10	12.5	£347.08	£347.08	321	94	227	£2,521.97
24	7	D0883030014C	267	£27.54	3	£7,353.18	20	10	12.5	£294.13	£294.13	98	32	66	£1,817.64
25	8	C78810742A	360	£16.87	3	£6,073.20	20	10	12.5	£242.93	£242.93	7	43	0	£0.00
26	9	D0862060018Y	163	£33.26	3	£5,421.38	20	10	12.5	£216.86	£216.86	65	20	45	£1,496.70
27	10	C78810761A	567	£8.43	3	£4,779.81	20	10	12.5	£191.19	£191.19	3	68	0	£0.00
28	11	LE02	396	£11.09	3	£4,391.64	20	10	12.5	£175.67	£175.67	0	48	0	£0.00
29	12	B78812001B	458	£7.10	4	£3,251.80	40	15	6.25	£260.14	£195.11	15	101	0	£0.00
30	13	KN552130	10	£319.90	4	£3,199.00	40	15	6.25	£255.98	£191.99	2	2	0	£0.00
31	14	A0906030015	18	£150.22	4	£2,703.96	40	15	6.25	£216.32	£162.24	8	4	4	£600.88
32	15	B78810721A	749	£3.44	4	£2,576.56	40	15	6.25	£206.12	£154.59	251	165	86	£295.84
33	16	D0991020012	164	£14.60	4	£2,394.40	40	15	6.25	£191.55	£143.66	104	36	68	£992.80
34	17	D0862070019Y	60	£35.25	4	£2,115.00	40	15	6.25	£169.20	£126.90	39	13	26	£916.50
35	18	D0978040014	35	£57.63	4	£2,017.05	40	15	6.25	£161.36	£121.02	91	8	83	£4,783.29
36	19	A78810601E	450	£4.20	4	£1,890.00	40	15	6.25	£151.20	£113.40	1117	99	1018	£4,275.60
37	20	B78818AE	35	£49.57	4	£1,734.95	40	15	6.25	£138.80	£104.10	14	8	6	£297.42
38	21	C78810762A	199	£7.44	4	£1,480.56	40	15	6.25	£118.44	£88.83	54	44	10	£74.40
39	22	D0753100033	75	£15.36	4	£1,152.00	40	15	6.25	£92.16	£69.12	34	17	17	£261.12
40	23	D1017040014	10	£95.36	4	£953.60	40	15	6.25	£76.29	£57.22	3	2	1	£95.36
41	24	KDB300600	8	£93.75	5	£750.00	80	20	3.125	£120.00	£60.00	6	3	3	£281.25
42	25	A0889030013	52	£9.59	5	£498.68	80	20	3.125	£79.79	£39.89	1	21	0	£0.00
43	26	B30880112C	700	£0.45	5	£315.00	80	20	3.125	£50.40	£25.20	566	280	286	£128.70
44	27	B30880113C	105	£1.18	6	£123.90	160	25	1.5625	£39.65	£12.39	125	78	47	£55.46
45		Totals				£213,512.81			310.94	£6,221.24	£6,126.70				

Enter these formulae

Using Excel 5.10, add Actual Stock figures in Column L.

Cell M18 and copy down to M44	= ROUND((C18/$B$2)*(G18+H18),0)
Cell N18 and copy down to N44	= IF(L18-M18<=0,0,L18-M18)
Cell O18 and copy down to O44	= N18*D18
Cell N6 and copy down to N14	= DSUM($E$17:$O$44,O$17,$A$5:$A6)-SUM(N$5:N5)

The practical application of *k*-curve

Introduction

This chapter brings together the tools and discussions from the previous chapters. We have examined the strengths and weakness of MRP as a planning system and know that we must manage the parameters. We have also discussed the various tools and techniques that can be used for determining the optimum inventory level, some of which look at individual part numbers and others look at managing groups of parts. What we now need to do is to link the need to change parameters to the approaches for determining the optimum inventory in an efficient and effective way. In this chapter we will explore how to develop an inventory plan for a business based on the *k*-curve approach, to show how this link can be easily made and implemented.

The four steps to this planning process were earlier in the book. They were:

- Understand your current inventory position – *How much have I got?*
- Determine the business targets that relate to inventory – *What do I have to achieve?*
- Create inventory plan – *How difficult will this be and what must I do?*
  - Plan group planning (*k*-curve)
  - Consolidate plan
- Implement the plan – *What actions must I do to achieve the plan?*

In this chapter we will take the four steps of inventory planning and show how we can apply the *k*-curve approach to the process. This will show how we can create an inventory plan, based on *k*-curve and how this plan can be linked, in a practical way, into your MRP system.

Figure 6.1 shows the overall inventory planning roadmap for the process, with links to the relevant chapters in the book. We have developed Figure 6.1

FIGURE 6.1   Overall planning process roadmap

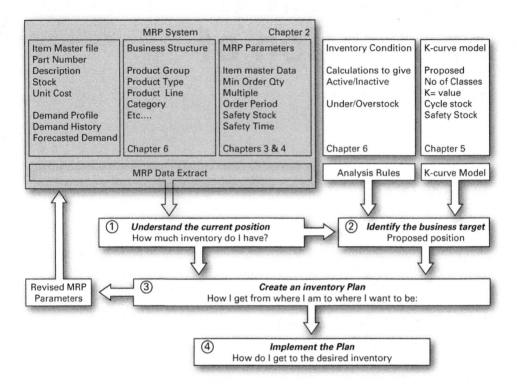

from Figure 3.19, where we will use the k-curve logic as the enabler to 'identifying the business targets'. The chapter will look in detail at each of the four steps and, using a practical scenario, demonstrate the creation of an inventory plan.

Looking at Figure 6.1 we can see that to complete these steps we first need to extract data from the company's MRP planning system. Second, identify analysis rules to analyse the data to establish a current position and then apply the k-curve model to 'identify the business targets' and show how these can meet. Having 'created an inventory plan' we need to detail the actions required to achieve the plan. This detail needs to be expressed in two ways: first, the revised MRP parameters and second the business actions needed to 'implement the plan' address the issues identified during the analysis and planning process.

The best way to demonstrate the application of this technique is to use a real inventory planning situation. In this chapter we will use a database of about 5,000 parts, available from the online resources, which we shall call our scenario Division X. Should you wish, you will be able to follow the planning process and examples and then take a closer look at the data to aid your understanding.

By working through an example we want to show how to tackle the issue raised in Chapter 1, Figure 1.3, which is related to the implementation of inventory reduction programmes that are driven from the global senior management targets. Thus for our working example we shall assume that our management has requested a 20 per cent inventory reduction within the next 12 months. We will show how, when planning Division X, the tools identified in Chapter 4 which looked at planning parts individually can be used. We will then show how *k*-curve can plan a group of parts as described in Chapter 5. We know that in a real business we would want to subdivide the parts into groups because we cannot adopt a one size fits all approach. Therefore when planning Division X we will look at how we can 'spread' the inventory reduction across the business. We will look at analysis techniques that allow you to understand the current position for a given group of parts and then create an exchange curve that will allow you to match the target inventory level and thus determine the *planning rule set* for that group of parts. Finally, we will step through the creation of a consolidated plan. As in previous chapters where it is appropriate we will show the Excel logic, however there is still a need for the reader to fully understand their own MRP system as each system has its own way of planning. Thus the use of Division X will show how to navigate the roadmap shown in Figure 6.1.

The scenario is as follows: Division X currently has £9.5 million of inventory, which is well managed and has a stock turn of around 10 turns. The business is doing well and predicts a cost of sales for the coming year of just below £100 million. The senior management would like to capitalize on the strong sales by reducing the inventory by 20 per cent. Thus our challenge is to achieve a planned stock level for year-end of £7.6 million.

Understand your current inventory position: how much have I got?

The first stage in any planning process is to understand where you are. There are three elements:

- First, identify the current position: this is the obvious start point, ie how much inventory do we have and where is it? This is a simple list of the quantity on the shelf, the unit cost, location (if appropriate) and its status: is it good stock, is it available for use, is it new or refurbished?

- Second, and almost as important, is to know what the MRP system is planning at the moment. This is so that we understand what inventory the MRP system is planning. These are normally located in the 'item master data' and should not be too difficult to extract. They are, typically, MOQ, multi, order period, safety quantity, safety time, lead-time, shelf life (if appropriate). These are important since they are the parameters used by MRP to raise purchase/manufacturing orders, which in turn drive deliveries into stores and the inventory held. We know from the discussions in Chapter 3 that if these are not managed they can cause significant problems in non-compliance. Thus in order to understand where we are we will need to broaden our data gathering to cover not just the actual stock but also to determine the current inventory related MRP parameters and thus the planned inventory level. We know from earlier chapters that there is a direct relationship between the inventory and demand (both historic and projected demand for the coming year). In order to understand what MRP is trying to do we need to identify the inventory-related parameters that sit within the MRP system.

- Most business will have developed reporting structures that divide the business into reporting groups. These are often based on MRP 'product groupings' and these help to segment the business performance data to match the structure of the business. Finally we need to determine the demand. It would be useful to determine both the past demand (historic) and the future demand (forecast). The importance of the historic demand will make it easier to understand why some parts are being held in stock, and the forecast will make it easier to determine the ideal level of future demand.

In combining these elements we will get a much clearer picture of the current inventory position rather than a simple list of all the inventory, with the highest inventory item at the top of the list, as often suggested when using Pareto. To enable this analysis we will need to establish a database/spreadsheet which we can use as the basis of the analysis. The data described above can be detailed into the following list of data elements:

- Item master data
  - part number, description
  - cycle stock parameters
    - lot size
    - minimum order quantity, multiple quantity;
    - economic order quantity – if defined
    - order period (in days, confirm if five-day week or seven days)
  - safety stock parameters
    - safety stock quantity
    - safety time
  - lead-time
    - manufactured
    - purchased
    - additional lead-times if used
- Business structure/reporting
  - product group, type, category
- Inventory module data
  - number in stock
    - available
    - allocated
    - quarantine
  - unit cost (to be used for all valuations)
  - location
  - warehouse
- Demand data
  - historic usage for previous years (three years)
  - projected demand
    - usage for 12 months if possible
    - or as far into the future as is valid, then prorate to be equivalent to 12 months' demand
    - or use the historic demand as a representation for future demand

This is quite an exhaustive list and may not be easily assembled, however it is worth persisting in assembling this data into a single database (eg Excel workbook) as it will form the basis of the inventory plan. Demand is often a difficult area to determine and it may require some ingenuity with Excel or a skilled IT technician to extract the required data. Ideally it is useful to look back at least three years and to get the forecast that will cover the next 12 months. Once the database is established it can also be used on a regular basis in the future for tracking the current performance, thus it should be reasonable to justify the considerable IT effort if needed.

Inventory overview

Once we have collected the above data we will want to present in a form that identifies the current inventory position. In order to utilize the database we need to calculate some key values:

- MRP cycle stock – this evaluates the MRP parameters to determine the cycle stock.
- Number of batches – using the cycle stock to give an estimate of the number of batches.
- MRP safety stock – this evaluates the MRP parameters to determine the safety stock.
- Inventory condition (A) – this identifies the basic state of the inventory.
- Inventory condition (B) – this identifies where the inventory is in the saw-tooth.

The detailed layout of the database is shown in Excel 6.1 and is positioned in Figure 6.1 as the core of the main feed into 'Understand the current position'.

MRP cycle stock and safety stock

The first step to correctly interpreting the MRP parameters is to estimate what the MRP system would calculate when creating a planned order. To understand the logic applied by the MRP system we have used the typical logic applied by most MRP systems. It is important to check the exact logic that your MRP system uses as there may be subtleties in the way it interprets the individual parameters.

Excel 6.2 shows the logic for creating the cycle stock; typically MRP will calculate the demand for a specified order period, and then test to see if a minimum order quantity and multiple quantity need to be applied. If no order period is applied it is usually one day of demand. Thus if all the parameters are set to zero it should return a value equivalent to one day of demand.

EXCEL 6.1 Structure of database and logic used

A	B	C	D
1 A	Part Number	Database	
2 B	Standard Cost		
3 C	STOCK		
4 D	Annual Demand Quantity		
5 E	MIN_QTY		
6 F	MAX_QTY		
7 G	ORD_MULT		
8 H	SFTY_TIME		
9 I	ORDER_PER		
10 J	SFTY_STOCK		
11 K	Product Group		
12 L	MRP Cycle Stock Quantity	Excel 6.2	
13 M	MRP Safety Stock Quantity	Excel 6.4	
14 N	MRP Over/Under Qty	Excel 6.7	
15 O	No of MRP batches	Excel 6.3	
16 P	Actual Stock Value	=B2*C2	
17 Q	Annual Demand Value	=B2*D2	
18 R	MRP Cycle Stock Value	=B2*L2	
19 S	MRP Safety Stock Value	=B2*M2	
20 T	MRP Net Overage Value	=B2*N2	
21 U	Days of Overage	Excel 6.8	
22 V	Plan Group	=VLOOKUP(K2,'Table 6.6'!A:B,2,FALSE)	
23 W	Active / Inactive	Excel 6.5	
24 X	Active Condition	Excel 6.6	
25 Y	Value Class		
26 Z	Class Cycle Days		
27 AA	Class Safety Days	Excel 6.9	
28 AB	Proposed No of Batches		
29 AC	Proposed Cycle Quantity		
30 AD	Proposed Safety Quantity		
31 AE	Proposed Cycle Stock Value	=B2*AC2	
32 AF	Proposed Safety Stock Value	=B2*AD2	
33 AG	Cycle Stock Difference	=L2-AC2	
34 AH	Safety Stock Difference	=M2-AD2	
35 AI	Cycle Stock Value Difference	=B2*AG2	
36 AJ	Safety Stock Value Difference	=B2*AH2	

Open new Excel workbook. Create sheets with names Database, *k*-curve.
Copy Excel 5.10 into *k*-curve.
Copy Database from online resources to Database columns A to K.

EXCEL 6.2 Estimating cycle stock logic

L2=IF((D2/'k-curve'!$B$2)*IF(I2<=1,'k-curve'!$J$2,I2)<=E2,E2,ROUNDUP(((D2/'k-curve'!$B$2)*IF(I2<=1,'k-curve'!$J$2,I2))/IF(G2=0,1,G2),0)*IF(G2=0,1,G2))

NB
Column B is Demand
Column I is Order period
Column E is Minimum Order Quantity
Column G is Order Multiple
Cell reference **'k-curve'!$B$2** is the number of work days in the year
Cell reference **'k-curve'!$J$1** is Planner consolidation factor (default setting is 5 days)
For calculating **demand / day the assumption is there are 260 working days in a year, with a 5 day week**
When applying this equation in Excel substitute the appropriate Column references
Assumes 1st line of data is Row 2

=IF((D2/'k-curve'!$B$2)*IF(I2<=1,'k-curve'!$J$2,I2)<=E2			
Test to see if **Order Period Qty** is Greater than MOQ			
Order period must be 1 not 0			
	True	**False**	
	E2,		
		ROUNDUP(	
		(((D2/'k-curve'!$B$2)*IF(I2<=1,'k-curve'!$J$2,I2))	/	IF(G2=0,1,G2)	,0)
		Order Period Qty	**Multiple**	
		Order period must be 1 not 0	**Must be 1 not 0**	

Apply the Multiple to Quantities over MOQ by dividing and then rounding by the multiple

Correct for where Multiple is 0, which logically means 1.	*IF(G2=0,1,G2))
	Multiple

EXCEL 6.3 Logic for calculating the number of batches

O2=IF(D2=0,0,ROUNDUP(D2/L2,0))				
NB				
Column D is Demand				
Column L is Calculated Order Quantity				
When applying this equation in Excel substitute the appropriate Column references				
Assumes 1st line of data is Row 2				
=IF(D2=0,	True			
	0, No demand = no batches		False	
		ROUNDUP(		
			D2/L2 Demand divided by Order Qty	,0))

EXCEL 6.4 Estimating additive safety Stock logic

M2=ROUNDUP(J2+(H2*D2/'k-curve'!$B$1),0)					
NB					
Column D is Demand					
Column H is Safety Time					
Column J is Safety Stock Quantity					
Cell reference 'k-curve'!$B$1 is the number of work days in the year					
For calculating demand / day the assumption is there are 260 working days in a year, with a 5 day week					
When applying this equation in Excel substitute the appropriate Column references					
Assumes 1st line of data is Row 2					
ROUNDUP(					
Add the Safety Quantity and Safety Time and round up the result.	J2 **Safety Stock Qty**	+	+(H2*D2/'k-curve'!$B$2) **Safety Time * Demand / Day**	,0)	

Once we know the estimate of the order size we can calculate the numbers of orders per year for each product by dividing the demand by the order size. Excel 6.3 shows the excel logic for calculating the number of batches based on the cycle stock.

The next element to determine is the safety stock. Excel 6.4 shows the logic here is slightly different as there are a number of key variations in logic that will need to be understood. The three options are:

1 Additive Safety Stock = Safety Time + Safety Quantity

2 Min Safety Stock = Lower of Safety Time or Safety Stock

3 Max Safety Stock = Higher of Safety Time or Safety Stock

It will need to be confirmed which is in use by the MRP system. The example is based on additive safety stock.

The next addition to the database is to determine the condition of the stock. This is divided into two stages: the first is to identify if the part is valid and active; the second is how much inventory there is compared with the plan level.

Active/inactive inventory

To be able to identify whether an item is active and inactive we need to consider three attributes: stock, demand and unit cost. The range of options for these three attributes and how the eight combinations can be classified are shown in Table 6.1.

TABLE 6.1 Inventory condition (A)

Name	Description	Stock	Demand	Cost
Active	Stock with Demand and Cost	Y	Y	Y
	No Stock with Demand and Cost	N	Y	Y
Inactive	Stock with No Demand but Cost	Y	N	Y
Dormant	No stock, No Demand but Cost	N	N	Y
Threat	Stock and Demand but No cost	Y	Y	N
	Stock with No Demand and No Cost	Y	N	N
	No Stock with Demand but No Cost	N	Y	N
Invalid	No stock, No Demand and No Cost	N	N	N

The inventory value will reside in the first two categories; dormant parts will indicate the number of parts in the database not being used. The threat category is important as it indicates that there are parts that cannot be valued and could potentially be a problem. These may be new products where the value has not been assigned, parts where the value has been written down to zero or an error. A possible logic statement that can be used to identify the inventory categories is shown in Excel 6.5.

A typical current position is shown below based on an excel pivot table from the Division X database in Table 6.2.

EXCEL 6.5   Logic tree for identifying inventory condition (A)

W2=+IF(B2>0,IF(D2>0,"Active",IF(C2>0,"Inactive","Dormant")),IF(D2>0,"Threat",IF(C2>0,"Threat","Invalid")))								
NB								
Column B is Unit Cost								
Column D is Demand								
Column C is Stock								
When applying this equation in Excel substitute the appropriate Column references								
Assumes 1st line of data is Row 2								
=+IF(B2>0, Cost	True					False		
Cost and Demand	IF(D2>0, Demand	"Active",	False			False		
Cost but No Demand test for Stock			IF(C2>0, Stock	"Inactive",	"Dormant")),			
No Cost but Demand						IF(D2>0, Demand	"Threat",	False
No Cost and No Demand test for Stock							IF(C2>0," Stock	Threat",	"Invalid")))

In this sample we can see that there is a total inventory of £9.5 million held in 4,953 parts.

Active

There are 3,991 active parts representing an inventory of £8.7 million, with demand of £86.9 million.

Inactive

About 809 parts are 'inactive' with a value of £789K. This inactive inventory is not contributing to the business and if the demand used in the analysis represent the next 12 months demand suggests that it will still be there in 12 months. More importantly, if the business target is based on reducing the inventory by say 20 per cent or £1.8 million then it will be made more difficult as at least 8 per cent of the inventory will still be there in a year's time.

Dormant

The next category is 'dormant'. Here we see just a few parts listed, however looking across we can see that the MRP parameters show some safety stock; if these parts are truly dormant then we should ensure that all the parameters in MRP are removed.

Threat

The next category, 'threat', shows that we have 126 parts that have no unit cost, but have quantities of stock, demand and MRP parameters. This is a dangerous situation as it means that first the actual stock and demand

TABLE 6.2 Division X analysis of inventory condition (A) using excel pivot table of the database

Row Labels	Count of Part Number	Sum of Actual Stock Value	Sum of STOCK	Sum of Annual Demand Value	Sum of Annual Demand Quantity	Sum of MRP Cycle Stock Value	Sum of MRP Cycle Stock Quantity	Sum of MRP Safety Stock Value	Sum of MRP Safety Stock Quantity
Active	3,991	£8,667,068	31,505,499	£86,900,221	196,810,241	£3,426,309	18,381,142	£3,441,748	6,589,762
Dormant	13	£0	0	£0	0	£0	0	£88	200
Inactive	809	£789,365	1,538,343	£0	0	£92,879	399,380	£8,595	2,761
Invalid	14	£0		£0	0	£0	0	£0	0
Threat	126	£0	300,022	£0	338,311	£0	6,831	£0	18,270
Grand Total	4,953	£9,456,433	33,343,864	£86,900,221	197,148,552	£3,519,188	18,787,353	£3,450,432	6,610,993

values are understated and second MRP is potentially ordering materials without knowing the cost. This can be because these are new products, or alternatively the stock has been written down. In both cases it is important to know what these parts are and ensure that they are costed at the earliest opportunity.

Invalid

The last group are 'invalid'. These parts are the deadwood and in data terms are clogging up the system. These are often excluded from reports so will go unnoticed. In summary, looking at the overview report can already give a lot of information about the parts being managed.

Inventory vs plan level: the good, bad and ugly

The next stage is to use the MRP parameters to determine the overall health of the active stock, and take a closer look at the inactive. In Figure 4.13 we identified the different conditions of inventory, underage, overage optimum and how these are related to the cycle stock and safety stock. We can therefore easily classify the active stock into the seven categories specified in Table 4.14. To classify the stock we will need to create a classification column in the database. The logic for determining the inventory condition is shown in Excel 6.5.

The same essential logic can be used to determine the amount of stock that is in overage and underage. This will help in the evaluation of the current stock position. Excel 6.6 shows the logic.

The final piece of logic is to determine how long the overage will last, as discussed previously in Figure 4.15 (see page 000), and extended in Excel 6.8 to show the logic for determining overage test and number of days.

Once we have added this logic to the database we can begin the process of analysis. Excel has an excellent pivot table which will make analysis very easy.

In this analysis we are only concerned with the active inventory. Looking at Table 6.3 we can see that active stock is £8.7 million and cost of sales of £89.6 million, which confirms the turnover of 10. On the surface this is very respectable. If we are able to achieve the optimum inventory (½ Cycle + Safety stock), of £3.426m / 2 + £3.441m = £5.154m it would give us an inventory well below our target of £7.6 million and a possible stock turn of 17.8.

EXCEL 6.6 Logic for determining the inventory condition (B)

X2=+IF(P2=0,"Shortage",IF(P2<S2,"Underage",IF(P2<(S2+R2),"Optimum",IF(P2<2*(S2+R2),"Overage",IF(P2<Q2,"Severe Overage",IF(P2<2*Q2,"Excess","Surplus"))))))

NB
Column P is Stock Value
Column Q is Demand value
Column R is Cycle Stock Value
Column S is Safety Stock Value
When applying this equation in Excel substitute the appropriate Column references
Assumes 1st line of data is Row 2

=+IF(P2=0, Stock Value = 0	"Shortage",					
Stock Value is less than Safety		IF(P2<S2, "Underage",				
Stock Value is less than Maximum Stock (Cycle + Safety)			IF(P2<(S2+R2), "Optimum",			
Stock value is less than twice Maximum Stock (Cycle + Safety)				IF(P2<2*(S2+R2), "Overage",		
Stock Value is less than one years demand					IF(P2<Q2, "Severe Overage",	
Stock Value is less than 2 years demand						IF(P2<2*Q2, "Excess", "Surplus"))))))

EXCEL 6.7   logic for determining over and under stocks

N2=IF(C2-L2-M2>0,C2-L2-M2,IF(C2-M2>0,0,C2-M2))
NB
Column C is Stock Quantity
Column L is Cycle Stock Quantity
Column M is Safety Stock Quantity
When applying this equation in Excel substitute the appropriate Column references
Assumes 1st line of data is Row 2
Explanation of Underage / Overage see Figure 4.13

=IF(C2-L2-M2>0,		True	False		
Overage is quantity of stock over maximum	C2-L2-M2,				
Test to identify for underage or optimum value			IF(C2-M2>0,	0, If inventory is within optimum range result is 0	C2-M2)) Underage

EXCEL 6.8   Logic for determining overage days

U2=ROUNDUP(IF(N2<=0,0,IF(D2=0,0,(N2+L2)/(D2/'k-curve'!$B$1))),0)
NB
Column D is Demand
Column L is Cycle Stock Quantity
Column N is The Over/Under Quantity
Cell reference 'k-curve'!$B$1 is the number of work days in the year
When applying this equation in Excel substitute the appropriate Column references
Assumes 1st line of data is Row 2
Explanation of Underage / Overage see Figure 4.13

=ROUNDUP(					,0)
	IF(N2<=0,	True	False		
Test for Overage	0,				
Test for Demand		IF(D2=0,	True	False	
Calculates number of days till minimum stock, i.e. next delivery is due			0,	(N2+L2)/(D2/'k-curve'!$B$1)))	

Shortage

Looking first at shortages there are 917 parts, which is approximately
22 per cent of the number of parts. It is reasonable to assume that not all
are causing line stoppages, but they represent a significant workload for
the planners, which will no doubt be the focus of the production and
shipping meetings. What is interesting is that if all these parts were to
become available it would increase the inventory by £565K.

TABLE 6.3 Division X analysis of Active Inventory Condition (B) using excel pivot table of the database

Row Labels	Count of Part Number	Sum of Actual Stock Value	Sum of Annual Demand Value	Sum of MRP Cycle Stock Value	Sum of MRP Safety Stock Value	Sum of MRP Net Overage value
Active	3,991	£8,667,068	£86,900,221	£3,426,309	£3,441,748	£3,533,615
Shortage	917	£0	£22,508,495	£560,652	£285,347	–£285,347
Underage	258	£546,555	£19,195,417	£516,009	£1,003,133	–£456,538
Optimum	671	£896,920	£11,362,098	£1,142,240	£412,624	£0
Overage	511	£2,736,574	£18,696,292	£694,928	£1,205,286	£836,360
Severe Overage	1,096	£3,335,642	£14,679,458	£431,901	£510,086	£2,393,655
Excess	138	£422,478	£312,317	£29,171	£17,186	£376,122
Surplus	400	£728,858	£146,145	£51,408	£8,087	£669,364
Grand Total	3,991	£8,667,068	£86,900,221	£3,426,309	£3,441,748	£3,533,615

Underage

Next underage items: these are not yet causing problems in production/sales, however the 'safety' is being utilized and the focus should be to ensure that the stock is delivered on time. Ideally the stock should be £1.261 million (£0.516 / 2 + £1.003 million) but it is currently only £0.546 million, some £456K short, the net result of getting the shortages and underage under complete control would be an increase in inventory of £1.0 million.

Optimum

The optimum stock should be £0.983 million (£1.142m / 2 + £0.412m) but is £0.896 million, thus is running slightly under. It is worth noting that only 10 per cent of the inventory is in optimum.

Overage

If we now look at the overage, here we have said that overage only occurs above maximum, so the amount of overage should be measured from the maximum stock, Cycle Stock + Safety Stock, thus the maximum is £1.9m and £0.836 million is the actual overage. In the discussion in Chapter 4 we understood overage was to be expected; this is, however, counterbalanced by the understocks. These over and understock values really represent the problems of balancing the supply and demand and they are to be expected in most businesses. The lower the value the more control the business has over its supply and demand.

Overage days

It is useful to be able to evaluate overage in terms of the number of days of overage, particularly when identifying where to focus, for example we may have a part with £10,000 of overage that will take five days to consume, and another £10,000 part that the overage will take 50 days to consume. There is really no case for action on the first part, where as it would be wise to investigate and ensure that no further orders were received for the second for at least 50 days.

Severe overage, excess and surplus

What is more of a problem is the remaining overstock conditions: severe overage, excess and surplus, although these values will take a lot longer to resolve and should be of significant interest to the organization. The severe overage, when the maximum stock of £0.941 million is removed is £2.393 million, and represents the bulk of the overstock problem.

Next, if we look at the excess, the correct working level for which is only £31K, £0.376 million is in 'excess', which means that this stock will take at least 12 months to be consumed.

Similarly for surplus the correct level is only £34K which means that the 'surplus' of £0.669 million is going to take at least two years to be consumed.

If we were to take the inventory conditions of severe overage, excess and surplus and investigate the top 10 per cent (only 170 items), we would get a very clear picture of the causes and thus actions to be put in place to improve the problem.

CASE STUDY   Comment

What we have found with clients is that there are numerous reasons why they are overstocked. There are two examples that come to mind: first, a company was managing a difficult contract where the supply for a particular motor was likely to put the project at risk. It was decided to purchase the entire estimated demand of 1,000 motors at £500. When the squeeze was put on inventory having £500,000 of insurance stock on an inventory of £3 million meant that finding inventory reductions is significantly harder as 10 per cent of £3 million is £300,000, whereas the true opportunity should be based on £2.5 million or £250,000, not only that but the £500,000 was going to take several years to be consumed. In the second, during a long period of drought a company decided to purchase water storage tanks – needed to enable their equipment to be used during the hose pipe ban. The 25 tanks were purchased at £6,100 each, at which point the weather broke, the hose pipe ban lifted and only three were ever utilized. The result was that the £134,000 of stock, which was 10 per cent of the £1.4 million businesses stock, remains waiting for next drought; meanwhile it limits the ability to reduce stock. In both cases the initial purchases were for sound business reasons, but when creating targets for inventory reduction it has to be accepted that these inventory items cannot be included. These inventory items need to be identified and classified as 'strategic stock' and handled outside the working stock.

In summary, through some simple analysis we can get a good view of our current position and make sure that when we set inventory reduction targets that we take into account inventory that can be reduced and specifically exclude those that for strategic reason we have decided to hold. This will result in credible targets and realistic plans. In summary, we would show the high level analysis as described for Division X in Table 6.4.

Determine the business targets that relate to inventory: what do I have to achieve?

All businesses need to plan and this will often follow an annual cycle; as the business year ends there is a frenzy of activity to meet the business targets set for that year, whether they be the sales, production or inventory targets.

CASE STUDY

When working for IBM I recall a number of New Year Eve's being disturbed, as the plants inventory manager I was called in to adjudicate on the last minute arrivals from our sister plants, who were trying to reduce their inventory by shipping early, whilst conversely we were refusing to receive early deliveries to ensure that we met our inventory targets. Businesses are driven by planning, targets and the creation of action plans to ensure delivery of the target.

A progressive business will begin the planning process before the end of the year and each department gets their targets and objectives. These are typically expressed at a high level and the departmental managers are expected to deploy the targets to a lower level; each business will have its own pro-gramme for this deployment.

- Quality functional deployment.
- Lean six sigma.
- Hosin Kanri.
- PDCA (Plan, Do, Check, Action).

TABLE 6.4 Division X Current inventory position report with management comments

Inventory	No of parts	Value	Over/Under Value	Comment/Action
Active	**3,991**	**£8,667,068**	**£3,533,615**	
Shortage	917	£0	–£285,347	22% of parts to be improved
Underage	258	£546,595	–£456,538	
Optimum	671	£896,920	£0	10% of parts
Overage	511	£2,736,574	£836,360	All overage 50% of stock
Severe Overage	1,096	£3,335,642	£2,393,655	Severe demand changes in July on Far East
Excess	138	£422,478	£376,122	
Surplus	400	£728,858	£669,364	Strategic stock = £450 for critical supply = £100 AB123455 Project Alpha
Inactive	**809**	**£789,365**	**£746,592**	£200 for Cancelled Project Alpha, alternate use being investigated by engineering
Dormant	**13**	**£0**	**–£88**	
Threat	**126**	**£0**	**£0**	100 new products being introduced costs due by M/E by mid Jan
Invalid	**14**	**£0**	**£0**	
Grand Total	**4,953**	**£9,456,433**	**£4,280,119**	

Overall position has improved since last year, overage running at 50% of all stock key focus will be improvement in shortage control, overage management and disposal/reuse of Project Alpha stock

The common feature is that they will look to link the actions of the business to the business targets to ensure that the focus is directed at what needs to be achieved. This effort is always in addition to the challenge of managing the day-to-day operations. Thus it is important to ensure that the inventory actions will assist in producing a more effective operation of the business system.

Inventory management from the top

As we stated in the introduction, senior management typically express the inventory target as a simple number, either × per cent or £y. For the operations manager we need to determine how this is to be achieved, which necessitates a detailed analysis of where we are and what is possible. The pressure within the business are often such that there is a constant pressure downwards on inventory and the need to consistently improve our 'on time performance' to the customer/manufacturing operation. These provide the key challenge to any manager responsible for inventory, often expressed as simple statements that completely belie their complexity.

> Quotes from Plant Inventory Manager at IBM in 1980s
> 'You can reduce the inventory as much as you like ... but don't stop my production.'
> 'Reduce the inventory by 10 per cent but you must not fail to service the customer.'
>
> Quotes from case study research conducted during Inventory Management Research Thesis
> 'Don't purchase any safety stock.'
> 'Only purchase A & B Components.'
> 'The Maximum stock cover must be no greater than six weeks.'
> 'Base batch sizes on 1–2 weeks of components or a practical minimum will be set to compensate for set-up times.' (Relph, 2006)

If we are going to avoid the scatter-gun approach we need to be able to express the global targets in detail. Fortunately business often naturally divides the business into sub-groups – these will provide the best basis for inventory planning.

Identifying different groups

These sub-groups can often reflect what the business manufactures, or consider manufacturing process key stages such as:

- raw materials;

- components;

- sub-assemblies;

- machined parts/moulded parts; and

- finished products.

These stages fall into three types of process: purchased, manufactured and finished goods stock. In addition to these groups we may need to consider the phase that the part is in its product lifecycle. If our business is retail the natural groupings would essentially be based on finished goods stock that has been purchased. Thus they will have the same constraints; in addition to product lifecycle the following may be important considerations for managing the stock levels:

- product categories;

- volatility of demand;

- criticality to customer; and

- source.

And finally, if our business were a Repairs and Maintenance business, it would be similar to Manufacturing as it will contain manufacturing stages, however we could also consider:

- criticality to customer;

- reliability of product;

- field population; and

- availability of replacement parts.

All these factors may or may not affect the way in which the inventory should ideally be planned. If these groupings are summarized it is possible to identify which factors will require different inventory planning rule sets. Table 6.5 shows how they affect the rule set components.

Once the business structure is defined we can begin to break down the inventory target. If the business structure can be expressed by utilizing particular data fields from MRP it will make the planning task much simpler. Business always tend to divide inventory into sub-groups, which are often used for reporting status and summarizing the business position. MRP systems will often provide data fields to facilitate the creation of these sub-groups. Product group, product type, product line, product class, planner, buyer, category are just a few examples. The prime purpose of these fields is

TABLE 6.5 Product grouping considerations

Group	No of Classes	Cycle Stock	Safety Stock	Capability/ Throughput
Purchased	Product Range Spread of Annual Spend		Service level required	Resource Technology
Manufactured				Tools Line changeover
Finished Goods		Maximise customer variety		Variability
New Product			Respond to initial demand	
End of Life			Minimize stock investment	
Customer Critical			Maximize service level through statistical safety stock	
Volatile Demand			Statistical Safety Stock to respond to demand volatility	

to enable management reporting and target setting. We will utilize these to form the basis of the plan groups as we develop the inventory plan. The issue will be that each of the plan groups must first relate to the way management wish to see the inventory and second that the parts within the group can be managed in the same way. If not, we may need to further divide the 'management groups' to make plan groups that can be set using the k-curve technique, eg A Class, Far East etc... New products, Dying Products, Machined or Purchased. Before commencing the next stage it is important to resolve two questions:

- Can I present and track the plan in a way that the management will recognize?

● Can I plan each group with a common set of rules for cycle stock, safety stock and overage?

Once the plan group decisions have been made we can progress to the next stage of planning.

In our scenario Division X we have used the Product Group (Column K) in the database and identified plan groups (Column V) based on the definition of the planning groups as shown in Table 6.6.

The plan groups initially reflect the management reporting structure but also will be used by the *k*-curve planning tool to identify the target inventory levels.

TABLE 6.6   Plan group structure for division X product codes

Product Code/Plan Group					
Group 1 UK	Group 2 Europe	Group 3 Asia	Group 4 End of Life	Group 5 New Products	Group 6 Field Spares
1	5	11	8	27	38	15
2	6		14	28		23
3	7		18	53		41
13	10		19	57		
			20	65		
			21	67		
			22	96		
			24	97		
			25	98		
			26	99		

Excel Formula
Create a sheet called 'Table 6.6' with the Product Code an column A and Plan Group in Column B
V2 =VLOOKUP(K2,'Table 6.6'!A:B,2,FALSE)

Create inventory plan: *how difficult will this be and what must I do?*

Apportioning inventory target

In Chapter 3 we looked at the business problem of specifying a business target and being able to determine a credible plan, and then execute the plan, and implement in the business system. This requires the tricky problem of looking at a total number of parts being managed and then determining how to spread the inventory reduction over the total inventory. Once we have identified in the database our plan groups we can summarize the inventory by plan group. We can now review the current inventory position of the Division X for each Plan Group based on an extension of Table 6.1 as shown in Table 6.7 below.

Table 6.7 shows the summary evaluating the stock, demand, current MRP parameters and the number of batches. The 'plan group' with the highest demand will be the most important to plan. If management are asking to achieve a 20 per cent reduction, that would mean finding £1.89 million. We can see that Group 1 is by far the largest demand, closely followed by Asia and Europe. We know from Table 6.3 that there is a significant amount of overstock; we should focus on the severe overage as this could be significantly reduced within the year. The excess should also be gone within the year, however we can assume that at least half the surplus will remain. The inactive stock will not reduce unless specific actions are taken to dispose of the stock as, at present, the MRP system see no use for the parts.

To be able to provide targets for each group we can present the inventory condition by plan group. The results for Division X are shown in Table 6.8. If we look at the analysis we can see that Group 1 and Group 3 have relatively small amounts of inactive, whereas Group 2, Group 4 and Group 6 are 20 per cent, 72 per cent and 17 per cent respectively. Group 4, End of life, suggests problems with managing falling demand. New products inactive could be an indication that the demand for the products is not yet visible in the MRP system. From this analysis we can consider how we would express the targets for each plan group. Table 6.9 shows the possible considerations for Division X.

TABLE 6.7 Division X showing plan groups and current status

Row Labels	Count of Part Number	Sum of Actual Stock Value	Sum of Annual Demand Value	Sum of MRP Cycle Stock Value	Sum of MRP Safety Stock Value	Sum of MRP Net Overage value	Sum of MRP No of MRP Batches
Group 1 UK	2,976	£5,864,409	£72,595,010	£2,575,729	£2,219,416	£2,430,787	102,508
Group 2 Europe	626	£611,355	£3,982,919	£226,140	£225,153	£299,893	13,859
Group 3 Asia	176	£1,883,980	£8,096,729	£473,799	£899,438	£653,571	2,747
Group 4 End of Life	826	£591,228	£674,632	£162,483	£25,785	£524,629	7,919
Group 5 New Products	65	£7,495	£156,282	£5,722	£9,159	-£3,496	2,148
Group 6 Field Spares	284	£497,966	£1,394,649	£75,314	£71,481	£374,735	4,661
Grand Total	4,953	£9,456,433	£86,900,221	£3,519,188	£3,450,432	£4,280,119	133,842

TABLE 6.8 Division X inventory plan groups and inventory condition

Sum of Actual Stock Value	Column Labels						
Row Labels	Group 1 UK	Group 2 Europe	Group 3 Asia	Group 4 End of Life	Group 5 New Products	Group 6 Field Spares	Grand Total
Active	£5,717,780	£488,958	£1,881,810	£164,176	£261	£414,083	£8,667,068
Shortage	£0	£0	£0	£0	£0	£0	£0
Underage	£458,612	£26,844	£54,487	£1,456		£5,196	£546,595
Optimum	£673,462	£54,009	£132,935	£11,514		£24,999	£896,920
Overage	£1,487,822	£123,095	£1,081,979	£18,425		£25,253	£2,736,574
Severe Overage	£2,588,716	£146,998	£359,083	£42,804		£198,041	£3,335,642
Excess	£183,539	£9,359	£146,742	£8,062	£62	£74,713	£422,478
Surplus	£325,628	£128,653	£106,584	£81,914	£199	£85,881	£728,858
Inactive	£146,629	£122,397	£2,169	£427,052	£7,234	£83,883	£789,365
Grand Total	£5,864,409	£611,355	£1,883,980	£591,228	£7,495	£497,966	£9,456,433

TABLE 6.9   Division X plan group strategy

Plan Group	Plan Group Inventory Curve Strategy
Group 1 – UK	Target for 20%+ ££4.5m
Group 2 – Europe	Target for 20%+ £390k Investigate Surplus and Inactive
Group 3 – Asia	Target 20%+ £1.5m, minimum safety of 20 days on all products
Group 4 – End of Life	Minimise safety stocks
Group 5 – New products	Investigate 4 & 6 Class curves, mirror Group 1 settings, ensure parts transferred as to Groups 1,2 & 3 when stable
Group 6 – Spares	Maintain at £500k, need to support products in field

Plan group planning (k-curve)

The next stage is to identify for each group the ideal k-curve for each plan group. Building on the Excel 5.10 model we can extend the summary section to cover the current inventory, active and inactive, and evaluate the values of the current MRP parameters and number of batches for each group. These extra fields are defined in Excel 6.1 and the logic for each element has been described in this chapter. The revised layout is shown in Excel 6.9 with the required formula for the summary tables. The DSUM Excel feature has been utilized to allow each plan group to be separately analysed and planned by the addition of the 'plan group' in Column A. Once the planning is complete the data will need to be copied and pasted to a separate sheet to summarize into a total plan.

As discussed in Chapter 5 the first step is to determine which number of classes and cycle stock policy is best for the group of parts. For Plan Group 1 UK, we assume that we have completed this work and concluded that a 6 Class policy as shown in Excel 6.9 is to be used for the plan. Once this decision is made, the remaining decisions of safety stock and overage can be made. This will establish a working model for Plan Group 1 UK; the value of k can be varied as shown in Chapter 5 and the results collated. In addition,

EXCEL 6.9 Division X product group 1 – inventory plan by class

Work Days	250
X Value	140

Minimum Cycle   5 Days

Plan Group	Value Class	Planning Rules				Base Data		MRP – Current parameters			Actual Performance			Proposed Inventory				
		Class Limit	Class Cycle Days	Class Safety Days	Overage %age	No of Parts in Class	Annual Demand Value	No of MRP Batches	MRP Cycle Stock Value	MRP Safety Stock Value	Actual Stock Value	MRP Net Overage value	Overage %age	Proposed no of Batches	Proposed Cycle Stock Value	Proposed Safety Stock Value	Planned Overage	Total Inventory
Group 1 UK	1	£175,000	5	5	10%	82	£37,961,380	3,942	£803,526	£986,251	£1,527,061	£270,452	18%	4100	£759,598	£759,598	£126,599.71	£1,265,997
Group 1 UK	2	£43,750	10	5	20%	231	£19,992,268	9,927	£525,329	£682,592	£1,667,875	£690,471	41%	5775	£776,601	£388,707	£194,251.92	£971,260
Group 1 UK	3	£10,938	20	10	25%	491	£10,814,534	19,682	£521,148	£400,417	£1,325,122	£613,509	46%	6383	£866,706	£434,290	£289,214.28	£1,156,857
Group 1 UK	4	£2,734	40	15	30%	598	£3,468,360	22,748	£379,035	£112,470	£711,269	£404,572	57%	4186	£555,908	£209,293	£208,820.24	£696,067
Group 1 UK	5	£684	80	20	40%	524	£782,846	17,386	£213,966	£29,501	£271,262	£156,132	58%	2096	£251,095	£63,109	£125,770.74	£314,427
Group 1 UK	6	£0	160	25	50%	879	£175,621	27,795	£90,659	£7,113	£215,191	£166,284	77%	1758	£113,766	£19,424	£76,307.47	£152,615
Group 1 UK	7	£0				0	£0	0	£0	£0	£0	£0	0%	0	£0	£0	£0.00	£0
Group 1 UK	8	£0				0	£0	0	£0	£0	£0	£0	0%	0	£0	£0	£0.00	£0
Group 1 UK	9	£0				171	£0	1,028	£42,066	£1,071	£146,629	£129,368	88%	0	£0	£0	£0.00	£0
						2976	£72,595,010	102,508	£2,575,729	£2,219,416	£5,864,409	£2,430,787		24,298	£3,323,675	£1,874,421	£1,020,964	£4,557,223
						4953	£86,900,221	133,842	£3,519,188	£3,450,432	£9,456,433	£4,280,119		31,262	£4,144,453	£2,277,029		

Enter these formulae

Cell C6 to C14 => = IF($D7=0,0,+$B$1*$B$2/($D6*$D7))
Cell G6 to G14 => = DCOUNTA(Database!A:AF,Database!A$1,$A$5:$B6)-SUM(G$5:G5)
Cell H6 to H14 => = DSUM(Database!$A:$AF,Database!$Q$1,$A$5:$B6)-SUM(H$5:H5)
Cell I6 to I14 => = DSUM(Database!$A:$AF,Database!$O$1,$A$5:$B6)-SUM(I$5:I5)
Cell J6 to J14 => = DSUM(Database!$A:$AF,Database!$R$1,$A$5:$B6)-SUM(J$5:J5)
Cell K6 to K14 => = DSUM(Database!$A:$AF,Database!$S$1,$A$5:$B6)-SUM(K$5:K5)
Cell L6 to L14 => = DSUM(Database!$A:$AF,Database!$P$1,$A$5:$B6)-SUM(L$5:L5)

Cell M6 to M14 => = DSUM(Database!$A:$AF,Database!$T$1,$A$5:$B6)-SUM(M$5:M5)
Cell N6 to N14 => = IF(L6=0,0,M6/L6)
Cell O6 to O14 => = DSUM(Database!$A:$AF,Database!$AB$1,$A$5:$B6)-SUM(O$5:O5)
Cell P6 to P14 => = DSUM(Database!$A:$AF,Database!$AE$1,$A$5:$B6)-SUM(P$5:P5)
Cell Q6 to Q14 => = DSUM(Database!$A:$AF,Database!$AF$1,$A$5:$B6)-SUM(Q$5:Q5)
Cell R6 to R14 => = S6-(P6*0.5)-Q6
Cell S6 to S14 => = ((P6*0.5)+Q6)/(1-F6)

FIGURE 6.2 *k*-curve chart showing inventory opportunity

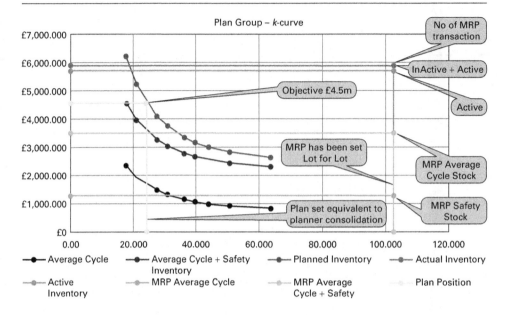

we can identify the current position from the MRP summary data. There is a lot of information to evaluate and showing the results on the chart in a single view would make it easier to understand the current position and evaluate the feasibility of the target inventory level. The required layout to create a plan exchange curve, using the XY Chart format, is shown in Excel 6.10.

Figure 6.2 shows the exchange curve and identifies the extent of the opportunity.

If we look at Figure 6.2, which shows Group 1 for Division X, we can see the *k*-curve and compare with the current MRP settings and actual and active inventory. What can be seen is that it should be possible to meet the objective as the current number of batches processed suggest that there are a lot of parts, which have possibly been set to lot for lot. This can be confirmed by an examination of the Division X database. This analysis shows us that 544 of the 2,976 parts in Plan Group 1 UK have an order period set to one day. This will mean that the planners must be making the batching decisions as they plan, rather than to a pre-defined set of rules. This can be verified by finding out how many transactions are actually being processed by each plan group; this may be 'goods in' if they are all purchased or the assembly line if they are manufactured. A case study example of this is detailed below.

EXCEL 6.10 Data layout for the creation of the plan group *k*-curve Figure 6.2

For each value of *k*, copy/paste values the following
No of orders $= O15$
Average Cycle $= P15/2$
Average Cycle + Safety Inventory $= P15/2 + Q15$
Planned Inventory $= S15$

	U	V	W	X	Y	Z	AA	AB	AC	AD
19	K	No of Orders	Average Cycle	Average Cycle + Safety Inventory	Planned Inventory	Actual Inventory	Active Inventory	MRP Average Cycle	MRP Average Cycle + Safety	Plan Position
20	10	63,708	£813,580	£2,299,059	£2,608,139					
21	20	50,769	£907,256	£2,426,996	£2,808,948					
22	30	44,025	£991,283	£2,545,447	£2,994,282					
23	40	39,770	£1,066,903	£2,653,040	£3,163,512					
24	50	36,473	£1,141,608	£2,764,115	£3,336,749					
25	75	30,955	£1,315,361	£3,022,191	£3,740,740					
26	100	27,566	£1,466,517	£3,249,683	£4,098,118					
27	200	20,978	£1,941,282	£3,953,224	£5,230,120					
28	300	17,732	£2,344,936	£4,553,653	£6,208,707					
29	MRP	102,508				£0	£0	£0	£0	
30		102,508				£5,864,409	£5,717,780	£1,287,865	£3,507,280	
31		0				£5,864,409	£5,717,780	£1,287,865	£3,507,280	
32	Plan Position	24,298								£0
33		24,298								£4,557,223
34		0								£4,557,223

From the summary table
MRP No of Orders $= I15$
Actual Inventory $= L15$
Active Inventory $= L15 - L14$
MRP Average Cycle $= J15/2$
MRP Average Cycle + Safety $= J15/2 + K15$

From the summary table
Plan Position No of Orders $= O15$
Actual Inventory $= S15$

Enter these formulae

Select range V19:AD34, Insert Chart type XY to create Figure 6.2

CASE STUDY   Kidde Graviner

Figure 6.3 shows a chart from Kidde Graviner where this issue was identified. When discussing the issue with the planners it was found that they were consolidating the lot for lot orders; a detail analysis was able to show the effect of the consolidation where it was found that they were producing a result similar to the *k*-curve recommendation. The client then instituted a project which included training the staff on MRP parameter management and followed through with providing the planners with tools to help with the correct batching rule decisions.

FIGURE 6.3   Consolidation of lot for lot recommendations

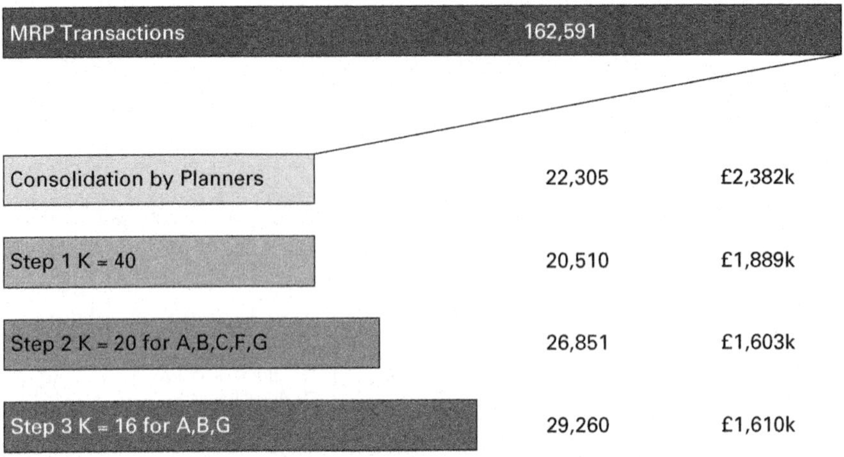

MRP Transactions	162,591	
Consolidation by Planners	22,305	£2,382k
Step 1 K = 40	20,510	£1,889k
Step 2 K = 20 for A,B,C,F,G	26,851	£1,603k
Step 3 K = 16 for A,B,G	29,260	£1,610k

Reproduced with kind permission of Kidde Graviner

Once we have compared the curve to the current position we can look at the opportunity: if we were to set the initial position such that the current cycle stock were to remain the same we would make a significant reduction in the workload as significantly fewer batches would be processed. This gives a plan position and represents a setting of $k = 140$. The model shows the cycle and safety stock decisions and comparisons between the current MRP values and the proposed values; overall the planned level corresponds with the current level. However, looking further at the curve we can see that the amount of cycle stock would increase, when compared to the current, whereas the safety stock recommended by the k-curve is slightly lower than the current MRP settings. The key challenge for Division X will be the how to deal with the order period of 1 days for 544 parts which appear to be the Class 1 to 3 parts. The planned overage level of £1.0 million will allow sufficient headroom for the overage but by referring back to Table 6.8 we can see that there will need to be a focus on severe overage to ensure the plan is met. Group 1 has a fair share of the 20 per cent inventory reduction at £1.2 million. This process needs repeating for the remaining plan groups and then consolidated into a total plan.

Consolidating the plan

Once the current position is established for each of the plan groups they can in turn be planned using the *k*-curve model for each of the plan groups as in Figure 6.2, working from highest inventory to lowest. This will easily identify the gap, which can then be prioritized until a consensus on the proposed plan is achieved. This will mean that for each plan group a statement like Excel 6.9 can be determined. The total lines from each individual analysis can then be consolidated into a total plan as shown in Table 6.10. This can be viewed as three separate tables:

- planning rules;
- MRP current parameters; and
- proposed inventory.

In describing the plan for each group we have now determined the target, identified where the key issues are and will have begun to understand the areas for concern.

In addition to the detail plan group numbers, they will need to prepare a summary statement which accounts for the inactive inventories and determine projections for the excess and surplus. An example is shown in Table 6.11.

What is also vital will be an assumptions statement. This needs to record the key assumptions that have been taken when building the plan and should include assumptions related to:

- The demand for each plan group over the plan period:
  - *It is expected that UK business will remain steady.*
  - *The Far East business will grow by 10 per cent.*
- The disposal of the inactive stock:
  - *Finance have approved a budget of £500,000 for scrap of inactive materials.*
- The consumption of surplus and excess:
  - *Outlook for Excess by Y/e is a reduction to £100,000.*
  - *Outlook for Surplus by Y/e is a reduction to £400,000.*
  - *Assumes no change in the Alpha Project consumption of Motors.*
- The management of supply/demand:
  - *Overage performance will reduce severe overage to £1.5.*
  - *Training of staff on supply demand management 1Q.*
  - *S&OP meeting to be held monthly from Jan.*

TABLE 6.10 Total plan by plan group – detail

Plan Group	Planning Rules					Base Data	
	k-value	Class Limit	Class Cycle Days	Class Safety Days	Overage %age	No of Parts in Class	Annual Demand Value
Group 1 UK	140	6 Class	5,10,20,40,80,160	5,5,10,15,20,25	10,20,25,30,40,50	2976	£72,595,010
Group 2 Europe	140	6 Class	5,10,20,40,80,160	5,5,10,15,20,25	10,20,25,30,40,50	626	£3,982,919
Group 3 Asia	100	6 Class	5,10,20,40,80,160	20,25,30,35,40,45	10,20,25,30,40,50	176	£8,096,729
Group 4 End of Life	150	6 Class	5,10,20,40,80,160	0,0,0,0,5,5	10,20,25,30,40,50	826	£674,632
Group 5 New Products	100	4 Class	5,10,20,80	5,5,10,20	10,20,30,50	65	£156,282
Group 6 Field Spares	150	6 Class	5,10,20,40,80,160	5,5,10,15,20,25	10,20,25,30,40,50	284	£1,394,649
Total						4953	£86,900,221

TABLE 6.10 *continued*

Plan Group	Base Data		MRP – Current parameters				Actual Performance		
	No of Parts in Class	Annual Demand Value	No of MRP batches	MRP Cycle Stock Value	MRP Safety Stock Value		Actual Stock Value	MRP Net Overage Value	Overage % age
Group 1 UK	2976	£72,595,010	102,508	£2,575,729	£2,219,416		£5,364,409	£2,430,787	41%
Group 2 Europe	626	£3,982,919	13,859	£226,140	£225,153		£611,355	£299,893	49%
Group 3 Asia	176	£8,096,729	2,747	£473,799	£899,438		£1,883,980	£653,571	35%
Group 4 End of Life	826	£674,632	7,919	£162,483	£25,785		£591,228	£524,629	89%
Group 5 New Products	65	£156,282	2,148	£5,722	£9,159		£7,495	–£3,496	–47%
Group 6 Field Spares	284	£1,394,649	4,661	£75,314	£71,481		£497,966	£374,735	75%
Total	4953	£86,900,221	133,842	£3,519,188	£3,450,432		£9,456,433	£4,280,119	45%

TABLE 6.10 *continued*

Plan Group	Base Data			Proposed Inventory			
	No of Parts in Class	Annual Demand Value	Proposed No of Batches	Proposed Cycle Stock Value	Proposed Safety Stock Value	Planned Overage	Total Inventory
Group 1 UK	2976	£72,595,010	24298	£3,323,675	£1,874,421	£1,020,964.35	£4,557,223
Group 2 Europe	626	£3,982,919	2530	£296,040	£131,149	£109,534.36	£388,703
Group 3 Asia	176	£8,096,729	2694	£270,861	£732,277	£172,896.41	£1,040,604
Group 4 End of Life	826	£674,632	1135	£83,815	£2,858	£26,723.99	£71,490
Group 5 New Products	65	£156,282	171	£9,382	£4,374	£3,779.09	£12,844
Group 6 Field Spares	284	£1,394,649	898	£107,055	£45,423	£38,684.75	£137,635
Total	4953	£86,900,221	31,726	£4,090,827	£2,790,503	£1,372,583	£6,208,499

TABLE 6.11   Summary plan combining active and inactive data

	Actual	Plan	Inactive
Group 1 UK	£5,864,409	£4,557,223	£146,629
Group 2 Europe	£611,355	£388,703	£122,397
Group 3 Asia	£1,883,980	£1,040,604	£2,169
Group 4 End of Life	£591,228	£71,490	£427,052
Group 5 New Products	£7,495	£12,844	£7,234
Group 6 Field Spares	£497,966	£137,635	£83,883
Total	£9,456,433	£6,208,499	£789,365
Total			£6,997,865
Scrap Disposal			–£500,000
Severe Overage			£750,000
Excess			£100,000
Surplus			£500,000
Total Plan			£7,847,865
Saving			£1,608,568
Target			£1,890,000

The importance of keeping a clear record of the assumptions is that if there are any changes to them, which result in a significant effect on inventory, then it will provide an important audit trail.

Implement the plan: what actions must I do to achieve the plan?

Creating the deployment plan

Now that we have created this plan statement, which is the result of a technical analysis we need to be able to articulate how we can implement this plan. There are three types of actions that we are required to organize:

- deployment of the inventory actions;
- deployment of the capability actions; and
- deployment of the MRP parameter actions.

Create deployment plan for inventory actions

Planning the *inactive/surplus/excess*

In the initial analysis we identified the inactive, surplus and excess inventories. We know that these are the longer-term problems and will take most of the year ahead to resolve. We need to ensure that there is a regular focus throughout the year to keep the focus. When starting this process for the first time the history of why parts got into the situation may not be known, however if this process is managed on a monthly basis with new items being identified as they occur the easier it will be to get the story and if possible take corrective actions.

What is important with the inactive parts is to understand if they are truly wanted, that is why having up to three years history will be useful. It may be that the parts have only just stopped being used or that they have not been used for a long time. Whichever is true once it has been confirmed that the parts are not wanted, then they should be disposed of. This is not a trivial process; it is not as simple as putting the parts into a skip. The engineering and finance departments will need to be closely involved to ensure that parts are scrapped in an effective and controlled way.

For the surplus and excess the most urgent action is to ensure that no further stock is being bought. Next the validity of the future demand needs to be understood to be sure that the stock will be used up. Looking at alternative usage of the parts as well as getting the sales team to focus on the products will all help. The database can be used to identify the inactive parts and identify a hit list based on the highest values. Our experience is to avoid producing long lists which will invariably not be completely actioned. A good rule is to only list one page and list the highest value first. For example:

Inactive inventory report for Division X

- All items over £5,000 of stock.
- Total report value £325,000 of £789 inactive stock (41 per cent).
- Total items listed 36 items of 810 (4 per cent).
- This would provide a good start to the achievement of the business target to dispose of £500,000.

Create a deployment plan for the capability actions

The deployment plan for capability needs to look at the business process side of the business to create a credible plan. In the Division X example, the issue of order period being set to one day has a significant effect on Plan Group 1. There will be good reasons why this happened and a 'capability project' should be established to understand why this decision was made. The Kidde Graviner case study shows how this issue was resolved in a particular client. The project will not directly benefit the inventory level, however it will ensure that the planners make the most effective use of their time and their decisions will sit within the guidelines required to achieve the proposed inventory level. It may be that what is required is to increase the capability of a particular manufacturing or supply chain process; in these cases it would be appropriate to use Lean implementation tools, some of which are described in Richards and Grinsted (2013). This book provides a simple guide to the many Lean tools that can be used to identify problems and focus on providing solutions.

Create deployment plan for MRP parameter changes

The *k*-curve analysis is based on making a decision about the cycle stock and safety stock; first at an aggregate then by inventory classing this decision is then made for each part which essentially reverses the aggregating process. Once we have made decisions for the number of classes and the value of k, we have in effect set the cycle stock and safety stock for each item.

The importance of parameter maintenance in MRP

In Chapter 2 we identified the importance of maintaining parameters. What is important here is that we can use the MRP parameters, calculated for each plan group to re-tune MRP to drive the business towards the new inventory plan. We know from earlier discussion about the planning process that unless we change the parameters the results that MRP produces will not change. We also know from Chapter 3 that keeping parameters up to date has a beneficial effect on compliance. The challenge is how to implement parameters for 5,000 parts. We know from Excel 6.2 and Excel 6.3 that there are at least five parameters that affect the cycle and safety stock; this means that there are 25,000 parameters that we potentially need to change. We could adopt an approach of uploading all the new parameters to the system. This would be potentially reckless as it takes no account of the reason why the parameters are currently set to their values in the first place. The second issue is more sensitive: the planner has traditionally been responsible for making the parameter decisions, and could easily resent advice from a computer/management system. They may argue that each decision has to be examined on the individual item and cannot be applied as blanket rules. Both are extremely valid points and ignoring them would mean taking a considerable risk.

There are two different strategies that we have found work well and can be adopted to facilitate implementation of MRP parameter change.

Guide the planner

The first is to provide a reference guide, which the planner can be asked to consider when making parameter decisions.

This table is a simple set of guidelines as shown in Excel 6.1 that will allow the planner to make the final decision within a set of rules that corresponds to the inventory plan, which will in effect drive the MRP parameters in the required direction. This has proved very effective with experienced planners.

Request planner permission

An alternate, slightly more prescriptive approach, which requires more effort, is to produce a report which compares the current parameters with the proposed parameters and identifying parts where there is a difference. As we rebalance the inventory the MRP parameter differences can be either an increase or a decrease, and if all the difference were listed would cover most parts, so rather than listing all parts, which would be rejected as too much work, we can create an exception report to identify the highest value changes. If we consider our database we can use difference and value filters to focus on the most important changes. Table 6.12 shows a simple action report which has identified the top eight increases and top eight decreases in the cycle stock.

TABLE 6.12 Planner action report

Part Number	Standard Cost	STOCK	Annual Demand Quantity	Min Quantity	Max Quantity	Order Multiple	Safety Time	Order Period	Safety Stock	MRP Cycle Stock Quantity	MRP Safety Stock Quantity	Value Class	Class Cycle Days	Class Safety Days	Proposed Cycle Quantity	Proposed Safety Quantity	Cycle Stock Difference	Safety Stock Difference
AB00711	£8.66	2,592	39,225	36	0	36	10	5	0	792	1,569	2	10	5	1,569	785	-777	784
AB00741	£5.02	15,860	50,480	0	0	5,292	30	5	0	5,292	6,058	2	10	5	2,020	1,010	3,272	5,048
AB00759	£15.59	1,384	21,843	16	0	16	10	5	0	448	874	2	10	5	874	437	-426	437
AB00827	£10.34	36	32,400	36	0	36	10	5	0	648	1,296	2	10	5	1,296	648	-648	648
AB00845	£22.74	324	15,063	90	0	18	10	5	0	306	603	2	10	5	603	302	-297	301
AB00919	£5.32	3,640	3,024	0	0	3,700	30	5	0	3,700	363	4	40	15	484	182	3,216	181
AB00921	£5.94	11,410	23,427	0	0	3,700	30	5	0	3,700	2,812	2	10	5	938	469	2,762	2,343
AB01931	£46.75	48	336	0	0	416	25	5	0	416	34	4	40	15	54	21	362	13
AB01935	£13.67	238	927	0	0	1,440	25	5	0	1,440	93	4	40	15	149	56	1,291	37
AB02342	£4.74	2,466	65,784	0	0	0	10	5	0	1,316	2,632	2	10	5	2,632	1,316	-1,316	1,316
AB02952	£8.04	6	390	0	0	2,142	30	5	0	2,142	47	5	80	20	125	32	2,017	15
AB03279	£1.89	1,339	71,318	0	0	13,320	0	5	20	13,320	20	2	10	5	2,853	1,427	10,467	-1,407
AB03288	£1.08	11,622	278,671	0	0	0	0	5	0	5,574	0	2	10	5	11,147	5,574	-5,573	-5,574
AB03685	£0.55	8,874	40,895	0	0	560	10	250	0	41,440	1,636	4	40	15	6,544	2,454	34,896	-818
AB04203	£9.13	0	36,624	0	0	0	0	5	0	733	0	2	10	5	1,465	733	-732	-733
AB04481	£7.92	4,779	42,581	60	0	60	10	5	0	900	1,704	2	10	5	1,704	852	-804	852

EXCEL 6.11   Planner table based on Excel 5.4 with added columns

	A	B	C	D	E	F	G	H	I	J
1	k Value	120								
2	Working Days	250								
3										
4										
5	Value Class	Cycle Days	Class Limit	Max Order value	Minimum Order Value	Class Safety Days	Maximum Safety Value	MOQ Round to nearest	Multi to nearest	Overage %age
6	1	5	£72,000	N/A	£1,440	5	£1,440	1	1	10%
7	2	10	£18,000	£2,880	£720	5	£360	1	1	20%
8	3	20	£4,500	£1,440	£360	10	£180	1	1	25%
9	4	40	£1,125	£720	£180	15	£68	10	10	30%
10	5	80	£281	£360	£90	20	£23	10	10	40%
11	6	160	£0	£180	£0	25	£0	100	100	50%
12	7									
13	8									
14	9									

Enter these formulae

Maximum Order Value   D7 = B7*(C6/$B$2)   B, F and J from k-curve
Minimum Order Value   E6 = B6*(C6/$B$2)   H & I Manager Decision
Maximum Safety Value   G6 = F6*(C6/$B$2)

Parameter investigation report for Division X

Top 16 Parts with Cycle Stock changes

8 Parts with Cycle stock reduction	= £139k
8 parts with Cycle Stock increases	= £ 52k
Net reduction	= £ 87k

Top item	Reduction £19,782	Increase £6,754
Part Number	= AB03279	= AB00345
Annual demand	= 71,317	= 15,063
MOQ	= 0	= 90
Multiple	= 13,320	= 0
Order Period	= 5 days	= 5 days
Proposed Cycle stock		
Class	= 2	= 2
Order Period	= 10 days	= 10 days
Cycle Quantity	= 2,853	= 603

For AB03279 – what is clear here is the multiple is very high, the recommendation is to reduce this by a factor of five. Reducing this to the proposed value would potentially save £20,000 of inventory so it would be worthwhile spending time investigating and if necessary negotiating a reduction in batch size. It may be that this parameter was set some years ago when the demand for the product was higher – the multiple will create an order for 50 days of stock. There is also a possibility that it could even be a typo, as the 1,320 would match the order period of five days.

For AB00345 we can see it would be possible to increase the order period to reflect that this part is a Class 2 part; this will possible counterbalance the fact that we will be increasing the number of batches of AB03279.

What can be seen from the above example is that the implementation does not always require a wholesale review of all the parameters? Although all the parameters may be adjusted the inventory effect of many is quite small by focusing on high value, both up and down we can have the greatest impact for a small effort. If we analyse the Division X data based on the plans we have created then we can see in Table 6.13 that 68.5 per cent are under ±£1,000 and 94.2 per cent under ±£5,000. Thus it is clear that we would only need to really focus on a small percentage to make significant impact.

CASE STUDY   Hozelock

Hozelock first implemented the approach by generating and reviewing the exception report, and examining the items, identifying where they disagreed with the recommendations they were able to improve the selection criteria. Once this process had been completed for a couple of years there was sufficient confidence in the report output that the reported items were uploaded directly to the MRP system.

Linking the inventory plan to MRP parameters

The importance of this part of the process cannot be overstated, as traditionally parameter maintenance has been seen as key cause of failure in MRP implementations. By using the *k*-curve process to determine a recommended position

TABLE 6.13

Value of Change	No of Parts Affected	Percent of Parts Affected
20,000	11	0.2%
10,000	23	0.5%
5,000	216	4.4%
1,000	99	2.0%
500	503	10.2%
0	2260	45.6%
−500	628	12.7%
−1,000	1172	23.7%
−5,000	41	0.8%
−10,000	0	0.0%

we are providing a challenge to the status quo. Without this challenge it is unlikely to expect all but the most diligent planners to continuously review their parameters. From the earlier discussions in Chapter 2 and 3 on non-compliance we can see how well-maintained parameters help to improve compliance. This process of feeding the output of the planning process back into MRP to close the loop between the inventory planning process and thus driving the execution of the planning system. Thus we now have a process that can take a top-down request for inventory reduction and generate a detailed part level plan that can quickly and efficiently focus on the 'inventory' issues.

It is important to note that the process described in this chapter is focused on inventory principally based on value – the actions are identified based on value. The operations manager will always have to apply the 'local' knowledge and not all the recommendations will be readily accepted.

Summary

In this chapter we have looked in detail at the inventory planning process and how the business targets, which are usually set at a high level, can be taken and broken down, analysed and rational decisions made that will result in a credible plan. Once the plan is confirmed, the data used to create these plans can be converted into detailed actions both specific, by part number and where necessary business process actions. The problem first described in Chapter 1 in Figure 1.3 remains a key headache for most operations managers today. The focus of this chapter has been to utilize the established theories and build (Excel-based) models that enables the operations manager with help from IT professionals to create a detailed inventory model and express inventory at both detail and summary levels. The model can then be used as a basis for rational planning and finally provide detail level instructions and reporting of key actions. The overall architecture is summarized in Figure 6.4. The model has three components:

- database;
- pivot table; and
- *k*-curve model.

The key function and relationship of the modules can be summarized as follows:

The database

The database is structured:

- The extracted data from the MRP system (Excel 6.1).
- The MRP rules for evaluating the current parameters (Excel 6.2 to Excel 6.4).
- The analysis rules for identifying what is:
  - Active and inactive (Excel 6.5)
  - Over and understock (Excel 6.7 and Excel 8.8)
  - Business reporting rules (Table 6.10)
- The *k*-curve logic applying the *k*-curve model to the extracted data (Excel 6.9).
- Differences – identifying the difference between current and proposed (Excel 6.1).

The database can be used to create detail part number level reporting for the current position and implementation action reports using the standard Excel filter feature.

FIGURE 6.4 Architecture of the Excel inventory model

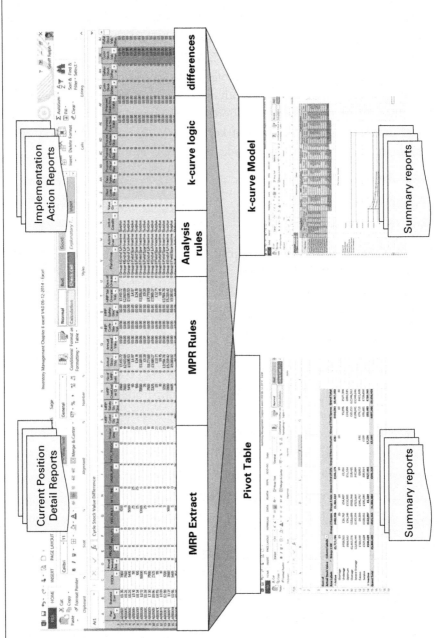

Pivot table

This utilizes the standard Excel feature to provide an analysis tool that can summarize the database. The summaries can be used to create summary level reports, both to summarize the current position and the proposed plan.

The k-curve model

The *k*-curve model, shown in Excel 6.9, summarizes the data from the database and allows the planner to:

- evaluate the most appropriate number of classes;
- evaluate the cycle stock, safety stock policies;
- compare current position to the *k*-curve; and
- set the appropriate target.

The calculated plans can then be copied and collated into a total plan.

Final comment

The chapter has progressed through the four key steps of planning inventory:

- Understand your current inventory position – *How much have I got?*
- Determine the business targets that relate to inventory – *What do I have to achieve?*
- Create inventory plan – *How difficult will this be and what must I do?*
  - Plan group planning (*k*-curve)
  - Consolidate plan
- Implement the plan – *What actions must I do to achieve the plan?*

In step one we show the importance of understanding what we have got and how by understanding what MRP parameters are doing and why we have got what we have. We know that the business targets will be given and represent our planning challenge. We have shown how we can calculate a plan based on the data available. And finally we have looked at both the specific, ie how to identify detail actions and the wider issues of getting the planning team to adopt a new process.

The journey we have taken through this book with you so far, and in particular through Chapters 5 and 6, have brought us to an important destination. We are at the point where you, should you so wish, should be able to plan and optimize your company's inventory using the *k*-curve methodology. We believe that this is an excellent achievement and that you now have in your hand something that should be truly valuable to your company. To further demonstrate the fact that the *k*-curve inventory planning journey is beneficial in business is shown in the case studies described in the final chapter. The final chapter will take a closer look at the success/failures that we have experienced and the lessons learnt.

Plan cycle checklist

- Understand your current inventory position – *How much have I got?*
  - MRP settings
  - determine inventory condition
  - active–inactive
  - over/understock
  - actual throughput rates
  - what is the business structure
  - list plan groups in descending order
  - add commentary and compare with previous assumptions
- Determine the business targets that relate to inventory – *What do I have to achieve?*
  - identify business targets
  - inventory
  - service level
  - identify constraints – limits to batch throughput rates
  - what is the business structure and where is the priority
  - allocate target to each group
  - list assumptions about targets and business direction
- Create inventory plan – *How difficult will this be and what must I do?*
  - plan group planning (*k*-curve)
  - separate active and inactive inventory
  - create scenario curves for active inventory
  - determine which curve is most effective
  - add safety stock policy – either days or statistical or hybrid
  - add overage limits
  - generate overall *k*-curve
  - identify current actual position
  - add actual inventory and number of batches

  – identify best scenario and value of *k*
  – consolidate plan
  – create consolidated plan of all plan groups
  – create plan for inactive, excess, surplus
  – identify gap between plan and actual
  – identify improvement required for each plan group
  – list assumptions about each group plan
- Implement the plan – *What actions must I do to achieve the plan?*
  – create parameter list for input to MRP
  – create deployment plan for capability improvement
  – create deployment plan for inventory actions
  – list assumptions about implementation challenges

Notes

Dupernex, S (1993) Improving inventory performance using *k*-curve methodology, Masters, Sunderland University

Dupernex, S (1997) Inventory parameter management and focused continuous improvement for repetitive batch manufacture, PhD thesis, Aston University

Relph, G (2006) Inventory management in business systems, PhD thesis, Manchester University

Richards, G and Grinsted, S (2013) *The Logistics and Supply Chain Toolkit*, Kogan Page, London

Wild, T (2002) *Best Practice in Inventory Management* (2nd edn), John Wiley, Oxford

Case study examples and what to do next

Introduction

This book has discussed the many facets of inventory management in business systems. And for those of you who have considered every chapter – even the scary maths – as well as for those of you who have skimmed much of the book, it's time to bring it all together with examples of how it's used in the real world.

The journey through the book has five milestones:

1 We have considered both the business needs as they relate to inventory and the systems together and separately:

- The business needs:
    - availability of inventory – place, time, quantity and quality;
    - to minimize inventory costs;
    - inventory to be well managed – ie planned, controlled, balanced.
- The systems:
    - are used to communicate and coordinate throughout the business;
    - are used to plan and manage the complexity;
    - are used to control – both the physical control in warehousing and elsewhere, and the control of data so that it matches the actual physical parts;
    - are used to balance real time progress and situations.

2 How inventory impacts the business at strategic, tactical and operational levels, as well as in many parts of the business from commercial to production and customer service to operations.

3 How inventory needs to be planned as effectively as possible to ensure best value add – reasonable cost for the greatest benefit.

4 We've considered that there are several ways to effectively plan inventory, including Pareto, inventory matrices, EOQ, but that ultimately we believe that the best way is the use of k-curve methodology.

5 We've talked about how systems assist us, the people, planning and decisions come from us. We've talked about the best way of using MRP within ERP systems to implement our plans, exploding the plans down from the independent demand into the dependent, detailed levels. It is quite likely that inventory planning decisions will be carried out outside MRP – using the methods talked about in the preceding point – and these decisions are then fed back into the ERP systems.

There's been some scary maths in this book. However, it's not necessary for everyone to get into the maths because it's the output from the methods that brings the value to the business.

This chapter briefly revisits some of the key steps along this journey and looks at case studies along the way.

What does the future hold?

What is happening in businesses today?

The business focus continues to manage the cash flow in the business. This requires continuous improvement on all aspects of inventory management as a key driver of the cash flow. The need to continuously improve puts ever more pressure on the effective use of business tools to manage the supply chain. Technology advances have significantly improved the interconnectivity of the supply chain. An understanding of the inventory within your business is key, in particular when we consider the high level business numbers and how they relate to the detailed inventory at part and parameter level, how to identify and drive down overstock, and how to optimize cycle stock without reducing it too far to a point where the business would become anorexic. It is still the case that most businesses rely on some form of planning system, of which ERP packages, cloud based or otherwise, are still the most common with MRP remaining at the core of these systems.

MRP relation to ERP

Since MRP still sits in the centre of most ERP systems, even though it may be enhanced by advanced planning, both rely on planning parameters. There may have been many significant developments and advances in the capabilities of ERP and the planning function in MRP. What continues to surprise us when visiting companies is that parameters – specifically those that define the cycle stock, safety stock and lead-times remain manually planned? This means that the business planning system is subject to planners making thousands of individual decision that are, in effect, not linked. If you recall Figure 2.9, the ERP configuration which shows that MRP is at the heart of the operations which shows just how fundamental these decisions are to the correct operation of the planning process and the ERP functions that then rely on those decisions.

Current management of MRP

A recent study of MRP parameter management practices over the last two decades by Jonsson and Mattsson (2006) is shown in Table 7.1 and shows that 64 per cent of lot sizing parameters are still set by the planner, which is a high and significant proportion. Of the three categories, planners/ operations managers will argue that lot-for-lot is a Lean approach and therefore a good thing. What is worth challenging is that lot-for-lot requires the planner to review at the time of ordering. We need to question whether

TABLE 7.1 Frequency of company using each lot-sizing method (Jonsson and Mattsson, 2006)

Method Identifier	Lot-sizing Method	Percentage of companies
A	Lot-for-lot	24
B	Experience-based number of periods covered	29
C	Experience-based Fixed Quantity	11
D	EOQ	31
E	Dynamic optimization method	5

(A, B, C bracketed = 64)

this is a good thing or a bad thing – or perhaps a bit of both. Is it that the 'setting of ordering parameters to "lot for lot"' gives the planner a sense of control and adding value, since it offers them the chance to review quantity at time of ordering and then to consolidate with other orders using skill and expertise. However, in reality this is a false sense of control since it forces the planner to review every order placed, whether each individual order is a useful use of their time or not, creating additional workload for an already busy planner. The result is that 64 per cent of the decisions are experienced-based. Without negating the benefit of this experience, just consider the difficulties in getting a group of planners making in the region of 30,000 decisions to remain rational and coordinated.

In spite of a wealth of knowledge and experience business systems implementations are still failing and for the same reasons. In Table 2.4 in Chapter 2 we summarised the many studies since the 1980s which show that the underlying cause of failure and thus the CSF (Critical Success Factors) for good ERP implementations remain the same.

The three-legged stool supporting inventory management

In Chapter 1 we refer to the three-legged stool of control, balance and planning where any one fails the whole process fails.

Control

In Chapter 1 we discussed the technological tools like bar-code and RFID that are used to improving the accuracy. If we consider the complexity described in the Airbus case study in Chapter 3 we can see that it would be common to need to pick a list of 100 parts. Were we to accept a 90 per cent chance of the items being correct, we know that failure is guaranteed as can be seen in Table 7.2. That is why very high levels of accuracy equivalent to PPM need to be applied. It is important to apply the same philosophy used for product quality to the quality of parts data, for example six-sigma and parts per million.

Balance

As systems increase their ability to update more often – or even go real time – it is much easier to provide the planner with up-to-date information and instructions as to what needs to be done to keep the inventory in balance. We know that as technology improves both interconnectivity and the speed of reaction times, the time needed to rebalance inventory according to the

TABLE 7.2   Probability of picking a kit with 100 parts

Accuracy of Data	Probability of shortage free Kit of 100 parts	No of Failures per Million
90.0000%	0.003%	100,000
95.0000%	0.592%	50,000
99.0000%	36.603%	10,000
99.9000%	90.479%	1,000
99.9990%	99.999%	10
99.9999%	99.999%	1

plan should also decrease. This doesn't, however, decrease the time needed to plan for optimum inventory. Sadly the increased efficiency of these systems has seen a reduction in the numbers of planners in the organizations, leaving them little time to 'think' and truly plan the products they are responsible for.

Planning

There is a much higher level of education/skills available and needed in the planning community. However, as Table 7.1 shows, inventory planning is still largely determined by the planner skill and judgement we believe that this remains the key inefficiency in managing MRP effectively. By giving the operations managers the ability to ensure that planners are working to common rules and guidelines we are not de-skilling the planner, but linking the high level plans to the detail decision. For most companies MRP is only successful when the painstaking detailed adjustments carried out by planners is aligned to the common goal of the business. As Einstein said, the definition of insanity is 'doing the same thing over and over again and expecting different results.' In this context:

1 If you do not change MRP parameters how can you expect the inventory level that MRP is driving the business towards to change?

2 If you do not change how parameters are calculated – ie moving from individual decisions to coordinated decisions that relate the

value and importance of parts to one another – how can you expect to influence the direction of travel?

3 If you do not link the high-level target to the detail parts, how can you expect to exert any power over MRP and the inventory level that MRP is driving the business towards?

Batch, safety, lead-time

In Chapter 3 we explained how MRP is critically dependant on three decisions being made:

- Batch: How much?
- Safety: How important is it to protect against service level failure – from both supply side and customer demand?
- Lead-time: How long must I allow for the resupply of the item?

The option is to plan inventory within MRP or to manage 'ad-hoc' often using Excel or home-grown reports designed by the planner. Lack of confidence in the system is a key reason why planners often plan outside the system. If these plans are not loaded back into the system, including changes to parameter settings, the recommendations then made by the system are likely to be incorrect.

CASE STUDY   Toiletries

Our Planning system did not plan so we created our own report... It takes the Gross requirement – subtracts the stock and then the orders. When it has done that it places new orders... Why do not use the MRP module... What is MRP...? Investigation of the system showed the module was available. Planners were trained and the old system – which was found to be incorrect – was switched off.

The normal approach to recommendations is that the planner can make changes as they see fit. However, unless these changes to forecasts, orders and other system created instructions are followed up with changes to the parameters, data and managing the settings that drive the transactions, the system will continue to diverge away from the physical world.

It is only by measuring and reporting on the numbers and types of changes made in the system – the non-compliance – that the 'correctness' of the system can be understood.

Non-compliance/compliance

The compliance approach to recommendations was discussed in Chapter 3. It basically measures how close the recommendations made by the system are to what is considered by the planner to be correct, which in turn translates into how useful the system is and how much the planner trusts its recommendations.

CASE STUDY Pumps

We worked with a client who had just implemented SAP in 17 plants worldwide. When their compliance level was analysed it was found to be as low as 25 per cent. When the planners were challenged they stated: 'We have no time to maintain our parameters because we are too busy firefighting.' The improvement project created a 'parameter sickie', which in effect meant that the planner was assumed not to be available and his colleagues covered for him as though he were sick. This gave the planner time and space to properly review the parameters, based on an analysis of their non-compliance. This returned huge benefits, with compliance increasing from 25 per cent to 75 per cent in six weeks and eventually to 90 per cent.

Why the *k*-curve approach is really different

Business-case-driven inventory planning

We have talked throughout the book about the need to understand the business, the need to drive costs down and the implication of this at detailed, part level. It is important for a business to know when to stop – when its stock turns are high enough and when its inventory levels should no longer be decreased. It is to be expected that there will be a continued and relentless pressure on inventory, but there is a fine line between lean and anorexic.

FIGURE 7.1 Typical lean implementation approach (Slack, Chambers and Johnston, 2010)

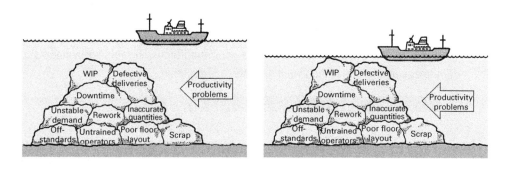

Inventory initiatives, unless properly handled, can often create a failure cycle:

> Reduce inventory – service level fails – production disrupted by short-term priority – safety re-applied – loss of confidence of customer demand falls – pressure to reduce inventory.

This failure cycle is difficult to break. But by utilizing the k-curve method, reductions can be made progressively in planned stages, rather than the typical vertical drop often caused by simply removing all the safety stock.

Lean approach to inventory reduction

Traditional Lean thinking can lead a company into danger, if the philosophy of removing the water to expose the rocks is followed blindly. When the rocks (the business problems) are exposed the business will need to improve the process. The assumption is that there is time to improve the process before each exposed rock causes a significant problem, which could potentially sink the boat (the business). If this is followed to the letter then lowering the inventory *will* cause problems in the business. Case note 3 details a case in point. Figure 7.1 shows the typical Lean approach as a ship in rocky waters.

CASE STUDY   Automotive

A new manufacturing manager wanted to focus the organization on Lean production. His strategy was to remove all safety stock from the products in order to reduce the inventory in the process. As is the case in most complex moulding equipment the production equipment was subject to failure. Although the organization was focused on improving these failures the effect was that production was disrupted. These disruptions would normally have been smoothed out by the safety stock. With the removal of the safety stock more emergency changeovers needed to be arranged, which in turn reduced capacity utilisation and finally decreased the customer service level. Only when the safety stock was put back into the process could the organization focus on real improvements to the equipment rather than wasting time on firefighting.

The *k*-curve approach to inventory reduction

Another example is of a client who manufactures front and rear bumpers for the automotive industry. This company used the *k*-curve approach and focused on capability improvements hand in hand with the inventory reductions. In this case study, the company didn't expose any 'rocks', since the problems were identified and resolved before the inventory reductions had reached the critical levels:

CASE STUDY   Automotive

The company moulded and painted front and rear bumpers for a number of local automotive manufacturers. They would receive the pull signal four hours prior to the required sequenced delivery. In order to improve flexibility and reduce inventory they completed an inventory – capability analysis using *k*-curve. The study used a particular safety stock algorithm that took account of the batch size and supply reliability and demand variation. The study showed that as the batch sizes reduced there was a point when the safety stock increased in order to protect for the risk of supply failure. This clarified that unless the processes were reliable, and it was known that the paint colour changeover was particularly problematic, then it was unwise to lower the safety stock further. This case study was presented at Manufacturer Live in 2004 and subsequently published in *The Manufacturer* in August 2004. The punch line was simple: 'If the paint changeover process is not capable don't take the inventory out, but when process becomes capable then take inventory out.'

FIGURE 7.2   Comparison of lean and inventory capability on
a k-curve

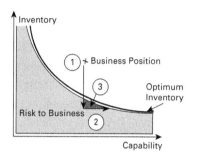
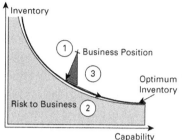

1. Lean / Agile initiatives
   'take out inventory expose the rocks'
2. Fix the process problems.
3. Result – business exposed whilst
   earning new skills

1. Optimised Inventory – understand and balance
   inventory with capability
2. Continuous process improvement synchronising
   inventory reduction with increased capability
3. Result – business protected whilst learning new skills

In summary, if you contrast the two approaches:

- The pure Lean approach is take out the inventory to find the problem, then fix it (ie the left-hand side of Figure 7.2).

- The k-curve approach is to balance the inventory with the capability and then remove inventory as the improvement in capability is achieved (ie the right-hand side of Figure 7.2).

You can see that while you may still use the Lean techniques to solve the capability problems, linking the inventory reductions to the improvements rather than using the reduction to expose the problems is a much safer path.

Where has it succeeded/failed

It succeeded because:

CASE STUDY   An aerospace company

When working with an aerospace company, as part of doctoral research by Relph (2006). The case study work carried out during the research led to a project to implement the k-curve approach through the use of DIOS, which was embedded into BaaN. The project succeeded because it was supported and sponsored by the General Manager and led by a highly experienced MRP user.

Pilot/implementation

In 2004 the company had recently completed the implementation of a new ERP system which was not achieving the expected inventory benefits. The volatility of the market was driving the inventory value up. There were significant challenges in controlling the supply chain. The research project had shown the benefits of a formalized approach to planning inventory at the item level. There were difficulties in translating inventory planning objectives from senior management to the detailed level needed by the planning function.

Approach

The underlying business processes were analysed and processes' breakages were determined.

The project wanted to integrate the parameter management processes with the planning objectives. It was identified that embedding the *k*-curve planning engine into the MRP process and using it to drive parameter change actions directly to the planner would bring order and structure to the parameter maintenance process. Figure 7.3 shows a typical action screen.

FIGURE 7.3   Baan screen showing AIM action codes

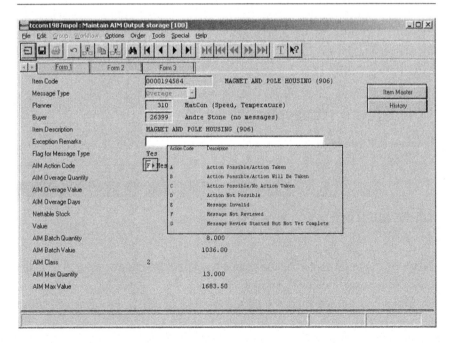

Summary of benefits to date

The use of *k*-curve methodology was embedded into the ERP system. Parameter evaluation and exceptions were calculated weekly and delivered to the planners as actions via the ERP system. The improved inventory planning processes reduced overage and was a significant contributor to the 25 per cent reduction in inventory.

CASE STUDY   EDF – setting up systems correctly

Background

The Supply Chain and Logistics group of EDF Energy Networks, a major power supplier in the UK, were having difficulty implementing their Inventory Optimization Software as an add-on to their SAP system. The initial implementation and re-implementation had not succeeded and as a result the system was not being used by the planners.

Project objective

The project examined the processes, organization and technology. The *k*-curve methodology was used to analyse the existing settings. These settings were challenged and an alternative set of values proposed. The organization and in particular the planners' non-compliance was investigated. By examining the reasons for their non-compliance the project was able to identify process improvements and training to help ensure that the software was properly understood. In particular, the parameter settings were reviewed to ensure that they were in alignment with the business targets.

The outcome

The project identified a revision to the current parameter settings and approach. It also identified where there were opportunities to increase compliance by focusing on high-value components. The manager's view of the completed project was:

> The main aim was to reduce the inventory value while improving service to our customers The structured manner in which the final report was submitted along with the suggested project plan will enable myself and my team to implement and track progress moving forward.
>
> (Paul Farmer, Inventory Demand Manager)

CASE STUDY

When to stop

Kidde Graviner

Business background

Kidde Graviner is part of Hamilton Sundstrand/UTC. In 2010 it was weathering the downturn well. Sales in 2008 were £28.7 million to 414 customers and the business balance was 70 per cent into the aerospace market and 30 per cent into the vehicle market. The S&OP process was able to identify 70 per cent of demand was known at start-of-month. The customer lead-time was 8–16 weeks for build. The expected spares lead-time for aerospace was much shorter. Kidde used Forth Shift to manage manufacturing and inventory. In addition, there was extensive use of Excel spreadsheets for forecasting. The business had between 10,000 and 20,000 part numbers, with 190 suppliers accounting for approximately £9.6 million spend of which approximately £5.6 million was inter-company trading. Like many companies Kidde had an active and successful business improvement initiative called ACE: (Achieving Competitive Excellence) in operation.

Business performance

- Over the last three years stock turns had been increased from 3.5 to 5.
- 'This has taken the low hanging fruit.'
- Kidde Graviner held safety stocks for some customers.
- £2,700k stock today split:
    - £2,000k in Raw Materials
    - (including £500k safety);
    - £600k is WIP;
    - £100k is FGS (2,500 items)

Project scope

The project wanted to identify the effort required to achieve the stock turn of 10 by end of 2011, estimating that it would significantly increase activity across many of the current improvement initiatives. Kidde wanted to understand how to accelerate the rate of improvements by thinking outside the box, prioritizing and obtaining new skills.

Outcome

The goal of the inventory capability study was to address the challenge of achieving a stock turn of 10. The project identified that some of the product areas had achieved optimum inventory and process capability; these were sunset products where there was no business benefit in focusing on further improvement. The optimal parameter settings for the sunrise products were identified using k-curve, and analysis of the capability requirements identified a path that would achieve the goal of stock turn of 10. Based on sales forecasts for 2010–2012 it required the inventory to reduce to less than £1.6 million by Y/E 2012. The project identified process weaknesses which were translated into 17 capability improvement projects. The 17 projects were then divided into three groups: inventory drivers, capability enablers and ACE improvements (ACE was the corporate improvement programme). A key capability enabler project was MRP Parameter training, which covered both the use of k-curve methodology and non-compliance as a MRP management process. The key success was a clear understanding of the relationship between the inventory and capabilities in the business and a re-focus on the effective use of MRP.

CASE STUDY   Training: Morrison's

Background

Morrison's is a well-known UK retailer who was implementing a new ERP system as part of a five-year IT improvement programme. Morrison's were particularly keen to ensure that the staff were properly trained in the use of the new system as it represented a significant change in the business operation, through automation of the ordering process. The ERP systems provider was contracted to provide the transactional training. Morrison's identified that there was an additional need to provide 'theoretical training' for the planning team to ensure that they understood the mechanics of the transactions and the reasons behind this. The training covered the operation of the forecasting and planning processes and the key requirements for managing the parameter settings.

Outcome

The training programme was initially developed and piloted using a group of the senior planners and first line management to confirm that the level of complexity in the material was appropriate for the target audience. All the planners were asked to complete a 'test' to determine their knowledge of supply chain planning principles. The planners were tested again at the conclusion of the training and an average improvement of 10 per cent on their test score was achieved. As expected, the planners were then able to approach the new system with confidence and were able to adjust to the new role easily. What was not so expected was that it almost completely removed the 'fear of job loss' associated with the new systems as the planners were able to see that the benefits of the automation was to enable them to become planners and not just order processors.

Where implementation projects failed

It is always easy to talk of success, but not so easy to talk of failure. This example is from a company which was making equipment for trains and tanks. The company had a mature MRP implementation, but due to staff turnover the level of MRP understanding within the business had declined. In addition there was a significant focus on working capital reduction and inventory reduction was seen as a significant component. The project initially focused on MRP training and followed through with analysis of the inventory using *k*-curve. The project developed inventory plans and identified the need to focus on non-compliance. The initial success of the project was not sustained due to a combination of senior management and planning manager changes. There was a strong solo mentality within the organization which meant the required level of inter-departmental cooperation was not forthcoming. Once the management support for the project waned the planners quickly reverted back to the old habits.

What are the real blockers?

Because planners have always been depended on to set parameters it is easy for them to feel threatened if given any external help or advice.

CASE STUDY   Electro-mechanical

In one of the four 26-week case studies conducted during the research for the *Inventory Management in Business Systems*, during the discussions with the planners about their parameter management practices, they stated 'we change parameters regularly'. However, part of the research had monitored the MRP database for 13 weeks prior to involvement of the planners and the data showed that not one parameter had been changed during these 13 weeks. The following 13 weeks parameters were changed based on the recommendations of *k*-curve based reports. At the concluding reviews when discussing the parameter changes the planners view was 'we would have made that change anyway' (Relph, 2006).

This shows that planners in general see that making the parameter decision is part of their raison d'etre, and removing this decision can appear a direct threat to their job security. Thus, when implementing, a more softly softly approach is more likely to deliver success, as the Hozelock study shows.

CASE STUDY   Hozelock

The implementation of the *k*-curve methodology implemented in stages. This was first recommended to planner who approved adjustment. Second, when confidence in output had been achieved, recommendations were uploaded, after management review of summary report.

Lesson learnt

The key learning points from this project were:

- maintain the management commitment;
- keep a sustained focus on embedding the new practices; and
- ensure that all departments understand and support the MRP improvements.

Software application

There are a wide range of software products that focus on inventory optimization. A majority still use Pareto ABC classification, Runner-Repeater-Stranger and Volatility to classify the parts. In addition, these advanced optimization tools use forecasting, forecast error and statistical safety stock to manage safety stock levels. However, they will still rely on the planner to specify the batch size. To our knowledge there are only two software products which explicitly use k-curve methodology in their inventory optimization approach.

DIOS (dynamic inventory optimization software)

IBM developed inventory management software based on the k-curve methodology in the mid-1990s in UK and Swiss offices. It was used by IBM Consulting to support consulting projects and the software was also made available to clients.

CASE STUDY Mann+Hummel

Mann+Hummel is a major German retailer which is quoted by IBM as a case study.

The implementation: a classic supply chain dilemma

In reviewing its operations, Mann+Hummel management team noticed that its central distribution centre was 'out of balance'. The centre was carrying excess inventory, but it was missing its targeted customer service levels. The company gave IBM a goal: identify upwards of 15 per cent to 30 per cent in inventory reductions – freeing up valuable working capital, and keep order line service levels at 97 per cent or above for all products. IBM was also asked to study the effect that other factors might have on the facility's inventory, such as shorter production lead times, stock build-ups that occur before production holidays and expected increases in market share.

Benefits

IBM was able to show how Mann+Hummel could lower its current stock by 30 per cent using DIOS while keeping customer service levels at 97 per cent and reducing order lines for production per year by 18 per cent. The resulting benefits quoted were:

- Reduced inventory levels and material handling costs.
- Increased customer service level performance.
- Improved demand forecasting. (IBM, 2014)

  www.ibm.com/solutions/sap/us/en/solution/U117139L02890Z46.html

Amis-delta

Inventory Matters developed amis-delta, an inventory planning tool based on k-curve principles, in 2008. It is used both as a consulting tool and operationally by clients.

CASE STUDY   Hozelock

This case study starts back in 2002 when Hozelock wanted to improve service levels to their customers. Hozelock work in the demanding UK DIY retail sector, and wanted to reduce lost business and improve the seasonal planning process.

Background

Hozelock were a mature MRP user with an established system. Lean/agile manufacturing techniques were established but the management wanted further service levels improvement. There was a recognition that the business needed to be 'make to stock' driven to meet the demands of their customers. Forecast was owned by the sales function, the quality was unreliable as the product demand was highly influenced by the weather. The planners were using arbitrary parameters policies and did not believe the forecast from sales. Supply/demand planning was not fully synchronized with significant manual progressing activities.

Approach

With the help of Inventory Matters, the business took a critical look at existing business processes and identified where there were breakages in the processes and scope for improvement. A critical area was the maintenance of safety stock parameters which were causing visibility and capacity issues as there were large changes on a quarterly basis. The MRP planning cycle needed to be aligned to the customer demand cycle. The weakness of the quarterly MRP seasonal planning process was identified and understood. A detailed analysis of seasonal demand patterns based on three years history helped balance the distribution of the safety stocks.

A re-evaluation of safety stock techniques using *k*-curve methodology improved the visibility and capacity utilization. The use of *k*-curve was supported by the use of a planning tool based on *k*-curve methodology, called amis-*delta*. The development and implementation of the amis-*delta* monthly stock planning process improved the overall stock effectiveness. Initially the output from amis-*delta* was reviewed by the planners and if approved input by them into their MRP system. Once confidence had been built up the parameters were then uploaded directly into the planning systems.

Summary of benefits to date

There has been a significant and sustained reduction in lost business. There has also been an improved visibility of demand in the seasonal cycle, resulting in better utilization of stock and improved capacity planning.

Continuous evaluation and adjustment of safety stock parameters has become a routine practice, which helps to ensure that end of season stocks are minimized. The planning in amis-**delta** focuses on the 'B' Class parts, leading to higher MRP compliance. This in turn means that the business can focus on detailed manual planning of the A Class stock parts. Hozelock were the Winners of the Manufacturer of the Year Award 2009.

www.amis-delta.co.uk

Review of key points in the book

Inventory/MRP complexity

In the book we have examined the dilemma of planning at aggregate vs detail levels. It is an inescapable problem, if you have to reduce inventory by 20 per cent or £1 million, how to decide which parts to reduce. Most business will have thousands of parts and if they use MRP there are a number of parameters to adjust. In this book we have examined the two areas of focus:

- Overage – I have too much inventory.
- Planning – I plan too much inventory.

What is obvious is that you cannot identify if you have too much inventory unless you have already defined your target inventory level. To define the target level you need some form of economic model to know if you are planning for too much inventory. The 'exchange curve' shows that inventory can only be reduced by exchanging it for a faster process, which requires the business to be more capable. If you can define the plan level then MRP will help to manage overage, but the planner must comply with the recommendations.

Item level planning tools

In the book we have looked at the well-known and largely understood EOQ approach, which is often challenged and modified. The EOQ logic is fundamentally sound but lacks credibility because the key elements required are show to be indeterminate. Safety stock is often considered more theoretically solid ground: however, looking at the wide range of safety stock algorithms, which vary widely from simple to very complex, very quickly the data required to execute the formulae becomes too difficult to gather and maintain.

Aggregate planning tools

Pareto

The requirement of a business to plan from aggregate to item is facilitated by Pareto. Pareto is widely understood and used. It is one of the few inventory planning tools that is generally available as a planning tool in MRP. In the book we examine the Pareto weaknesses (Relph and Newton, 2014) and how they are resolved by developing the exchange curve principle.

Exchange curve and *k*-curve

The extension of Pareto into the *k*-curve methodology has been developed through the book, and an inventory planning model has been created to enable the reader to use the *k*-curve approach within their own business.

Inventory capability planning

In this chapter we have looked at how the *k*-curve approach can improve the Lean approach by ensuring that the capability is improved before the 'water is lowered', avoiding the business from floundering on the rocks. The *k*-curve approach takes fewer risks and can indicate when to stop. The four steps to inventory planning are summarized below.

Four steps to inventory heaven

- Understand your current inventory position – *How much have I got?*
  - What inventory is active and which of the active parts have I got too much of?
  - What inventory is inactive, how long has it been inactive, can I dispose of it or use it elsewhere? Is there a strategic reason why I acquired the inventory and is that reason still valid?

- Determine the business targets that relate to inventory – *What do I have to achieve?*
  - The business will of necessity need to reduce costs and inventory will invariably come into focus. Inventory targets are always broad-brush expressed as percentages or monetary values. To understand what the business needs to achieve the business needs to know where the constraints are. The constraints can be expressed as an inventory level or in the capability of the business processes.

- Create inventory plan – *How difficult will this be and what must I do?*
  - Plan group planning (k-curve). Using a combination of Pareto and k-curve, individual groups can be planned, and individual constraints for each group identified and listed in action plan. Thus each active group can then be planned separately.
  - Consolidate plan. These individual plans can be brought together before adding back the inactive stock to create a consolidated total plan.

- Implement the plan – *What actions must I do to achieve the plan?*

The planning process will have identified actions:

  - What parameters need changing?
  - Where am I overstocked?
  - Plan and agree disposal of inactive stock.
  - Where do I need to improve the process?

The plan is supported by a detailed list of assumptions that will ensure that when changes happen the plan can be adjusted with confidence.

Summary

The intention in writing this book is to promote the k-curve planning approach. We believe that the approach addresses the current business issues facing most operations managers. The book aims to provide the tools and techniques that are available and presents the k-curve as a viable alternative approach. We have included detailed Excel instructions which enable the reader to construct an Excel-based model capable of enabling the methodology to be used.

We hope that there has been a clear demonstration though the business cases that the k-curve process has achieved many business benefits. These have been illustrated through the paths both to success and failure. We sincerely hope that we have shown that this is not a scary process, because once calculated the 'inventory – capability curve' is easy to understand and the output needed to drive MRP can be easily extracted from the planning tool. This will leave the reader very much in control of their inventory management.

Notes

ElSayed, M S, Hubbard, N J and Tipi, N S (2013) Evaluating Enterprise Resource Planning (ERP) post-implementation problems in Egypt: Findings from case studies of governmental, multinational and private Egyptian organizations, Logistics Research Network

IBM (2014, 6 November) IBM Dynamic Inventory Optimization Solution. Retrieved from IBM & SAP: www.ibm.com/solutions/sap/us/en/solution/U117139L02890Z46.html

Jonsson, P and Mattsson, S (2006) A longitudinal study of materials: Planning applications in manufacturing companies, *International Journal of Operations Production Management*, **26**, pp 971–95

Relph, G J (2006) Inventory management in business systems, PhD thesis, Manchester University

Relph, G J and Newton, M (2014) Both Pareto and EOQ have limitations; combining them delivers a powerful management tool for MRP and beyond, *International Journal of Production Economics*, **157**, pp 24–30

Slack, N, Chambers, S and Johnston, R (2010) *Operations Management*, Financial Times/Prentice Hall, London

APPENDICES

Appendix A

Sample parts for exercises in part number order:

TABLE A.1

Count	Part Number	Annual Usage or Demand	Actual Stock	Cost Per Part	Annual Spend Value £	Actual Stock Value
25	A0889030013	52	1	£19.59	£1,018.88	£19.59
14	A0906030015	18	8	£150.22	£2,703.97	£1,201.77
19	A78810601E	401	1117	£5.20	£2,085.20	£5,808.40
26	B30880112C	700	566	£1.19	£835.28	£675.38
27	B30880113C	650	125	£1.18	£767.00	£147.50
15	B78810721A	749	251	£3.44	£2,579.83	£864.54
3	B78810741A	1012	75	£18.50	£18,722.00	£1,387.50
1	B78811ZD	1324	58	£42.84	£56,726.63	£2,485.00
12	B78812001B	458	15	£7.10	£3,250.36	£106.45
2	B78812ZF	987	20	£41.87	£41,325.69	£837.40
20	B78818AE	35	14	£59.41	£2,079.36	£831.74
8	C78810742A	360	7	£16.87	£6,071.97	£118.07

TABLE A.1 *continued*

Count	Part Number	Annual Usage or Demand	Actual Stock	Cost Per Part	Annual Spend Value £	Actual Stock Value
10	C78810761A	567	3	£8.43	£4,780.58	£25.29
21	C78810762A	230	54	£8.44	£1,941.66	£455.87
22	D0753100033	75	34	£22.84	£1,713.04	£776.58
9	D0862060018Y	163	65	£33.26	£5,420.88	£2,161.70
17	D0862070019Y	60	39	£38.98	£2,338.96	£1,520.32
7	D0883030014C	267	98	£27.54	£7,354.28	£2,699.32
18	D0978040014	39	91	£57.63	£2,247.62	£5,244.45
16	D0991020012	164	104	£14.60	£2,393.59	£1,517.89
23	D1017040014	15	3	£104.23	£1,563.49	£312.70
24	KDB300600	8	6	£193.37	£1,546.99	£1,160.24
13	KN552130	10	2	£319.98	£3,199.83	£639.97
11	LE02	396	0	£11.09	£4,393.19	£0.00
6	LE763	781	321	£11.11	£8,679.28	£3,567.29
4	N6554004M0256	523	75	£35.08	£18,346.42	£2,630.94
5	SK98751	46	10	£316.19	£14,544.64	£3,161.88
	Totals				£218,630.61	£40,357.77

Appendix B

Sample parts for exercises in highest to lowest spend:

TABLE A.2

Count	Part Number	Annual Usage or Demand	Actual Stock	Cost Per Part	Annual Spend Value £	Actual Stock Value
1	B78811ZD	1324	58	£42.84	£56,726.63	£2,485.00
2	B78812ZF	987	20	£41.87	£41,325.69	£837.40
3	B78810741A	1012	75	£18.50	£18,722.00	£1,387.50
4	N6554004M0256	523	75	£35.08	£18,346.42	£2,630.94
5	SK98751	46	10	£316.19	£14,544.64	£3,161.88
6	LE763	781	321	£11.11	£8,679.28	£3,567.29
7	D0883030014C	267	98	£27.54	£7,354.28	£2,699.32
8	C78810742A	360	7	£16.87	£6,071.97	£118.07
9	D0862060018Y	163	65	£33.26	£5,420.88	£2,161.70
10	C78810761A	567	3	£8.43	£4,780.58	£25.29
11	LE02	396	0	£11.09	£4,393.19	£0.00
12	B78812001B	458	15	£7.10	£3,250.36	£106.45
13	KN552130	10	2	£319.98	£3,199.83	£639.97
14	A0906030015	18	8	£150.22	£2,703.97	£1,201.77
15	B78810721A	749	251	£3.44	£2,579.83	£864.54
16	D0991020012	164	104	£14.60	£2,393.59	£1,517.89

TABLE A.2 *continued*

Count	Part Number	Annual Usage or Demand	Actual Stock	Cost Per Part	Annual Spend Value £	Actual Stock Value
17	D0862070019Y	60	39	£38.98	£2,338.96	£1,520.32
18	D0978040014	39	91	£57.63	£2,247.62	£5,244.45
19	A78810601E	401	1117	£5.20	£2,085.20	£5,808.40
20	B78818AE	35	14	£59.41	£2,079.36	£831.74
21	C78810762A	230	54	£8.44	£1,941.66	£455.87
22	D0753100033	75	34	£22.84	£1,713.04	£776.58
23	D1017040014	15	3	£104.23	£1,563.49	£312.70
24	KDB300600	8	6	£193.37	£1,546.99	£1,160.24
25	A0889030013	52	1	£19.59	£1,018.88	£19.59
26	B30880112C	700	566	£1.19	£835.28	£675.38
27	B30880113C	650	125	£1.18	£767.00	£147.50
	Totals				**£218,630.61**	**£40,357.77**

USEFUL WEBSITES

www.cilt.co.uk
www.iomnet.co.uk
www.im3l.co.uk

INDEX

Numbers in *italics* refer to figures or tables.

CPSIA information can be obtained at www.ICGtesting.com
Printed in the USA
BVOW09s0829070715

407725BV00002B/4/P